LIFE IN CHRIST

Register This New Book

Benefits of Registering*

- ✓ FREE **replacements** of lost or damaged books
- ✓ FREE **audiobook** – *Pilgrim's Progress*, audiobook edition
- ✓ FREE information about new titles and other **freebies**

www.anekopress.com/new-book-registration

*See our website for requirements and limitations.

LIFE IN CHRIST

Lessons from Our Lord's
Miracles and Parables

The Miracles of Our Lord
Volume 7

Charles H. Spurgeon

We love hearing from our readers. Please contact us
at www.anekopress.com/questions-comments with
any questions, comments, or suggestions.

Life in Christ, Vol. 7
© *2022 by Aneko Press*
All rights reserved.
Revised edition 2022

Please do not reproduce, store in a retrieval system, or transmit in any form or by any means – electronic, mechanical, photocopying, recording, or otherwise, without written permission from the publisher. Please contact us via www.AnekoPress.com for reprint and translation permissions.

Scripture quotations are from The Authorized (King James) Version. Rights in the Authorized Version in the United Kingdom are vested in the Crown. Reproduced by permission of the Crown's patentee, Cambridge University Press.

Cover Design: Natalia Hawthorne
Cover Painting: Matt Philleo
Editors: Ruth Clark and J. Martin

Aneko Press
www.anekopress.com
Aneko Press, Life Sentence Publishing, and our logos are trademarks of
Life Sentence Publishing, Inc.
203 E. Birch Street
P.O. Box 652
Abbotsford, WI 54405

RELIGION / Christian Life / Spiritual Growth
Paperback ISBN: 978-1-62245-822-6
eBook ISBN: 978-1-62245-823-3
10 9 8 7 6 5 4 3 2 1
Available where books are sold

Contents

Ch. 1: The Withered Hand 1

Ch. 2: Jesus Angry with Hard Hearts 19

Ch. 3: Jesus, Not a Ghost 35

Ch. 4: Mr. Fearing Comforted 53

Ch. 5: The History of Little Faith 69

Ch. 6: Hope in Hopeless Cases 87

Ch. 7: A Desperate Case – How to Meet It 103

Ch. 8: "If You Can" 121

Ch. 9: Faith Omnipotent 137

Ch. 10: All Things Are Possible 155

Ch. 11: Faith's Dawn and Its Clouds 173

Ch. 12: Conflict 189

Ch. 13: The Devil's Last Throw 205

Charles H. Spurgeon – A Brief Biography 223

Other Similar Titles 227

Chapter 1

The Withered Hand

And, behold, there was a man which had his hand withered. . . . Then saith he to the man, Stretch forth thine hand. And he stretched it forth; and it was restored whole, like as the other. (Matthew 12:10, 13 KJV)

Note well the expression. Jesus *went into their synagogue: And, behold, there was a man which had his hand withered* (emphasis added). A mark is set, as it were, in the margin, as if it were a notable fact. That word *behold* is a sort of note of exclamation to draw attention to it. *Behold, there was a man which had his hand withered.* In many congregations, if there should step in someone of the great and mighty of the land, people would say, "Behold, there was a duke, an earl, or a bishop there." But although there were some great ones occasionally in our Savior's congregation, I find no notes of admiration about their presence, no "beholds" inserted by the Gospel writers as if to call attention to their appearance. No doubt if there were in a congregation some person of known intelligence and great learning, who had earned to himself a high degree, there are persons who would say, "Do you know that Professor Science or Doctor Classic was present at the service?" There would be a "behold" put to that in the memories of many. There were persons well learned, according to the learning of the day, who came to listen to Christ, but there are no "beholds" put about their having been present. Yet in the synagogue there was a poor man whose hand had been withered, and we are called upon to note the fact.

It was his *right* hand which was withered (Luke 6:6), the worse of the two for him, for he could scarcely follow his handicraft or earn his bread. His best hand was useless, his breadwinner failed him. I have no doubt he was a very humble, obscure, insignificant individual, probably very bad off and in great poverty, because he could not work as his fellow craftsmen could, but not a man of any rank, or learning, or special intelligence. His being in the assembly was in itself nothing very remarkable. I suppose he had been accustomed to going to the synagogue as others of his townsmen did; yet the Holy Spirit takes care to mark that he was present, and to have the word *behold* hung out like a signal, that it might be regarded as a special subject for consideration that the crippled man was there.

And today, dear friends, it matters very little to the preacher or to the congregation that *you* are here, if you are some person of note or consequence; for we make no note of dignitaries here, and attach no special consequence to anyone in this place where the rich and the poor meet together. But if you happen to be here as a needy soul wanting a Savior, if you happen to be here with a spiritually withered hand so that you cannot do the things that you want, and you are wanting to have that hand restored to you, there shall be a "behold" put to that, and especially shall it be doubly emphatic if today the Master shall say to you, "Stretch out your withered hand," and if the divine power shall restore that hand and a deed of grace shall be accomplished.

> He did not want any greatness in anybody there, but some poor needy one in whom he could display his power.

What our Lord wanted on that particular Sabbath morning was somebody to work upon, somebody whom he might heal and so defy the traditional legality of the Pharisees who said that it was wrong to heal on the Sabbath day. Christ did not want their health that morning; he looked out for their sickness that he might illustrate his healing power. He did not want any greatness in anybody there, but he did want some poor needy one in whom he could display his power to heal. And that is just the case today. If you are rich and increased in goods and have need of nothing, my Master does not want you. He is a physician, and those who practice the healing art look out for sickness as their sphere of operation. If we were to tell a wise physician about a town where nobody was sick, but everybody enjoyed perfect health, he would not settle there unless he wished to retire from practice. My Master does not come into the assemblies where all feel themselves quite content with themselves, where there are no blind eyes, no deaf ears, no broken hearts, and no withered hands; for what do such folks need with a Savior? He looks around and his eye fixes itself upon pain, upon necessity, upon incapacity, upon sinfulness, upon everything to which he can do good; for what he wants in us mortals is the opportunity to do us good and not a pretense on our part that we can do him good.

I begin with this because my talk today will be very simple, and it will only be meant for those of you who want my Lord and Master. Those of you who do not need him can go; but you that want him, it may be you shall find him today, and there shall be the record kept in heaven, not of those who were here who said, "We see," nor of those who said, "Our hand is strong and skillful for labor," but of blind ones who shall say, "Thou Son of David, open our eyes," and of withered ones who shall today stretch out their withered hands in obedience to his divine command. I do not know that our crippled friend when he went to the synagogue that morning expected to get his withered hand healed. Being, perhaps, a devout man, he went there to worship, but he got more than he went for. And it may be that some of you whom God means to bless today do not know what you have come here for. You came because you somehow love the ordinances of God's house, and you feel happy in hearing the gospel preached. You have never yet laid hold of the gospel for yourselves, never enjoyed its privileges and blessings as your own, but still you have a hankering after the best things. What if today the hour has come, the hour which sovereign grace has marked with a red letter in the calendar of love, in which your withered hand shall be made strong, and your sin shall be forgiven? What bliss if you shall go your way to glorify God because a notable miracle of grace has been worked in you! God grant it may be so done by the power of the Holy Spirit. I entreat those of you who love the Master to pray him to work wonders at this time upon many, and his shall be the praise.

First, we will say a little about the person to whom the command in our text is addressed. *Then saith he to the man, Stretch forth thine hand.*

This command was addressed, then, to *a man who was hopelessly incapable of obeying. Stretch forth thine hand.* I do not know whether his arm was paralyzed, or only his hand. As a general rule, when a thorough paralysis, not a partial one, takes place in the hand it seizes the entire member, and both hand and arm are paralyzed. We usually speak of this man as if the entire limb had been dried up, and yet I do not see either in Matthew, Mark, or Luke any express declaration that the whole arm was withered. It seems to me to have been a case in which the hand only was affected. We used to have, not far from here, I remember, at Kennington Gate, a lad who would frequently get on the step of the bus and exhibit his hands, which hung down as if his wrists were broken, and he would cry, "Poor boy! poor boy!" and appeal to our compassion. I imagine that his case was a picture of the one before us in which not the arm, perhaps, but the hand had become dried up. We cannot decide positively that the arm was still unwithered, but we may notice that our Lord did not say, "Stretch out *thine arm,*" but *thine hand,* so that he points to the hand as the place where the paralysis lay. If he had said, "Stretch out thine arm," as the text does not declare that the arm was dried up, we would have said that Christ bid him to do exactly what he was capable of doing, and there would have been no miracle in it. But inasmuch as he says, *Stretch forth thine hand,* it is clear that the mischief was in the hand, if not in the arm; and so it was putting him to do what he could not possibly do, for the man's hand was assuredly withered. It was not a sham disease. He had not made a pretense of being paralyzed, but he was really incapable. The hand had lost the moisture of life. The spirits which gave it strength had been dried out of it, and there it was a withered, wilted, useless thing, with which he could do nothing; and yet it was to such a man that Jesus said, *Stretch forth thine hand.*

This is very important for us to notice, because some of you under a burden of sin think that Christ does not save real sinners – that those people whom he does save are, in some respects, not quite so bad as you – that there is not such an intensity of sin about them as about your case, or if there is an intensity of sin, it is not such an utter hopelessness and helplessness as there is about you. You feel quite dried up and utterly without strength. Dear hearer, it is exactly to such as you that the Lord Jesus Christ directs the commands of the gospel. We are bidden to preach to you, saying, "Believe," or at other times, *"Repent, and each of you be baptized"; "Believe in the Lord Jesus Christ, and you will be saved"* – commandments not addressed, as some say they are, to sensible sinners, but to insensible sinners, to stupid sinners, to sinners who cannot, so far as moral ability is concerned, obey the commands at all. Such are bidden to do so by him, who in this case bid the man to do what he, naturally in and of himself, was quite incapable of doing. For you see that if he could stretch out his hand himself, there was no miracle needed, for the man's hand was not withered at all. But it is clear that he could not move his hand, and yet the Savior addressed him as if he could. In this I see a symbol of the gospel way of speaking to the sinner, for the gospel cries to him in all his misery and incapacity, "To you, even to you, is the word of this salvation sent." This very incapacity and inability of yours is but the space in which the divine power may be displayed, and because you are thus incapable, and because you are thus unable, therefore to you does the gospel come, so that the excellency of the power may be seen to dwell in the gospel and in the Savior himself, and not at all in the person who is saved.

> As soon as a man truly longs for salvation, then has salvation already come to him.

The command, then, which brought healing with it, was addressed to one who was utterly incapable. But, mark you, it came to *one who was perfectly willing,* for this man was quite prepared to do whatever Jesus bid him to do. If you had questioned him you would have found no desire to retain that withered hand – no wish that his fingers should remain lifeless and useless. If you had said to him, "Poor man, would you like to have your hand restored?" tears would have been in his eyes, and he would have replied, "Alas, that I would, so that I might earn bread for my dear children; that I might not have to go about begging, and have to depend upon the help of others, or only earn a hard crust with this left hand of mine. I wish above all things that I could have my hand restored!" But the worst thing about many unconverted people is that they do not want to be healed – do not want to be restored. As soon as a man truly longs for salvation, then has salvation already come to him; but most of you do not wish to be saved. "Oh," say you, "we truly wish to be saved." I do not think so, for what do you mean by being saved? Do you mean being saved from going down to hell? Everybody, of course, wishes that. Did you ever meet a thief that would not like to be saved from going to prison or being locked up by the policeman? But when we talk about salvation, we mean being saved from the habit of wrongdoing; being saved from the power of evil, the love of sin, the practice of folly, and the very power to find pleasure in transgression. Do you wish to be saved from pleasurable and gainful sins? Find me the drunkard who sincerely prays to be delivered from drunkenness. Bring me an impure man who longs to be pure. Find me one who is a habitual liar and yet longs to speak the truth. Bring me one who has been selfish and who in his very heart hates himself for it, and longs to be full of love and to be made Christlike. Why, half the battle is won in such cases. The initial step is taken. The parallel holds good in the spiritual world. The character I have in my mind's eye is the case of a soul desiring to be what it cannot be, and to do what it cannot do, and yet desiring it. I mean the man who cries in agony, *The willing is present in me, but the doing of the good is not.* "I would, but cannot, repent. My heart feels like a stone. I would love Christ, but alas, I feel that I am fettered to the world. I would be holy, but alas, sin comes violently upon me and carries me away."

> **He comes to you that want him, to you that are guilty.**

It is to such people that Jesus Christ's gospel comes with the force of a command. Will you be made whole, my friend? Then you may be. Do you desire to be saved from sin? You may be. Do you wish to be emancipated from the bondage of corruption? You may be. And this is the way in which you may be saved – *"Believe in the Lord Jesus, and you will be saved."* His name is called *Jesus,* for he shall save his people from their sins. He has come on purpose to do this to real sinners, and not to mere pretenders, for it is clear that he cannot save men from sins if they have none. He cannot heal withered hands if there are no withered hands to be healed. He comes to you that want him, to you that are guilty, to you whose hands are withered. Even to you is this glorious word of the good news proclaimed. God grant you grace to hear it believingly and to feel its power!

Secondly, I want to speak a little upon the person who gave the command. It was *Jesus* who gave it. *He* said, *Stretch forth thine hand.*

Did our Lord speak this in ignorance, supposing that the man could do so? By no means, for in him is abundant knowledge. He had just read the hearts of the Pharisees, and you may be sure that he who could read those subtle spirits could certainly see the outward condition of this patient. He knew that the man's hand was withered, and yet he said, *Stretch forth thine hand.* When I read in Scripture the command, *"Believe in the Lord Jesus,"* I am sure that Jesus Christ knows what he is saying. *Go ye,* said he, *into all the world, and preach the gospel to every creature* (KJV). Yes, to every creature. Suppose that some of his disciples had been very orthodox, and had come back and said, "Lord, was there not a mistake about the persons? Why preach to every creature? Are not some of them dead in sin? We would rather preach to character." I have heard some of Christ's professed servants say that to bid dead sinners to live is of no more use than to shake a handkerchief over the graves in which the dead are buried; and my reply to them has been, "You are quite right. Do not do it, for it is evident you are not called to it. Go home and go to bed. The Lord never sent you to do anything of the kind, for you acknowledge that you have no faith in it." But if my Master sent *me* as the herald of resurrection, and bid me to shake a handkerchief over the graves of the dead, I would do it, and I should expect that this poor handkerchief, if *he* commanded it to be shaken, would raise the dead, for Jesus Christ knows what he is doing when he sends his servants. If he does not send us, it is a fool's errand indeed to go and say, "You dead men, live!" But his commission makes all the difference. We are to say to the dead, "Awake, and Christ shall give you life." What, wake first, and then get life afterwards? I shall not try to explain it, but that is the order of the Scripture: *"Awake, sleeper, and arise from the dead, and Christ will shine on you."* If my Master puts it so, I am quite satisfied to quote his words. I cannot explain it, but I delight to take him in his own way, and blindly follow his every step, and believe his every word. If he bids me to say, *"Arise from the dead,"* I will gladly do it now. In the name of Jesus, you dead ones, live. Break, you hard hearts. Dissolve, you hearts of steel. Believe, you unbelievers. Lay hold of Christ, you ungodly ones. If he speaks by his ministers, that word shall be with power; if he speaks not by us, it is little matter how we speak. Well may the judicious brother say that there would be no use in *his* bidding the dead to arise, for he confesses that his Master is not with him. Let him, therefore, go home till his Master is with him. If his Master were with him, then he would speak his Master's word, and he would not be afraid of being called foolish. It is the Lord Jesus Christ who says to this man with the withered hand, *Stretch forth thine hand*.

To me it is a sweet thought that he is able to give power to do what he gives the command to do. Dear soul, when you are bidden to believe, and you stand with tears in your eyes and say, "Sir, I cannot understand, and I cannot believe," do you not know that he who bids you to believe can give you power to believe? When *he* speaks through his servants, or through his Word, or directly by his Spirit upon your conscience, he who bids you to do this is no mere man, but the Son of God, and you must say to him, "Lord, I beg you to give me now the faith which you do ask of me. Give me the repentance you do command"; and he will hear your prayer, and faith shall spring up within you.

Did you never notice, dear souls, Christ's way of doing his work? His way is generally this – first, to give the command, then to help the heart to turn the command into a prayer, and then to answer that prayer by a promise. Take these specimens. The Lord says, *"Make yourselves a new heart."* That is clearly a command. But by and by you find the psalmist David, in the fifty-first psalm, saying, *Create in me a clean heart, O God*. And then, if you turn to Ezekiel, you get the promise: *"I will give you a new heart."* First, he commands you; next, he sets you praying for the blessing; and then he gives it to you.

Take another; the command is, *"Turn back, turn back from your evil ways! Why then will you die, O house of Israel?"* Then comes the prayer, *"Bring me back that I may be restored"*; and then follows the blessed turning of which the apostle Paul speaks when he says that God has sent his Son to bless us by turning every one of us from his iniquity.

Take another case, and let it refer to cleansing. We find the Lord commanding us to *clean out the old leaven;* and immediately there comes the prayer, *Purify me with hyssop, and I shall be clean,* and then on the heels of it comes the promise, *"I will . . . smelt away your dross."* Or, take another kind of precept, of a sweeter sort, belonging to the Christian. You are continually told to sing, *"Sing praises to God, sing praises; sing praises to our King, sing praises."* In another place we meet with the prayer, *O Lord, open my lips, that my mouth may declare Your praise;* and in a third Scripture we have the divine promise: *"The people whom I formed for Myself will declare My praise."* See, then, the Master's way of going to work – he commands you to believe, or repent; he then sets you a-praying that you may be enabled to do it, and then he gives you grace to do it, so that the blessing may really come to your soul. For everywhere gospel commands are uttered by Christ himself to men's hearts, and they, receiving them, find the ability coming with the command.

"But he is not here," says one, "he is not here." Truly I say unto you in his name, he is here. His word is, *"Lo, I am with you always, even to the end of the age."* Till this dispensation shall be ended, Christ will be where the gospel is preached. Where his message is honestly and truthfully delivered with the Spirit of God, there Jesus Christ himself is virtually present, speaking through the lips of his servants. Therefore, dear soul with the withered hand, today Jesus himself says to you, *Stretch forth thine hand.* He is present to heal, and his method is to command. He now commands. O gracious Spirit, be present that men may obey.

It is time for a few words upon another point, and that is upon the command itself. The command itself was, *Stretch forth thine hand.* I notice about that command that it goes to the very essence of the matter. It is not, "Rub your right hand with your left"; it is not, "Show your hand to the priest, and let him perform a ceremony upon it"; it is not, "Wash your hand"; but it is, "Stretch it forth." That was the very thing he could not do, and thus the command went to the very root of the mischief. As soon as the hand was stretched out it was healed, and the command went directly to the desired mark.

Now, my Lord and Master does not say to any of you sinners today, "Go home and pray." I hope you will pray, but that is not the great gospel command. The gospel is *"Believe in the Lord Jesus, and you will be saved."* Paul stood in the dead of night, with the trembling jailer, who hardly understood his own question, when he cried, *"Sirs, what must*

I do to be saved?" and Paul, according to the practice of some, should have said, "We must have a little prayer," or "You must go home and read the Bible, and I must further instruct you until you are in a better state." He did nothing of the sort; but there and then Paul said, *"Believe in the Lord Jesus, and you will be saved."* There is no gospel preached unless you come to this; for salvation comes by faith, and by nothing short of it. That is just the difficult point, you tell me. Yes, and at the difficult point this command strikes and says, *Stretch forth thine hand;* or in the case of the sinner, *"Believe in the Lord Jesus."* For, remember, all that any of you ever do in the matter of eternal life, which has not faith in it, can be nothing after all but the effort of your carnal nature, and that is death. What can come of the movements of death but a still deeper death? Death can never produce life. Prayer without faith! What sort of prayer is it? It is the prayer of a man who does not believe God. Shall a man expect to receive anything of the Lord if he does not believe that God is, and that he is the rewarder of them that diligently seek him? "Oh, but I must repent before I believe," says one. What kind of repentance is that which does not trust God – does not believe in God? An unbelieving repentance – is it not a selfish expression of regret because of punishment incurred? Faith must be mixed with every prayer and every act of repentance, or they cannot be acceptable; and hence we must go right straight to this point, and demand faith, saying, "Believe and live"; *Stretch forth thine hand.*

That stretching forth of the hand was entirely *an act of faith.* It was not an act of sense. As a matter of sense and nature the man was powerless for it. He only did it because his faith brought the ability. I say it was a pure act of faith, that stretching out of the hand. "I do not understand as yet," says one, "how a man can do what he cannot do." But you will understand a great many other wonderful things when the Lord teaches you, for the Christian life is a series of paradoxes; and for my own part, I doubt an experience unless there is something paradoxical about it. At any rate I am sure that it is so – that I who can do nothing of myself can do everything through Christ who strengthens me. The

> All that any of you ever do, which has not faith in it, can be nothing but the effort of your carnal nature.

man who is seeking Christ can do nothing, and yet, if he believes on Christ, he can do everything, and his withered hand is stretched out.

But, in addition to its being an act of faith, it seems to me it was *an act of decision.* There sit the haughty, frowning Pharisees. Your imagination can easily picture those fine-looking gentlemen, with fringes on their garments and phylacteries across their foreheads. There, too, are the scribes all wrapped up in their formal array – very grave and knowing men. Persons were almost afraid to look at them; they were so holy, and so contemptuous. See, there they sit, like judges of an inquest, to try the Savior. Now, Christ does, as it were, single out this poor man with a withered hand to be his witness; and by his command he practically asks him which he will do – will he obey the Pharisees or himself? It is wrong to heal on the Sabbath day, say the Pharisees. What say you with the withered hand over yonder? If you agree with the Pharisees, of course you will decline to be healed on the Sabbath day, and you won't stretch out your hand; but if you agree with Jesus, you will be glad to be healed, Sabbath or no Sabbath. Ah, I see, you will stretch out your hand and break away from the tyrants who would keep you withered. The man did as good as vote for Christ when he stretched forth his hand. Many a soul has found peace when at last he has held up his hand and said, "Sink or swim, lost or saved; Christ for me, Christ for me! If I perish I will cling to his cross-foot, and to him alone will I look; for I am on his side, whether he will have compassion upon me or not." When that act of decision is performed, then comes the healing. If you hold up your hand for Christ, he will make it a good hand though now it is all paralyzed and drooping like a dead thing. Unworthy as you are, he has the power, as you hold up your hand for him, to put life into it, and to give you the blessing your heart desires.

I think I hear somebody say, "Oh, sir, you would not be praising me too much if you were to say that I do wish to be saved, and saved in Christ's own way; I would give my very eyes to love him." Ah, you need not lose your eyes; give him your trust, give him your soul's eyes. Look to him and live. "Oh, that I could be saved," says one; "How I long for it." May the Holy Spirit lead you to resolve in your own soul that you will not be saved by anybody but Christ. O that you would determine –

> He that suffered in my stead,
> > Shall my Physician be;
> I will not be comforted
> > Till Jesus comforts me.

When that is done, I do not doubt that through faith in the physician, you will be revived by divine power, and you will find healing at once.

So I will just lead you on, in the fourth place, to notice this man's obedience. We are told that he stretched forth his hand. Christ said, *Stretch forth thine hand.* Mark says, *And he stretched it out.* That is to say, he stretched forth his hand. Now, observe that *this man did not do something else in preference to what Jesus commanded,* though many awakened sinners are foolish enough to try experiments. Christ said, *Stretch forth thine hand, and he stretched it out.* If, instead of that, the man had walked across the synagogue and brought himself up to Christ, the Master would have said, "I commanded you to do no such thing. I commanded you to stretch forth your hand." Suppose he had then with his left hand begun to grasp the roll of the law as it stood in the synagogue, and had kissed it out of reverence – would that have been of any use? The Master would only have said, "I commanded you to stretch forth your hand." Alas, there are many, many souls that say, "We are bidden to trust in Jesus, but instead of that we will heed the means of grace regularly." Do that by all means, but not as a substitute for faith, or it will become a vain confidence. The command is, "Believe and live"; attend to that, whatever else you do. "Well, I shall take to reading good books; perhaps I shall get good that way." Read the good books by all means, but that is not the gospel. The gospel is *"Believe in the Lord Jesus, and you will be saved."*

Suppose a physician has a patient under his care, and he says to him, "You are to take a bath in the morning; it will be of very great service to your disease." But the man takes a cup of tea in the morning instead of the bath, and he says, "That will do as well, I have no doubt." What does his physician say when he inquires, "Did you follow my rule?" "No, I did not." "Then you do not expect, of course, that there will be any good result, for you have disobeyed me." So we, practically, say to Jesus Christ, when we are under searching of soul, "Lord, you bid me to trust you, but I would sooner do something else. Lord, I want to have horrible convictions; I want to be shaken over hell's mouth; I want to be alarmed and distressed." Yes, you want anything but what Christ prescribes for you, which is that you should simply trust him. Whether you feel or do not feel, you should just come and cast yourself on him, that *he* may save you, and he alone. "But you do not mean to say that you speak against praying, and reading good books, and so on?" Not one single word do I speak against any of those things any more than, if I were the physician I quoted, I should speak against the man's drinking a cup of tea. Let him drink his tea; but not if he drinks it instead of taking the bath which I prescribe for him. So let the man pray: the more the better. Let the man search the Scriptures; but remember, that if these things are put in the place of simple faith in Christ, the soul will be ruined. Let me give you a text; did you ever hear it quoted properly? *"You search the Scriptures because you think that in them you have eternal life; . . . and you are unwilling to come to Me so that you may have life."* That is where the life is – in Christ; not even in searching Scripture, good as the searching of Scripture is. If we put even golden idols into the place of Christ, such idols are as much to be broken as if they were idols of mud or idols of dung. It matters not how good an action is; if it is not what Christ commands, you will not be saved by it. *Stretch forth thine hand,* says he; that was the way by which the healing was to come. The man did nothing else, and he received a gracious reward.

Notice that *he did not raise any questions.* Now this man had a fair opportunity of raising questions. I think he might very fairly have stood up in his place and said, "This is inconsistent, good Master. You say to me, 'Stretch forth thine hand.' Now, you know that if I can stretch forth my hand there ails me nothing, and therefore there is no room for your miracle. And if I cannot stretch forth my hand, how can you tell me so to do?" Have you not heard some of our friends, who like to make jests of holy things, and to scoff at our doctrines of grace, declare that we teach, "You can and you can't; you shall and you shall not"? Their description is right enough, though meant to ridicule us. We do not object to their putting it thus if so it pleases them. We teach paradoxes and contradictions to the eye, if you only consider the letter; but if you get down into the innermost spirit, it is within these contradictions that the eternal truth is found. We know that the man is dead in trespasses and sins – steeped in spiritual and moral apathy, out of which he cannot raise himself; yet we by the Master's own command say, *"Awake, sleeper, and arise from the dead, and Christ will shine on you"*; or, in other words, we say to the withered hand, "Be thou stretched out," and it is done. The blessed result justifies that very teaching which in itself seems so worthy of sarcastic remarks.

Notice further that what the man did was that *he was told to stretch out his hand, and he did stretch out his hand.* If you had asked him, "Did *you* stretch out your hand?" perhaps he would have said, "Of course I did. Nobody else did." "Wait a minute, my good man. Did you *of yourself* stretch out your hand?" "Oh no," he would say, "because I have tried many times before and I could not, but this time I did do it." "Then how was it that you were able to do it?" "Jesus told me to do it, and I was willing, and it was done." I do not expect that he could have explained the rationale of it, and perhaps we cannot either. It must, indeed, have been a very beautiful sight to see that poor, withered, limp, wilted hand first hanging down, and then stretched out before all the people in the middle of the synagogue. Do you not see the blood begin to flow, the nerves gaining power, and the hand opening like a reviving flower? Oh, the delight of his sparkling eyes as at first he could only fix them upon the little finger and the thumb to see if they were really all alive! Then he turned, looked at that blessed One who had healed him, and seemed eager to fall down at his feet and give him all the praise! Even so, we cannot explain conversion and regeneration and the new birth, and all that; but we do know this, that Jesus Christ says, "Believe," and we believe. By our own power? No. But as we will to believe (and he gives us that will), there comes a power to do according to his good pleasure.

I look around me, wondering where the man is with the withered hand today, or where the woman is with the withered hand. To such I would say in my Master's name, "Stretch out that hand of yours." It is an optimistic moment. A great thing shall be done unto you. Believe it now. You have said formerly, "I never can believe." Now trust Jesus. Sink or swim, trust him.

> Venture on him, venture wholly;
>   Let no other trust intrude,
> None but Jesus
>   Can do helpless sinners good.

Our Lord Jesus never casts away a sinner who trusts in him. Oh, I would almost put it like this – If you do not feel that you can come, or ought to come, to Christ, being so unworthy, then steal in. Steal into his house of mercy, just as you have known a hungry dog to steal in where there has been something to eat. The butcher very likely would give him a kick if he saw him after a bone; but if he once gets it, he may as well make off with it and keep it to himself. There is this blessed thing about my Master – if you can get a crumb from under his table he will not take it from you, for he never casts out those that come. However they come, he neither turns them away nor takes back the blessing. He never says, "Come here, you sir, you have no right to hope in my grace." Remember the woman in the press that dared not come to Christ before his face, but who came behind him and touched the hem of his garment. She stole the cure from him, as it were, willy-nilly, and what did he say? "Come here, my woman, come here. What have you been doing? What right had you to touch my garment, and to steal a cure like this? A curse shall come upon you." Did he speak thus in indignation? Not at all, not at all! He bid her to come, and she told him the whole truth, and he said, *"Daughter, take courage; your faith has made you well."* Get at him, soul! Behind or before, push for a touch of him! Make a dash at him. If there be a crowd of devils between you and Christ, plow your way through them by resolute faith. Though you be the most unworthy wretch that ever trusted him, trust him now, that it may be told in heaven that there is a bigger sinner saved today than ever was saved before. Such a salvation will make Christ more glorious than he ever was; and if yours is a worse case than he ever touched with his healing hand to this day, well then, when he has touched and healed you, as he will, there will be more praise to him in heaven than he ever had before. O soul, I wish I

> Our Lord Jesus never casts away a sinner who trusts in him.

could persuade you to draw near to him, but my Master can do it. May he draw you by his great grace!

The last thing to consider is the result of this stretching out of the man's hand in obedience to the command. He was healed.

I have already tried to set before you the fact that the healing was *obvious;* it was also *immediate.* The man did not have to stand there a long time, but his hand was immediately healed; and yet the cure was *perfect,* for his hand was whole like unto the other, just as useful as his left hand had been, with all the extra dexterity which naturally belongs to the right hand. It was perfectly healed, though healed in a moment. You may depend upon it, that it was *permanently* healed; for, though I have heard it said that saved souls fall from grace and perish, I never believed it, for I have never read of any of the cases which our Lord cured that they became bad again. I never heard of a withered hand that was healed and was paralyzed a second time. Nor will it ever be. My Master's cures last forever. I remember seeing in the shop windows some years ago, that there was to be had within the shop a "momentary cure" for a toothache. I noticed after a few months that the proprietor of that valuable medicine, whatever it was, had discovered that nobody wanted a *momentary* cure, and so the word *momentary* was changed to the word *instantaneous,* which was a great improvement. I am afraid that some people's salvation is a momentary salvation. They get a sort of grace, and they lose it again. They get peace, and by and by it is gone. What is wanted is permanence, and there is always permanence in the work of Christ. *For the gifts and the calling of God are irrevocable,* and his healing is never revoked. O soul, do you see, then, what is to be had at this moment of Jesus? Healing for life, deliverance from the withering power of sin through life and through eternity. This is to be had by cheerful obedience to the matchless command: *Stretch forth thine hand,* or, in other words, "Trust, trust, trust."

Only this week I was talking with one who said he could not trust Christ, and I said, "But, my dear friend, we cannot have that. Could you trust *me*?" Yes, he could trust me. "Why can you trust me and not trust the Lord Jesus? I will put it the other way. If you said to me, 'I cannot trust you,' what would that imply?" "Why," said he, "it would mean, of course, that you were a very bad fellow, if I could not trust you." "Ah," I said, "that is exactly what you insinuate when you say, 'I cannot trust Jesus'; for *the one who does not believe God has made Him a liar.* Do you mean to say that God is a liar?" The person to whom I spoke drew back with horror from that consequence and said, "No, sir, I am sure that God is true." Very well then, you can certainly trust one who is true. There can be no difficulty in that; to trust and rest upon one whom you cannot doubt must follow as a matter of course upon your good opinion of him. Your belief that he is true is a sort of faith. Throw yourself upon him now. Just as I lean upon this rail with all my weight, lean like that upon the mercy of God in Christ Jesus. That is faith. If God's mercy in Christ cannot save you, be lost. Make it your sole hope and confidence. Hang on to your God in Christ Jesus as the vessel hangs upon the nail. As a man casts his whole weight upon his bed, so throw yourself unreservedly upon the divine love which was seen in Jesus, and is seen there still. If you do this you shall be saved. And I do not mean merely that you shall be saved from hell; for the power of faith, working in you by God the Holy Spirit, shall save you from loving sin any more. Being forgiven, you will henceforth love him who forgives you, and you will receive a new principle of action which shall be strong enough to break the bands of your old habits, and you shall rise into a pure and holy life. *So if the Son makes you free, you will be free indeed;* and free you shall be at once if now you trust him. The Lord grant his blessing, for Christ's sake. Amen.

Chapter 2

Jesus Angry with Hard Hearts

After looking around at them with anger, grieved at their hardness of heart, He said to the man, "Stretch out your hand." (Mark 3:5)

My text will really consist of these words: *After looking around at them with anger, grieved at their hardness of heart.* It is the divine Lord, the pitiful Jesus, the meek and lowly in heart, who is here described as being angry. Where else do we meet with such a statement while he was here among men? A poor man was present in the synagogue who had a withered hand. It was his right hand, and he who has to earn his daily bread can guess what it must be like to have that useful member dried up or paralyzed. In the same synagogue was the Savior, ready to restore to that hand all its usual force and cunning. Happy conjunction! The company that had gathered in the synagogue, professedly to worship God, would they not have special cause to do so when they saw a miracle of divine goodness? I can imagine them whispering one to another, "We shall see our poor neighbor restored today; for the Son of God has come among us with power to heal, and he will make this a very glorious Sabbath by his work of gracious power."

But I must not let imagination mislead me; they did nothing of the kind. Instead of this, they sat watching the Lord Jesus, not to be delighted by an act of his power, but to find something of which they might accuse him. When all came to all, the utmost that they would be able to allege would be that he had healed a withered hand *on the Sabbath*. Overlooking the commendation due for the miracle of healing, they laid the emphasis upon its being done on the Sabbath, and held up their hands with horror that such a secular action should be performed on such a sacred day. Now, the Savior puts very plainly before them the question, *"Is it lawful to do good . . . on the Sabbath?"* He put it in a form which only allowed one reply. The question could, no doubt, have been easily answered by these scribes and Pharisees, but then they would have condemned themselves, and therefore they were all as mute as mice. Scribes most skilled in splitting hairs, and Pharisees who could measure the border of a garment to the eighth of an inch, declined to answer one of the simplest questions about morals. Mark describes the Savior as looking around upon them all with anger and grief, as well he might.

You know how minute Mark is in his record: his observation is microscopic, and his description is graphic to the last degree. By the help of Mark's clear words you can easily picture the Savior looking around upon them. He stands up boldly, as one who had nothing to conceal, as one who was about to do that which would need no defense. He challenged observation, though he knew that his opposition to ecclesiastical authority would involve his own death, and hasten the hour of the cross. He did not defy them, but he did make them feel their insignificance as he stood looking around upon them all. Can you conceive the power of that look? The look of a man who is much given to anger has little force in it; it is the blaze of a wisp of straw, fierce and futile. In many cases we almost smile at the impotent rage which looks out from angry eyes; but a gentle spirit, like the Savior's, commands reverence if once moved to indignation. His meek and lowly heart could only have been stirred with anger by some overwhelming cause. We are sure that he did well to be angry.

Even when moved to an indignant look, his anger ended there; he only looked, but spoke no word of rebuke. And the look itself had in it more of pity than of contempt; or, as one puts it, "more of compassion than of passion." Our Lord's look upon that assembly of opponents deserves our earnest regard. He paused long enough in that survey to gaze upon each person, and to let him know what was intended by the glance. Nobody escaped the searching light which that expressive eye flashed upon each malicious watcher. They saw that to him their base conduct was appalling; he understood them, and he was deeply moved by their obstinacy.

Note well that Jesus did not speak a word, and yet he said more without words than another man could have said with them. His opponents were not worthy of a word; neither would more words have had the slightest effect upon them. He saved his words for the poor man with the withered hand; but for these people a look was the best reply. They looked on him, and now he looked on them. This helps me to understand that passage in the book of Revelation, where the ungodly are represented as crying to the rocks to cover them and the hills to hide them from the face of him that sat upon the throne. The judge has not spoken so much as a single word; not yet has he opened the books; not yet has he pronounced the sentence, *"Depart from Me, accursed ones"*; but they are altogether terrified by the look of that dignified countenance. Concentrated love dwells in the face of Jesus, the judge; but in that dread day, they will see it set on fire with wrath. The wrath of a lion is great, but it is nothing compared with that of the Lamb. I wish I had skill to describe our Lord's look, but I must ask the aid of your understandings and your imaginations to make it vivid to your minds.

When Mark has told us of that look, he proceeds to mention the mingled feelings which were revealed by it. In that look there were two things – anger and grief, and indignation and inward sorrow. *After looking around at them with anger, grieved at their hardness of heart.* He was angry that they should willingly blind their eyes to a truth so plain, an argument so convincing. He had put to them a question to which there could only be one answer, and they would not give it; he had thrown light on their eyes, and they would not see it; he had utterly destroyed their chosen pretext for opposition, and yet they would persist in opposing him. Evidently it is possible to be angry and to be right. Hard to many is the precept, *Be angry, and yet do not sin;* and this fact renders the Savior's character all the more admirable, since he so easily accomplished what is so difficult for us. He could be angry with the sin, and yet never cease to be compassionate toward the sinner. His was not anger which desired evil to its object; no touch of malevolence was in it. It was simply love on fire, love burning with indignation against that which is unlovely.

Mingled with this anger there was grief. He was heartbroken because their hearts were so hard. As Manton puts it, "He was softened because of their hardness." His was not the pitiless flame of wrath which burns in a dry eye; he had tears as well as anger. His thunderstorm brought a shower of pity with it. The Greek word is hard to translate. There is what an eminent critic calls a sort of *togetherness* in the word; he grieved with them. He felt that the hardness of their hearts would one day bring upon them an awful misery; and foreseeing that coming grief, he grieved with them by anticipation. He was grieved at their hardness because it would injure them; their blind enmity vexed him because it was securing their own destruction. He was angry because they were willfully rejecting the light which would have illuminated them with heavenly brightness, the life which could have accelerated them into fullness of joy. They were thus determinedly and resolutely destroying their own souls out of hatred for him, and he was angry more for their sakes than his own.

> Even when our Saviour grows angry with men, he is angry with them because they will not let him bless them.

There is something very admirable in our Savior even when we see him in an unusual condition. Even when he grows angry with men, he is angry with them because they will not let him bless them, because they will persevere in opposing him for reasons which they cannot themselves support, and dare not even acknowledge. If I had been one of the disciples who were with him in the synagogue, I think I should have burned with indignation to see them all sitting there, refusing to forego their hate, and yet unable to say a word in defense of it. I doubt not that the loving spirit of John grew warm. What a horrible thing that any creature in the shape of a man should act so unworthily toward the blessed Son of God, as to blame him for doing good! What a disgrace to our race, for men to be so inhuman as to wish to see their fellow man remain withered, and to dare to blame the gentle physician who was about to make him perfectly whole! Man is indeed at enmity with God when he finds an argument for hate in a deed of love.

Our first question is, *What was the cause of this anger and this grief?* Then let us ask, *Does anything of this sort rest in us?* Do we cause our Lord anger and grief? And thirdly, let us ask, *What should be our feeling when we see that something about us may cause, or does cause, him anger and grief?* Oh, that the Holy Spirit may bless this sermon to all who hear me this day!

What caused this anger and grief? It was their hardness of heart. To use other words, it was the callousness of their conscience, their lack of feeling. Their hearts had, as it were, grown thorny, and had lost their proper softness. The hand may furnish us with an illustration. Some persons have very delicate hands. The blind who read raised type with their fingers develop special sensitiveness, and this sensitiveness is of great value. But when men are put to pick oakum, or break stones, or do other rough work, their hands become hard and callous. Even so is it with the heart, which ought to be exceedingly tender, but through continuance in sin it grows callous and unfeeling. Use is second nature: the traveler's foot gets hardened to the way, his face becomes hardened to the cold, his whole constitution is hardened by his mode of life. Persons have taken deadly drugs by little and little till they have been hardened against their results. We read in history that Mithridates had used poison till at last he was unable to kill himself thereby, so hardened had he become. But hardening is of the worst kind when it takes place in the heart. The heart ought to be all tenderness, and when it is not, the life must be coarse and evil. Yet multitudes are morally struck with ossification of the heart. Do we not know some men in whom the heart is simply a huge muscle? If they have any hearts, they are made of leather, for they have no pity for anybody, no fellow feeling even for their relatives. God save us from a hard heart! It leads to something worse than death! A heart of flesh may be gone out of a man, and instead he may have a heart of stone. Scripture even calls it a heart *like flint* – unfeeling, unyielding, impenetrable, and obstinate. Those enemies of our Lord who sat in the synagogue that Sabbath day were incorrigible. They were desperately set on hating him, and they strengthened themselves in the resolve that they would not be convinced, and would not cease to oppose him, no matter what he might say or what he might do. Our Lord Jesus became angry, grieved, and sorrowful toward them.

What was their exact fault?

First, *they would not see,* though the case was clear. He had set the truth so plainly before them that they were obliged to strain their understandings to avoid being convinced. They had to draw down the blinds of the soul, and put up the shutters of the mind, to be able *not to see.* There are none so blind as those that will not see, and these were of that blindest order; they were blind people that had eyes and boasted that they could see, and therefore their sin was utterly without excuse. Ah, me! I fear that we have many around us still, who know but do not act on their knowledge; who do not wish to be convinced and converted, but harden themselves against known duty and plain right.

What was more, *what these people were forced to see they would not acknowledge.* They sullenly held their tongues when they were bound to speak. Does it not happen to many persons that the gospel forces itself upon their belief? They feel that they could not conjure up an argument against the divine truth which is set before them. The Word comes with such demonstration that it hits them with sledgehammer force; but they do not intend to acknowledge its power, and so they brace themselves up to bear the blow without yielding. They shut their mouths against the water of life which is held up to them in the golden cup of the gospel. No child could shut his teeth more desperately against medicine than they do against the gospel. Any man may take a horse to water, but ten thousand cannot make him drink; and this is proved in many a hearer of the Word. There sat these scribes and Pharisees. It is a wonder that the stones did not cry out against them; they were so doggedly determined not to admit that which they could not deny. Are there none of that breed among us still?

More than that, *while they would not see what was so plain, they were diligently seeking to spy out flaws and faults where there were none, namely, in the Lord Jesus.* So are there many who profess that they cannot understand the gospel, but they have understanding enough to fuss over it and cast slurs upon it. They have a cruelly keen eye for nonexistent errors in Scripture: they find this mistake in Deuteronomy, and the other in Genesis. What great wisdom, to be diligent in making discoveries against one's own eternal interests! The gospel of the Lord Jesus is man's only hope of salvation. What a pity to count it the height of cleverness to destroy our only hope! Alas for judgmental skeptics! They are as sharp-sighted as eagles against themselves, but they are as blind as bats to those things which make for their peace. These scribes and Pharisees tried to discover the undiscoverable, namely, some fault in Jesus, and yet they could not or would not see the wickedness of their own opposition to him.

They dared to sit in judgment upon the Lord, who proved himself by his miracles to be divine, and yet all the while they professed great reverence for God and for his law. Though they were fighting against God, *they made the pretense of being very zealous for him,* and especially for his holy day. This is an old trick of the Enemy, to fight true religion with false religion, to battle with godliness in the name of orthodoxy. This is a hollow sham, and we do not wonder that our ever-sincere and truthful Lord felt indignant at it. You will know yourselves whether you ever do this. I fear that many do. By their zeal for the externals of religion they try to justify their opposition to the vital possession of it.

Brethren, I pray that none of us may be hypocrites, for the Lord Jesus cannot endure such. He cares not for whitewashed sepulchers, but proclaims woe unto all false professors. Here let me give you a parable. In our fine old churches and cathedrals you see monuments raised to commemorate the dead. These are rich in costly marble and fine statuary, with here and there a touch of gold, and a Latin inscription flattering the dead. What a goodly show! Yet what does it all mean? Why, it means that corpses are underneath. Take down those marble slabs, remove a little earth, and you come to corruption and emotional awfulness. Graves are fitter for cemeteries than for the place which is consecrated to the living God. I do not mean by this any censure upon the tombs, which are well enough; I only use them as a parable. What shall I say of those men and women of whom they are the type and emblem? They are dead while they live, and have a form of godliness but deny the power of it; they present a fair outside, but secretly practice all manner of abominations. What have these to do in the church of God? What a horror to know that there are such in the assemblies of the saints! O my hearers, dread the hardness which would permit you to be hypocrites! Shun above all things that deadness of soul which makes a false profession possible, for this is very grievous to the Lord.

A hard heart is insensible, impenetrable, and inflexible. You can no more affect it than if you should strike your hand against a stone wall. Satan has fortified it and made its possessor to be steadfast, unmovable, always abounding in the works of sin. The enmity of such a heart leads it to resist all that is good; its hardness returns the efforts of love in the form of opposition. Our Savior saw before him persons who would oppose him no matter what he did, and who would not change their minds however they might be made to see their error. Let this suffice to explain the scene before us of our Lord grieved and angry.

I must now come closer to home, while I ask, Is there anything of this sort among us? Oh, for help in the work of self-examination!

Remember, we may grieve the Savior because of the hardness of our heart, and yet be very respectable people. We may go to the synagogue, as these did; we may be Bible readers, as the scribes were; we may practice all the outward forms of religion, as the Pharisees did; and yet the Lord Jesus may be grieved with us because of the hardness of our heart.

We may anger the Lord, and yet be strictly noncommittal. I dare say there are some here who are not Christians, and yet they never say a word against Christianity. They are strictly neutral. They judge that the less they think or say about this great matter the better. Jesus was angry that men should be silent when honesty and candor demanded speech from them. You must not think you are going to escape by saying, "I am not a professor." There can be no third party in this case. In the eternal world there is no provision made for neutrals. Those who are not with Jesus are against him, and they that gather not with him are scattering abroad. You are either wheat or tares, and there is nothing between the two. O sirs, you grieve him though you do not openly oppose him! Some of you are especially guilty, for you ought to be among the foremost of his friends. Shame on you to treat the Lord so harshly!

You may be very tender towards other people; in fact, you may have, like the old Jewish king, great tenderness towards everybody but the Lord. Did not Zedekiah say, *"The king can do nothing against you"*? I know many who are so fond of pleasing others that they cannot be

Christians. They have not the moral courage to oppose anyone for the truth's sake. O sirs, this may well make Jesus look upon you with anger and grief – that you should be so self-denying, so kind, and so considerate to others, and yet act so cruelly to him and to yourselves. To yourselves, it is a cruel kindness to save yourselves from speaking out. Your fear is driving you to spiritual suicide. To save a little present trouble you are heaping up wrath and judgment.

Alas, this hardness of heart may be in us, though we have occasional meltings! I think that man has a very hard heart who is at times deeply moved, but violently represses his emotions. He hurries home to his chamber greatly distressed, but in a short time he rallies and shakes off his fears. He goes to a funeral and trembles on the brink of the grave, but joins his merry companions, and is at his sins again. He likes to hear a stirring sermon, but he is careful not to go beyond his depth while hearing it. He is on the watch against his own welfare, and is careful to keep out of the way of a blessing. By a desperate resolve he holds out against the pressure of the grace of God, as it comes to him in exhortations and entreaties. He is often rebuked, but he hardens his neck; he is occasionally on the verge of yielding, but he recovers his evil firmness, and holds on to his way with a perseverance worthy of a better cause.

> Your outwardly moral man is often a hardened rebel against God.

How often have we hoped for better things for some of you! How often have you blighted those hopes! You must be very hard in heart to hold out so long. It shows a strong constitution when a man has frequently been near to death, and yet has recovered; and it shows an awful vitality of evil when you have been driven to the verge of repentance, and then have deliberately turned back to the way of evil, sinning against conscience and conviction.

Yes, and we may have this hardness of heart, and yet keep quite clear of gross sins. I have wondered at some men, how they have guarded themselves in certain directions, and yet have been lax in other matters. While they have gone to excess in sins against God, they have been scrupulous in avoiding wrong towards man. Their sins have not been stones, but sand. I hope they do not forget that "sand is heavy," and that a vessel can as easily be wrecked upon quicksand as upon a rock.

Your outwardly moral man is often a hardened rebel against God. His pride of character helps to harden him against the gospel of grace. He condemns others who are really no worse than himself. There is an abominable kind of caution which keeps some men out of certain sins; they are too mean to be wasteful, too fond of ease to plunge into risky sins. Many a man is carried off his feet by a sudden flood of temptation, and he sins grievously, and yet at heart he may be by no means so hardened as the cool, calculating transgressor. Woe unto the man who has learned to sin deliberately, and to measure out iniquity as if it were a lawful merchandise, to be weighed by the ounce and the pound! Why, sir, on account of the evident strength of your mind better things are expected of you. You cannot plead violence of passion, or feebleness of judgment. For you there will be reserved the deeper hell, though you escape present condemnation.

This hardness of heart may not overcome you to the full at present, and yet you may have grave cause to dread it. Hardness of heart creeps over men by insensible degrees. The most hard-hearted man in the world was not so once; the flesh of his heart was converted into stone little by little. He that can now curse and blaspheme once wept for his boyish faults at his mother's knee, and would have shuddered at the bare idea of falling asleep without a prayer. There are those about us who would give worlds to be free from the bondage of habit, so as to feel as they once did. Their soul is as parched as the Sahara, it has forgotten the dew of tears; their heart is as hot as an oven with evil passions, and no soft breath of holy repentance ever visits it. Oh, that they could weep! Oh, that they could feel! Repentance is hidden from their eyes. There remains nothing sensitive about them, except it be the base imitation of it which comes over them when they are in a sloppy state through strong drink. What calamity can be greater? What can be said of sin that is more terrible than that it hardens and deadens? Well did the apostle say, *Encourage one another every day, as long as it is still called "today," so that none of you will be hardened by the deceitfulness of sin.*

I cannot refrain from saying that among the hardened there are some who may be said especially to provoke the Lord. Among these we must mention those who, from their birth and education, received an unusually keen moral sense, but have blunted it by repeated crimes.

Those sin doubly who have had double light and special tenderness of nature. Judge, O you sons of the godly, whether there are not many such among you! Esau was all the more a *godless person* because he was a son of Isaac, he knew something about the covenant heritage, and he had certain fine touches of nature which ought to have made him a better man.

This is also true of those who have been indulged by Providence. God has dealt with them with wonderful favor; they have continued long in good health; they have been prosperous in business; their children have grown up around them; they have all that a heart can wish for. Yet God receives from them no gratitude; indeed, they hardly give a thought to him. Ingratitude is sure to bring a curse upon the man who is guilty of it. Alas, the ungrateful are numerous everywhere! Some who are well-known to me should have remembered the Lord, for he has granted them a smooth path, a full wallet, and sunshine to travel in. If there were an honest heart in you, your heart would cleave to the Lord in deep and hearty love. Silken cords of love are stronger with true men than fetters of iron are to thieves.

Let me not forget the obligations of others who have been often chastened, for this side of the question has its force also. Certain persons have endured many trials, have often suffered bodily pain, and have been brought at times to the verge of the grave; they have lost the beloved of their eyes with a stroke; they have followed their children to the grave; sorrows have been multiplied to them. Yet, after all, they are hard of heart. The fire of affliction has not softened their iron nature. Why should they be stricken anymore? They will revolt more and more. The Lord himself cries, *What shall I do with you, O Ephraim?* Long-suffering fails; mercy is weary. There are no more rods to use upon you; as the young bull kicks out against the goad, so do you resist the chastening of the Lord God. The Savior looks upon all such with that grieving anger of which the text speaks.

Alas! I dare not omit those towards whom the Savior must feel this anger very especially, because they have been the subjects of tender, earnest, and faithful ministry. I will not say much of my own personal ministry, which has been spent for years upon many of you; but assuredly if it has not affected you, it is not for lack of strong desire and intense longing to be of service to your souls. God is my witness that I have kept back nothing of his truth. I have never flattered you, neither have I occupied this pulpit to make it a platform for self-display. I have not shunned to declare unto you the whole counsel of God. But, apart from this, certain ones of you have had the tender ministries of a holy mother who is now with God, of a wise father who lives still to pray for you, of affectionate teachers who instructed you correctly, and of loving friends who sought your good. Father, your child has wooed you. Young man, your newly converted wife has agonized for you, and is agonizing even now. Very select have been the agencies used upon you. Choice and musical the voices which have endeavored to charm you. If these do not reach you, neither would you be converted though one rose from the dead. If Jesus himself were here again among men, how could even he reach you? If all the means he has already used have failed with you, I know not what is to be done with you. The Savior himself will, I fear, leave you; with a look of grief and anger he will turn from you because of the hardness of your heart. Stay, Lord Jesus, stay a little longer! Perhaps they will be won next time. Bid not your Spirit to take his everlasting flight. Do not swear in your wrath that they shall not enter into your rest, but be patient with them yet a little longer, for your mercy's sake.

We must now close. Oh, that my poor pleadings may not have been lost upon you! In many things which I have spoken there has been a loud voice to many of you; now hear me while I raise the question, What should be our feeling in reference to this subject?

First, *let us renounce forever the habit of quibbling.* These scribes and Pharisees were great word-spinners, critics, and faultfinders. They found fault with the Savior for healing on the Sabbath day. He had not broken God's law of the Sabbath; he had only exposed their error upon that point. If the Sabbath had not furnished an opportunity for objection, they would soon have found another, for they meant to object. One way or another, they resolved to contradict. Multitudes of persons in this present day are most effectually hardening their hearts by the habit of nitpicking. While others are struck by the beauty of the gospel which they hear, these people only remember a mispronunciation made by the preacher. Having commenced in this line they begin to sit in judgment on the gospel preached, and before long the Scriptures themselves are subjected to their alteration and correction. Reverence is gone, and self-sufficiency reigns supreme. They criticize God's Word. Any fool can do that, but only a fool *will* do it. They give themselves the airs of literary men; they are not like commonplace hearers, they require something more intellectual. They look down with contempt upon people who enjoy the gospel and are proving the power of it in their lives. They themselves are persons of remarkable mind, men of light and leading, and it gives them distinction to act the part of skeptics. They show their great learning by turning up their noses at the plain teachings of the Bible. It seems to be the great feature of a cultured man nowadays to wear a sneer upon his face when he meets with believers in inspiration. An idiot can attain in five minutes to a high degree of contempt of others; do not exhibit such folly. Pride of this sort ruins those who indulge it. To be unbelieving in order to show one's superiority is an unsatisfactory business. Let us never imitate that evil spirit who in the garden of Eden proved himself to be the patron and exemplification of all skeptics. Remember how he raised the question, *"Indeed, has God said?"* Forget not how he went further, and, like a sage philosopher, hinted that there was a larger hope: *"You surely will not die!"* said he. Then he proceeded to lay down a daring radical philosophy, and whispered, *"For God knows that in the day you eat from it your eyes will be opened, and you will be like God."* This old Serpent has left his trail on many minds in the present day, and you can see it in the slimy questions and poisonous suggestions of the age. Get away from nitpicking; it is of all labors the least remunerative.

Next, *let us feel an intense desire to submit ourselves unto the Lord Jesus.* If he be in the synagogue, let us ask him to heal us, and to do it in his own way. Let us become his disciples, and follow him wherever he goes. Yield yourselves unto God. Be as melted wax to the seal. Be as the water of the lake which is moved with every breath of the wind. All he wills is our salvation. Lord Jesus, let your will be done!

Let us be careful to keep away from all hardening influences, whether of books, or men, or habits, or pleasures. If there be any company which deadens us as to spiritual things, which hinders our prayers, shakes our faith, or dampens our zeal, let us get out of it, and keep out of it. If any amusement lessens our hatred of sin, let us never go near it; if any book clouds our view of Jesus, let us never read it. We grow hard soon enough through the needful contact with the world which arises out of workday life and business pursuits; let us not increase these evils. Shun the idler's talk, the scorner's seat, and the way of the ungodly. Shun false doctrine, worldliness, and strife. Keep clear of frivolity and trifling. Be in earnest, and be pure; live near to God, and remove yourself far off from the throne of iniquity.

Lastly, *use all softening influences*. Ask to have your heart daily rendered sensitive by the indwelling of the reviving Spirit. Go often to hear the Word; it is like a fire, and like a hammer breaking the rock in pieces. Dwell at the foot of the cross; it is there that tenderness is born in human hearts. Jesus makes all hearts soft, and then stamps his image on them. Entreat the Holy Spirit to give you a very vivid sense of sin, and a very intense dread of it. Pray often according to the tenor of Charles Wesley's hymn, in which he cries,

> Quick as the apple of an eye,
>   O God, my conscience make!
> Awake my soul when sin is nigh,
>   And keep it still awake.
>
> Oh, may the least omission pain
>   My well-instructed soul;
> And drive me to the blood again,
>   Which makes the wounded whole!

If such be the condition of our heart, our Lord will not be angry with us. He will look upon us with joy, and take delight in us.

So far I have kept to the text, bearing all the while the burden of the Lord. If it be not heavy-hearing to you, it is certainly painful-preaching to me. That same love which made the loving Jesus grieved has driven me to speak after this fashion. Not that I love men as much as he did; but a spark from his fire has kindled in my soul, and is burning there according to the measure of grace given. But now, let me indulge myself with a word of the gospel. Surely there are some of you who desire to lose your hardness. You are crying to yourselves,

> Heart of stone, relent! relent!
> Melt by Jesus' love subdued!

To you there is abundant cause of hope. He who made the heart can melt it. Job said, *"It is God who has made my heart faint."* It is the peculiar office of the Holy Spirit to renew our nature; indeed, he makes us to be born again, working on the behalf of our Lord Jesus, whose royal word is, *"Behold, I am making all things new."* The Holy Spirit can work in us conviction of sin, the new birth, faith in the Lord Jesus, deep contrition, and holy tenderness. Do you desire that it should be so? Will you join me in a silent prayer that his melting operations may at this moment be felt in your soul?

To you is the word of this salvation sent. The Lord God has undertaken to glorify himself in redeeming his people from all iniquity. He has entered into covenant with his chosen, and all who believe in his Son Jesus are recognized in that number. The covenant speaks in this manner: *"Moreover, I will give you a new heart and put a new spirit within you; and I will remove the heart of stone from your flesh and give you a heart of flesh"* (Ezekiel 36:26). See how this promise exactly meets your case! That kind of heart which you so greatly need shall be given

Remember that the Lord never speaks beyond his line; there is no boasting with him.

you, though indeed it is a miracle of miracles to do it. A new arm or leg would be a wonder, but what shall be said of a new heart? The spirit which you also so greatly require is to be bestowed; your whole tone, temper, and tendency shall be altered in an extraordinary manner. The Lord can drive out the evil spirit, and then he can renew your spirit, and fill your being with his own Holy Spirit. As for that nature which refuses to feel or yield, or break or bend, the Lord is able to take this altogether away. What an operation to perform, and yet leave the patient alive! *"I will remove the heart of stone from your flesh."* None but he that made the heart could execute such delicate surgery as this. Do you think that it can never be done in your case? Remember that the Lord never speaks beyond his line; there is no boasting with him. His arm has not grown short; he is still able to save unto the uttermost. When the old heart of stone is gone, the Lord can fill up the empty space with the most gentle and sensitive affections, even as he says, *"I will give you a new heart."* By this means we shall be made to stand in awe of God's Word; we shall tremble before him; we shall also feel a childlike gratitude, a filial love, and a holy obedience. Instead of needing to be struck with a hammer, we shall feel the slightest touch of the divine finger, and shall answer to the faintest call of the divine voice. What a change!

Now this is a matter of promise. See how the verse glitters with *"I will"* and *"I will."* The Lord, who is able to perform his word, has spoken in this fashion, and he will not run back from his promise. But please read the thirty-seventh verse of this thirty-sixth chapter of Ezekiel, and mark it well. *'Thus says the Lord God, "This also I will let the house of Israel ask Me to do for them."'* Will you not ask? Will you not ask the Lord to do this for you? If so, your prayer has begun to be answered. Your desire is a token that the stone is softening, and flesh is taking its place. O Lord, grant that it may be so! Believe in the Lord Jesus that he is able to do this unto you, and it shall be according to your faith.

Chapter 3

Jesus, Not a Ghost

When the disciples saw Him walking on the sea, they were terrified, and said, "It is a ghost!" And they cried out in fear. (Matthew 14:26)

Some of the richest comforts are lost to us for lack of clear perception. What consolation could be greater to the storm-tossed disciples than to know their Master was present, and to see him clearly revealed as Lord of sea as well as land? Yet because they did not discern him clearly, they missed the incomparable consolation. What is worse, at times the dimness of our perception will even turn the rarest consolation into the source of fear. Jesus is come, and in his coming the sun of their joy has risen, but they do not perceive it to be Jesus, and therefore thinking it to be a ghost, they are filled with alarm, and cry out in dread. He who was their best friend they were as much afraid of as though he had been the archenemy. Christ walking on the wave should have put all fear to rest, but instead, they mistake him for a ghost appearing amid the storm, and foreboding darker ill. They were filled with dismay by that which ought to have lifted them up with joy. Oh, the benefit of the heavenly eye salve by which the eye is cleared! May the Holy Spirit anoint our eyes with such. Oh, the excellence of faith which, like the telescope, brings Christ near to us, and lets us see him as he is! Oh, the sweetness of walking near to Christ, and knowing him with an assured, confident, and clear knowledge, for this would give us comforts which now we miss, and at once remove from us distresses which today unnecessarily afflict us.

The subject upon which I wish to speak will be indicated to you if I supply you with the outline of it first of all. The first topic will be this: *it is too common an error to make a ghost of Christ;* and, secondly, *we are most apt to do this when Jesus is most evidently revealed;* and therefore, thirdly, *from this spring forth our greatest sorrows;* and, fourthly, *if we could be cured of this evil, Jesus would rise very much in our esteem, and many other blessed results would be sure to follow.*

It is too common an error to make a ghost of Christ.

There are some who make a Christ of a ghost. I mean they take that to be their Savior which is but a delusion. They have dreamed so, they have excited themselves up to a high pitch of presumptuous naiveness, they have persuaded themselves into false comfort, and they make their excited feeling or fancy their Christ. They are not saved, but they think they are. Jesus is not known to them. They are unspiritual, they are not his sheep, and they are not his disciples, and yet they have put something up before their mind's eye which they think to be Christ; and their ideal of Christ, which is but a ghost, is Christ to them. A terrible error! May God save us from it and bring us to know the Lord in deed and in truth by the teaching of his Holy Spirit; for to know him is life eternal. But an equally and probably a more common error is to make a ghost of Christ. More or less we have all erred in this direction. Let me show you this for reproof and direction.

First, how often we have done this *in the matter of sin and the cleansing of it.* Our sin seems to us, when we are convinced of it, very real. Real indeed it is, for our offenses against God are no imaginary ones; we have really provoked him to wrath, and he is angry with us every day. The stain of sin is not on the surface only, the leprosy also lies deep within. Sin is a horrible evil, and when our spirits have been able to see the reality and the heinousness of it, they sink within us. But oh, what a glorious thing it is when we can with equal vividness see the actual cleansing from sin which Christ confers on all believers by his precious blood! To see the scarlet and to weep over it is well, but then to see that same scarlet vanish in the pure white of the atoning sacrifice is better.

Did you ever get as clear a perception of the second as you have of the first? It is a great blessing when God makes sin to be experimentally heavy to you so that you feel it, but it is a greater blessing still when the atoning blood is quite as vividly realized, and you see the bloody sweat drops of Gethsemane, and the pouring out of the life of the Redeemer upon Calvary, and the agonies unknown by which guilt was fully atoned for before the eternal throne. My brethren, when we are under concern of soul, or even after our first conviction, when sin returns heavily upon our spirits, our fears and terrors and alarms are real enough. No one dares to say to us then that we are in a state of nervous excitement about a fable; our danger then is right before us, as clearly as the flames are before some poor person imprisoned in a burning house. We are sure of the danger; we see it, we perceive it, we feel it in the very core of our nature. But there is salvation provided by the Redeemer. He took our sin upon himself, he suffered the punishment of it, and he has put the sin away. Believing in him our sin has gone, we have a right to peace, and we are fully warranted in standing before God and saying, *Who will bring a charge against God's elect?*

What we want is not to think of this as a dreamy thing, which may or may not be, but to realize it as a fact quite as sure, quite as certain as our distress and the sin which caused it. We are not to look through the storm upon the Savior and view him as though he were a will-o'-the-wisp, a ghostly thing, while the storm that surrounds us is real. **But we are to see a real Savior for real sin, and to rejoice in real pardon**, a pardon which has buried all our sins; and to see a real salvation, a salvation which has set our feet upon a rock beyond the reach of harm. Brethren, if we came to this point about sin we should have less of the groaning, or if as much of the groaning, we should still have more of the rejoicing. We lament for sin, and we do well. I hope we shall do so till we reach the gates of heaven. Sin can never be too much lamented or repented of; but at the same time we are not so to mourn over sin as to forget that Jesus died, and thereby canceled all our guilt. No, with every note of lamentation, lift up the joyful strain of triumph, for iniquity is gone, Christ has finished transgression, made an end of sin, and he that believes in him is not condemned, neither can he be, world without end.

The same remarks apply to *the matter of our acceptance with God after our pardon*. Dear brethren and sisters, if I may speak for the rest of you, our shortcomings in Christian duty are often very painfully real to our souls. We cannot preach a sermon, or offer prayer, or give charity, or do any service for our Lord but that we feel, when all is done, that we are unprofitable servants. The faults and imperfections of our service stare us in the face, and there is not a day we live but that we are compelled to say that we come very far short of what Christians should be. In fact, we are led sometimes to question whether we can be Christians at all, and very rightly are we anxious as to the truthfulness of our professions. When we come to the Lord's Table and examine ourselves, we find many causes of anxiety, and much reason for trembling of spirit. Looking through the whole course of our Christian career, shame must cover our face. We have good reason to say, *Not to us, O Lord, not to us, but to Your name give glory*. We cannot suppose ourselves able to take any glory, for our life has been so inglorious, so undeserving, and so hell-deserving. And there are some Christians to whom this state of things is very, very, very, very painfully conspicuous. They are of a desponding turn of mind, much given to looking within, and their inward corruptions and the outward displays thereof cause them continued anxiety and alarm.

My brethren, there is so much that is good about all this, that who shall condemn it? But at the same time the sacred balance of the soul must be maintained. Are my shortcomings real? Equally real is the perfect righteousness of Jesus Christ, in which all believers always stand. Are my prayers imperfect? Alas; but equally perfect and prevalent are the prayers and intercessions of my great Advocate before the throne. Am I defiled with sin, and therefore worthy to be rejected? Is that true? Equally true is it that in him is no sin, and his eternal merits have weight with the ever-blessed Father, and stand me in good stead as he, my representative and surety, stands before the throne. Yes, I am in myself unworthy, but I am accepted in the beloved. *"I am black."* "Yes," says the believer, "it is so"; add, however, the next clause: *"but lovely."* Equally sure it is that we are lovely, yes, in God's sight, we *have no spot or wrinkle or any such thing.* As God the Father sees us in Christ Jesus, he beholds no iniquity in us. Christ has put our blemishes away, and made us lovely in his comeliness; he sees everything that is lovely in us. Christ has bestowed his own beauty upon us, for he is made this day of God unto us wisdom, righteousness, sanctification, and redemption. All we need is in Christ. Our standing is safe in him, and the love of the Father towards us comes to us without diminishment at any time, despite our flaws and failures, through the perfection of the beloved One's acceptance. Now do not overcloud this fact. Do not look at the Lord your righteousness as a ghost; do not cry out as if you thought his work to be an impalpable something that comforts others but cannot comfort you. The work of Jesus is the grandest of all facts. O for faith to grasp it and rely upon it as such!

The principle applies next in *the matter of sanctification.* Very real and close to our souls, my brethren, is the flesh; it makes us groan daily, being burdened. Very close to home for us are our corruptions; these foes of our own household worry us too much to allow us to forget them. Very plain to us also are our temptations, they await us on all sides. And the inward conflict which comes of our fallen nature, and the temptations of Satan and the world – this too is very clear. We can no more doubt our conflicts than the wounded soldier doubts the bloodiness of the battle. All these things are evermore before our eyes to our grief. But I am afraid that here, too, Christ Jesus is often to us as merely an apparition, and not as a real sharer in our spiritual conflicts.

> You have corruptions within – this is a fact; but Christ is formed in you the hope of glory – this is an equal fact.

Do you not know, beloved, that Jesus Christ is touched with tender sympathy for you in all your temptations? Do you not understand that he has prepared provision for you in all your conflicts so that you may surely win the day? Do you not even yet expect to say, I have overcome through the blood of the Lamb? Will you not at this hour shout the anticipatory note of triumph, *Thanks be to God, who gives us the victory though our Lord Jesus Christ*? You have corruptions within – this is a fact; but Christ is formed in you the hope of glory – this is an equal fact. There is that in you which would destroy you, but there is also that implanted in you which cannot be destroyed – this is equally true. You are in the first Adam made in the image of the earthly, and over this you lament; but in the second Adam you already begin to bear the image of the heavenly, and you shall perfectly bear it before long. Can you not grasp this? Alas! we do not lay hold of these things, we do not get to say, as the apostle John did, *What we have seen with our eyes, what we have looked at and touched with our hands, concerning the Word of life.* Too much is this with us a doctrine to be accepted because we are taught it, a matter to be received because some other persons have experienced it, but too little is it a subject of inward living experience. For you and me to know by blessed realization that it is so, that the Holy Spirit sent forth from the Father is in us and with us, and that Christ will overcome our sin within us by the power of the cleansing water which flowed with the blood from his side, and will as much deliver us from the power of sin, as he has already saved us from the guilt of sin – this is heavenly experience indeed.

We must not forget to illustrate this state of mind also by the condition of many saints when *under trial*. How often when the storms are out, and our poor ship is filling, do we realize everything but what we should! We are like the disciples on the Galilean sea. The ship is real – ah, how the timbers creak! The sea is real – how the hungry waves leap up to destroy them! The winds are real – see how the canvas is torn to ribbons, how the mast bends like a bow! Their own discomforts are real – wet to the skin with the spray, and drenched, and cold are they all! Their dangers are real – the ship must certainly go down with all on board! Everything is real but the Master walking on the waves; and yet, beloved, there was nothing so real in all that storm as the Master. All else might be a matter of deception to them, but he was real and true. All else did change, and pass away, and subside into calm, but he remained still the same.

Now, observe how often we are in a similar condition. Our wretched circumstances, the bare cupboard, our bodily weakness, the loss of that dear child or parent, all the distresses that await us, the dread of bankruptcy, or poverty, all these seem real. But that word, *I am with you*, appears often in such circumstances to be a matter of belief certainly, but not a matter of realization. And that promise, *God causes all things to work together for good to those who love God, to those who are the called according to His purpose* – we dare not deny it, but we are not comforted by it to the degree we should be, because we do not grip it, grasp it, know it. The holy young men in the fire knew they were in the fire, but they were safe because they knew with an equal certainty that the Son of Man was there with them. And so in the furnace you know that *all discipline for the moment seems not to be joyful, but sorrowful;* know equally well that where Jesus is, the discipline – or trial – is blessed, and the affliction has a sweetness in it unknown to anything besides.

I shall only illustrate this in two other points. My dear brethren, in the matter of *death,* I do not know whether you can all think about death without a shudder. I am afraid there are not many of us who can. It is very easy to sing, when we are here on Sundays rejoicing with all our brethren,

> On Jordan's stormy banks I stand,
>   And cast a wishful eye.

I am afraid, yes, I am afraid we would rather live than die after all. A missionary told me the story of an old negro woman in Jamaica who used to be continually singing, "Angel Gabriel, come and take Aunty Betsy home to glory," but when some wicked chap knocked at the door in the dead of night and told her the angel Gabriel was come for Aunty Betsy, she said, "She lives next door." I am afraid it may possibly be so with us, that though we think we wish the waves of Jordan to divide so that we may be landed on the other shore, we linger on the bank shivering still. It is so. We dread to leave the warm precincts of this house of clay; we cast many "a longing, lingering look behind." But why is it? It is all because we realize the dying bed, the death sweat, the pangs, the glazing eye often never turns out to be reality, but we do not realize what are sure to be realities, namely, the angelic watchers at the bedside, waiting to act as a convoy to bear our spirits up through tracts unknown of purest heavens. We do not realize the presence of the Savior receiving saints into his bosom so that they may rest there until the trumpet of the archangel sounds. We do not really grasp the rising again

> From beds of dust and silent clay,
> To realms of everlasting day.

If we did, then our songs about dying would be more true, and our readiness to depart more abiding. For what is death? It is a pin's prick at the worst, often scarce at that, the shutting of our eyes on earth and the opening of them in heaven. So rapid is the departure of the saint, and the movement of the soul from the body here to the presence of the Lord yonder, that death is scarcely anything; it is swallowed up in victory. O for the realization, then, of Jesus, and death would lose all its sting.

And once again, and this is the last illustration I will give on this point, I am afraid that in *Christian work* we very often fall into the same style of doubt. Here is an enterprise, and immediately if we are wise we realize the difficulties. If we are something more than wise we exaggerate these difficulties and conclude that with our slender means we shall never be able to grapple with them. But ah! why is it that we so seldom think of the living, present Savior, who is the church's head? Calculate the forces of the church if you will, but do not forget the most important item of all: the omnipotence of the Lord her King. Reckon up if you will all the weaknesses of her pastors, and teachers, and evangelists, and members; but when you have done that, imagine not that you have calculated all her resources, for you have only considered the very fringe thereof; the main body and the strength of the church lies in the fullness of the Godhead bodily, which dwells in the person of Jesus Christ. Shall heathendom be real? Shall priestcraft be real? Shall Roman Catholicism be real? Shall the corruption of the human heart and the alienation of the human will be real? And shall I not equally realize the omnipotence of Christ in the realm of spirit, and the irresistible power of the Holy Spirit, who can turn men from darkness into light, and from the power of Satan unto God? Let not Christ be a ghost to his church. In her worst hours, though tossed like a ship in the storm, let her Lord, as he walks on the waves, be real to her, and she will do and dare right valiantly, and the results will be glorious. Thus much on the first point.

Secondly, the worst of it is that we make Christ a ghost most when he is most really Christ, most really revealed as the Son of the Highest.

Observe, my dear brethren, when our Lord Jesus Christ walked on the land by the seashore, that none of his disciples ever said, "It is a spirit." None of them said, "It is an apparition." Yet they did not see Christ when he walked on the shore, on *terra firma*; they saw his manhood, that was all. There was no more to be seen of Christ as he walked there than there is to be seen of any other – simply a man, no Godhead is there revealed. But when Christ walked on the waves, there was more of Christ visible than there was on the land; then they saw his manhood, but they also saw his Godhead, who could make the liquid waves bear him up. There was most of Christ to be seen, and yet then they saw the least.

Is it not strange that where he uncovers most, we see least, where he reveals himself most clearly, our unbelieving eye is least able to see? Yet, mark you, Christ is never so truly Christ anywhere as when he works beyond the ordinary course of nature. He is Christ if he takes a little child upon his knee and blesses it, but more of the Christ is seen when he puts his hand upon the girl and raises her from the dead, or calls Lazarus out of the tomb. He is the Christ when he speaks a gentle word to a sorrowing heart, but oh, what a Christ he is when he says, "Winds be hushed, and waves be still!" Then is his glory laid open to faith's strengthened eye. Truly he is most himself when he is most above all others; when, as high as the heavens are above the earth, so high are his thoughts above our thoughts, and his ways above our ways. And, brethren, we have never seen Christ unless we have seen him far above all others, and acting beyond the bounds of expectation and reasoning. The Christ is half hidden when he acts as another man. The whole Christ does not appear in the ordinary run of our affairs; it is in the extraordinary, the unusual, and the unexpected, that we view the glory of Christ, and see him fully. So it is that we refuse most to discern and glorify him when he is most openly displayed. Let me show my point.

Christ, I say, walking on the sea, is most of all Christ there, and yet his disciples do not perceive him; so in *the pardon of very great sin* you see the most of Christ. Yet whenever a man has fallen into a great sin, that is, a vile sin in the esteem of others, then he says, "Ah! now I cannot be forgiven this." Why, man, Jesus is most truly Jesus when he pardons grievous iniquity. The putting away of your little transgressions, as you have thought them to be, do you think this is all he came for – to redeem such as have a little bit fallen and a little bit transgressed? Is he a little Savior for little sinners to be little worshiped? Oh! but herein he comes to be Christ in deed and in truth, when bloody murders, black adulteries, scarlet blasphemies, and crimson filthinesses are all washed away by his blood. Then we see him as "a Savior and a great one," as one who is "mighty to save." Why is it that we will not discern him when he abundantly pardons? Why, my brethren, do we honor him as he should be honored, if we only think that the sentimentalism of sin is put away by him? If we acknowledge that the reality, the filthiness, the damnableness of sin is put away by Jesus, and trust him when our sins seem blackest, foulest, and most abhorrent, then we do him honor and see him to be the Christ he is.

So it is again *in great distresses* of the soul. It pleases God often after conversion to allow the fountains of the great deeps of our corruption to be broken up, and we never felt before as we do then. We had not expected this, and are overwhelmed with surprise to find ourselves such corrupt, such deceitful, such foul things. Then at the same time Satan will invade the heart with fierce temptations and diabolical insinuations, and, alas! our suspicious spirits will imagine that Jesus himself cannot help us in such a condition. Oh, but man, now is the time for the divine manifestation! Now shall you see the Christ. Do you suppose that the Lord Jesus comes only to speak peace to those who have peace already, or to give peace to those enduring a trifling disturbance of mind? Man, do you think Jesus a superfluity? Or do you imagine that he is only suited for little occasions? Be ashamed of such insinuations; for he reigns on high above tremendous storms; he rules the hugest waves and the most roaring floods. When all our nature is vexed, when our hopes are gone, and our despair is uppermost, it is amid the tumult of such a tempest that he says, *"Hush, be still,"* and creates a calm. Believe in the Christ who can save you when most of your temptations threaten to swallow you up. Do not think him to be only able to save when you are not in extremities, but believe him to be best seen when your uttermost calamities are near.

I might select many other cases as illustrating this, but I will run over one or two in rapid review. We are perhaps enduring an *unusually severe trial,* and need more than usual support; but we fearfully say, "I cannot expect to be supported under this affliction." Ah! your Christ is a ghost, then. If you saw him you would know that there is nothing too hard for him, that the sustenance of a soul, when it is at its lowest famine point, is easy enough work for the divine Consolator, and you would cast yourself on him believingly, and not act towards him as now you do. Yes, but you need great supplies for the present time of distress; your circumstances are trying to the last degree. Do not, now that you need great supplies, make Christ to be poor and limited in your esteem, but rather, like Abraham, say, *"God will provide."* Abraham, in extremity, when about to slay his son by God's command, finds that God intercedes, and the ram is found for a burnt offering. In your worst poverty Christ will intercede; Jesus will prove himself to be the Lord of heaven and earth. You shall see that in him all fullness dwells. Can you only rely upon Jesus in little and ordinary troubles? I know it is sweet to run to him in such times, but is he to be only an ordinary, fair-weather friend to cover you from little showers, and walk with you when a little gale is blowing? Will he refuse to be with you in stormy weather, or to cross with you upon the boisterous sea? O do not so miserably spirit away the Savior! Do not phantomise the Redeemer when you need him in every deed. You have real poverty, and a real cross, and real difficulties; now in the mount of the Lord shall it be seen that he is true to his word, and his name, Jehovah-Jireh, across the darkness of your need shall be written as with letters of fire.

In times of *great* danger, again, we sometimes gloomily mutter, "Now we shall not be preserved. Christ has kept us up till now, and we quite believe that he would do so if the circumstances of today were no worse than those of times gone by. But now we are extremely tempted, now we are violently attacked, now our sorrows multiply; will he help us now?" Dare you say, "Will he?" when you know that he cannot change? Dare you say, "Can he?" Is anything too hard for the Lord? Are you going to make your Savior into a mere appearance? He is a real Savior, lean on him; he will bring you safely through, cover you with his shield, and keep the fiery darts from you. He will not leave you or forsake you. Great deliverances! alas! we imagine that these will never occur. Jesus will not work these as formerly, so we wickedly imagine; and if they are worked, we are like Peter, who could not realize his escape from prison. He knew the saints had prayed for him, but when he was delivered from the prison and found himself in the street of the city, he could not think it was a fact; *he did not know that what was being done by the angel was real, but thought he was seeing a vision.* Often before God has delivered us, we have said, "It cannot be" – our Christ was only a spirit; and when he has delivered us we have said, "I do not understand it, I am overwhelmed with amazement." The fact is, that we do not get such a grip of Christ as to be assured that he is real, present, mighty, and gracious; or if we did, we should receive even his greatest deliverances as natural proofs of his goodness and greatness such as faith is warranted to expect. "Is it not surprising," said one, "that God should have heard my prayers and have been so gracious to me in providence?" "No," said an old saint, whose long experience had taught her more of the Lord, "it does not surprise me; it is just like him, it is his way with his people." Oh, to feel that great mercy is like him; that it is what we should expect of God, that he should give great deliverances, should walk the waters of our griefs, and instruct them to cease their raging! It is a blessed faith which enables us to recognize Jesus on the waters, and to say, "I know it is Jesus, for nobody but Jesus could act so wondrously. I might not have known him if I had seen him working in an ordinary way, or traveling like a common traveler, but here amid extraordinary seasons I expected his help. If I had never seen him before, I expected to see him now; and now that I do see him, I am not amazed, though I am delighted. I looked for him, and knew that when the need of him was greatest, his coming would be sure." When faith brightens the eye of hope with the flash of expectation, joy is not far away.

I will only add that if we will but realize Christ, our *great successes* – which will be sure to come – over spiritual foes within and over difficulties without, will again infallibly prove to us his reality. But the probabilities are that we shall think him not capable of giving us such great successes, and shall toil on despondingly when we ought to have rejoiced in the Lord.

As to our ultimate future, we have too often thought it will be hard *to die*. We have trembled at standing before the judgment seat. We have read of the day of judgment and thought, "How shall I bear it?" forgetting that we shall know our Redeemer better in death than before, and in the resurrection and in the glory that shall follow we shall see him more clearly revealed than now; and therefore we ought to think more of him and lean upon him in all the great concerns of eternity with a great, a confident, and a childlike faith.

But I must pass on to the third topic. Our greatest sorrows arise from our treating our Lord as unreal.

It is because of our weakening, vaporizing, and spiriting our Lord away, and making him into a myth so often, instead of gripping him with a commonsense, practical, firm, and realizing faith that we suffer so much from our troubles. For, brethren, it is a sad cause of trouble to have a phantom Redeemer, a Savior who cannot actually pardon sin when it comes to be great sin, a Savior who gives us only a little indefinite hope about our guilt, but does not literally put it away. This is the seedbed of all manner of evil weeds. I do not wonder if you are vexed with doubts and fears if you have not realized Christ. O that you would all learn to sing with Hart these precious lines:

> A Man there is, a real Man,
>   With wounds still gaping wide,
> From which rich streams of blood once ran,
>   In hands, and feet, and side.
>
> ('Tis no wild fancy of our brains,
>   No metaphor we speak;
> The same dear Man in heaven now reigns,
>   That suffered for our sake.)

> This wondrous man, of whom we tell,
> > Is true Almighty God;
> He bought our souls from death and hell,
> > The price, his own heart's blood.

Beware, my brethren, of resting content with anything short of faith in an actual, literal, and living Mediator, for nothing but reality will be of any use to you in the matter. Of course, with a phantom Savior for real sins, an apparition of a Redeemer for real bondage, you cannot find comfort. Of what use is the appearance of bread and the resemblance of water to famishing pilgrims in the desert? If you have a phantom helper for real woes, you are the worse for such help. If your Savior does not actually and practically support you in times of need, and supply your wants and console you under depression, then in what respects are you better off than those who have no helper at all? Jesus is a friend indeed. His grace, love, and presence are not fiction; of all facts they are most sure. If I have to carry a real load, and then have a ghost to assist me, I am in truth unassisted. We want true power, force, and energy in our helper, and all that faith sees in Jesus her Lord; but you will readily see how sorrows multiply where Jesus is lightly esteemed.

Besides, to some Christ is not only, as it were, an intangible spirit, but he is also really an indifferent, unfeeling spirit. Jesus to his disciples on the sea seemed as though he would have gone by them and left them to their fate, and we often imagine that our gracious Lord is unmindful of us. At any rate, we forget that he is tenderly mindful of our case. It did not strike you when you were so poor last week that Jesus knew it and was grieved for your affliction. You forgot, dear brother, when you were trembling as you went into the pulpit that Jesus knew you trembled, and would uphold you while bearing your testimony. Too seldom do we remember that

> In every pang that rends the heart
> > The Man of Sorrows bears a part.

Ah! good husband, you knew your wife pitied you, you noted well the teardrop when she saw your grief. Ah! dear child, you knew your mother sorrowed for you. Ah, but if you did but know Christ, you would know this too, that he never puts you to an unnecessary pain, nor ever tests you with an unneeded trial. There is a necessity for all things, and he has sympathy for you in all things.

Many a poor sinner even imagines Jesus to be an angry spirit, and he cries out for fear. He imagines that Jesus is wrathful and will reject him with indignation. Ah! you do not truly realize my Savior if you think he would ever reject anyone who came to him. When on earth what a real physician of souls he was! He mingled with publicans and sinners; he did not talk about them as people who ought to be looked after, but he actually went after them himself and permitted one of them to wash his feet with her tears, and wipe them with the hairs of her head. He was accustomed to touching diseased sinners with his finger as he healed them. He was not an amateur Savior; he did not come into this world to save us from hypothetical sin and imaginary trouble. There is nothing which is more overlooked, but which ought to be better remarked about our Lord, than his commonsense practicableness. He is utterly devoid of sham and pretense. He is always in the gospel history as real as the scenes of life around him; he never strikes you as theatrical and pretentious. May we all feel that he is really a loving Savior, a tender Savior, and a practical Savior to us. May you know him, may you realize him, and then your sorrows will either come to an end, or be accepted with thanksgiving.

Lastly, if we could but be cured of this desperate mischief, our Lord Jesus Christ would have a higher place in our esteem, and many other beneficial results would follow.

For, first, did you notice that after the disciples knew it to be Christ, and he came into the ship with them, they said, *"You are certainly God's Son"*? If you once realize Christ, you will know him in his person as you never will know him by all I can tell you, or by all you can read about him. You once read about a man, you saw his likeness in the *Illustrated London News,* you heard people talk about him, but at last you were in his company, and sat down with him, and then you said, "Now I know the man; I did not before." Oh, if you can realize Christ so as to draw near to him by faith, you will feel that you now begin to know him in truth, and, what is best, you will know him then with assurance. They said, *"You are certainly God's Son!"* You were persuaded that he is God by what you found in Scripture; but when you came to see him, when he became real to you, the doctrine of his deity needed no arguments to support it, for the truth that Jesus Christ is Lord is woven into your very being. He is the Son of God to you, if to no one else. What did those mariner disciples do when they saw that it was indeed Jesus who trod the wave? It is added, *Those who were in the boat worshiped Him.* You will never worship a phantom, an image, or an apparition. Know Jesus to be real, and immediately you prostrate yourself before him. Blessed God, blessed Son of Man, coming from heaven for me, bleeding for me, standing in glory, pleading for me, I had thought of you and heard of you, but now I see you; what can I do but worship you? It is the grasping of Christ that produces devotion; it is the mistiness of our thoughts about him that is the root of our undevout frames of mind. God give us a firm hold on Christ, and we shall instinctively adore him.

They not only worshiped Christ, but they also served him. Their worship was such that whatever he bid them to do, they did it, and the vessel was steered wherever he wanted until it brought him to the other side where he wished to go. Those who realize Christ are sure to obey him. I cannot obey that which floats before me like a cloud; but when I see the man, the God, and know him to be as real a person as myself, as much a matter-of-fact existence as my brother, then what he bids me to do I do; my obedience becomes real just in proportion as the Master who commands it becomes real to my soul. Then it is, dear friends, that we become humbled in spirit. No man realizes Christ without also realizing himself, and being bowed down in self-humiliation. *"I have heard of You by the hearing of the ear; but now my eye sees You; therefore I retract, and I repent in dust and ashes."* But with the humility comes a deep and profound joy and peace. With Christ in the vessel, known to be there, we smile at the storm; whether it continues or subsides we are equally peaceful now that we have realized that Christ is with us.

I do believe that the actualizing of their Lord is the main thing that Christians want; they require, first and foremost, a real Leader, they want to grasp his reality, and feel his actual power. And is it needful for this that he should come here in person? I trust not. If he were to appear today on this platform, and his servant should hide his head, you would say, "Behold the glorious sight, yonder is our Lord." I know your heads would bow to worship, and then you would open your eyes and gaze on him, and feast your souls with the sight, and then each one would say, "What can I do for him?" And if the condescending Master gave you each permission to come and spread offerings at the feet of the Crucified One, oh, what heaps of treasure would be brought! Each one would feel, "I do not have with me what I wish," but you would say, "Take all I have, my blessed Lord, for you have redeemed me with your blood." Is not he just as dear to you now, though unseen? Is not faith as mighty a faculty as sight? Is it not *the conviction of things not seen*? Is not Wesley's verse true?

> The things unknown to feeble sense,
>   Unseen by reason's glimmering ray;
> With strong, commanding evidence,
>   Their heavenly origin display.
>
> Faith lends its realizing light,
>   The clouds disperse, the shadows fly;
> The invisible appears in sight,
>   And God is seen by mortal eye.

Does not faith make Jesus as real to us as our sight would do? It should do so; I pray it may. And then see how true will be your consecration, how abundant will be your service, how ready your thanksgiving, how abounding your offerings! May God grant you grace to get into this true position, both you who are saints and you who still are sinners, for in having a real Christ you will have the reality of every good. God give it you for Jesus' sake. Amen and Amen.

Chapter 4

Mr. Fearing Comforted

"You of little faith, why did you doubt?" (Matthew 14:31)

It seems as if doubt were doomed to be the perpetual companion of faith. As dust accompanies the chariot wheels, so do doubts naturally cloud faith. Some men of little faith are perpetually enshrouded with fears; their faith seems only strong enough to enable them to doubt. If they had no faith at all, then they would not doubt, but having that little, and but so little, they are perpetually involved in distressing surmises, suspicions, and fears. Others, who have attained to great strength and stability of faith, are nevertheless, at times, subjects of doubt. He who has colossal faith will sometimes find that the clouds of fear float over the brow of his confidence. It is not possible, I suppose, so long as man is in this world, that he should be perfect in anything; and surely it seems to be quite impossible that he should be perfect in faith. Sometimes, indeed, the Lord purposely leaves his children, withdraws the divine inflowings of his grace, and permits them to begin to sink, in order that they may understand that faith is not their own work, but is at first the gift of God, and must always be maintained and kept alive in the heart by the fresh influence of the Holy Spirit. I take it that Peter was a man of great faith. When others doubted, Peter believed. He boldly declared that Jesus was the Christ, the Son of the living God, for which faith he received the Master's commendation, *"Blessed are you, Simon Barjona, because flesh and blood did not reveal this to you, but My Father who is in heaven."* He was of faith so strong that at Christ's command he could tread the billow and find it like glass beneath his feet, yet even he was permitted in this thing to fall. Faith forsook him, he looked at the winds and the waves and began to sink, and the Lord said to him, *"You of little faith, why did you doubt?"* It was as much as to say, "O Peter, your great faith is my gift, and the greatness of it is my work. Think not that you are the author of your own faith; I will leave you, and this great faith of yours shall speedily disappear, and like another who has no faith, you shall believe the winds, and regard the waves, but shall distrust your Master's power, and therefore shall you sink."

I think I shall be quite safe in concluding today that there are some here who are full of doubt and fear. Sure I am that all true Christians have their times of anxious questioning. The heart that has never doubted has not yet learned to believe. As the farmers say, "The land that will not grow a thistle, will not grow wheat"; and the heart that cannot produce a doubt has not yet understood the meaning of believing. He that never doubted the state of his condition – he may, perhaps he may, too late. Yes, there may be timid ones here, those who are always of little faith, and there may be also great hearts, those who are valiant for truth, who are now enduring seasons of despondency and hours of darkness of heart.

> If you believe a thing, you want evidence, and before you doubt a thing, you ought to have evidence too.

Now in endeavoring to comfort you today, I would remark that the text goes upon a very wise principle. If a man believes in anything, it is always proper to put to him the question, "Why do you believe? What evidence have you that what you believe is certainly correct?" We believe on evidence. Now the most foolish part of many men's doubts is that they do not doubt on evidence. If you should put to them the question, "Why do you doubt?" they would not be able fairly to answer. Yet mark, if men's doubts be painful, the wisest way to remove them is by simply seeing whether they have a firm basis. *"You of little faith, why did you doubt?"* If you believe a thing, you want evidence, and before you doubt a thing, you ought to have evidence too. To believe without evidence is to be credulous, and to doubt without evidence is to be foolish. We should have grounds for our doubts as well as a basis for our faith. The text, therefore, goes on a most excellent principle, and it deals with all doubting minds by asking them this question: *"You of little faith, why did you doubt?"*

I shall endeavor to exhort you on the same plan today. I shall divide my sermon into two parts. First, I shall address myself to those of you who are in great trouble with regard to *worldly circumstances;* you are God's people, but you are sorely tested, and you have begun to doubt. I shall then deal with you upon *spiritual matters;* there are some here who are God's true, revived, and living people, but they are doubting. To them also I shall put the same question: *"You of little faith, why did you doubt?"*

First, then, in worldly circumstances, God has not made for his people a smooth path to heaven. Before they are crowned they must fight; before they can enter the celestial city they must fulfill a weary pilgrimage. Religion helps us in trouble, but it does not permit us to escape from it. It is through much tribulation that we inherit the kingdom. Now the Christian when he is full of faith passes through affliction with a song in his mouth; he would enter the fiery furnace itself, fearless of the devouring flame; or with Jonah he would descend into the great deeps, unalarmed at the hungry sea. As long as faith maintains its hold, fear is a stranger; but at times, during various great and sore troubles, the Christian begins to fear that surely at last he shall be overcome, and shall be left to himself to die and perish in despair.

Now, what is the reason why you doubt? I must come to the plan of the text and put the great question, *"You of little faith, why did you doubt?"* Here it will be proper for us to ask, Why did Simon Peter doubt? He doubted for two reasons: first, because he looked too much to second causes, and secondly, because he looked too little at the first cause. The answer will suit you also, my trembling brother. This is the reason why you doubt, because you are looking too much to the things that are seen, and too little to your unseen Friend who is behind your troubles, and who shall come forth for your deliverance. See poor Peter in the ship – his Master bids him come; in a moment he casts himself into the sea, and to his own surprise he finds himself walking upon the billows. He looks down, and actually it is the fact: his foot is upon a crested wave, and yet he stands erect. He treads again, and yet his footing is secure. "Oh!" thinks Peter, "this is marvelous." He begins to wonder within his spirit what manner of man *he* must be who has enabled him thus to tread the treacherous deep. But just then, there comes howling across the sea a terrible blast of wind; it whistles in the ear of Peter, and he says within himself, "Ah! here comes an enormous billow driven forward by the blast; now, surely, I must, I shall be overwhelmed." No sooner does the thought enter his heart than down he goes, and the waves begin to enclose him. So long as he shut his eye to the billow, and to the blast, and kept it only open to the Lord who stood there before him, he did not sink; but the moment he shut his eye to Christ, and looked at the stormy wind and treacherous deep, down he went. He might have crossed the leagues of the Atlantic, he might have crossed the broad Pacific if he could but have kept his eye on Christ, and never a billow would have yielded to his tread. But he might have been drowned in a sheer brook if he began to look at second causes, and to forget the Great Head and Master of the universe who had bidden him to walk on the sea. I say, the very reason of Peter's doubt was that he looked at second causes and not at the first cause. Now, that is the reason why *you* doubt.

Let me just probe you now for a while. You are in despondency about worldly affairs; what is the reason why you are in trouble? "Because," say you, "I never was in such a condition before in my life. Wave upon wave of trouble comes upon me. I have lost one friend and then another. It seems as if business had altogether run away from me. Once I had a flood tide, and now it is an ebb, and my poor ship grates upon the gravel, and I find she has not water enough to float her – what will become of me? And, oh! sir, my enemies have conspired against me in every way to cut me up and destroy me; opposition upon opposition threatens me. My shop must be closed; bankruptcy stares me in the face, and I know not what is to become of me." Or else your troubles take another shape, and you feel that you are called to some eminently arduous service for your Lord, and your strength is utterly insignificant compared with the labor before you. If you had great faith it would be as much as you could do to accomplish it, but with your poor little faith you are completely beaten. You cannot see how you can accomplish the matter at all. Now, what is all this but simply looking at second causes? You are looking at your trouble, not at the God who sent your trouble; you are looking at yourselves, not at the God who dwells within you, and who has promised to sustain you. O soul! it would be enough to make the mightiest heart doubt, if it should look only at things that are seen. He that is nearest to the kingdom of heaven would have cause to droop and die if he had nothing to look at but that which eye can see and ear can hear. What wonder, then, if you are downcast, when you have begun to look at the things which always must be enemies to faith.

But I would remind you that you have forgotten to look to Christ since you have been in this trouble. Let me ask you, Have you not thought less of Christ than you ever did? I will not suppose that you have neglected prayer, or have left your Bible unread; but still, have you had any of those sweet thoughts of Christ which you once had? Have you been able to take all your troubles to him and say, "Lord, you know all things; I trust all in your hands." Let me ask you, Have you considered that Christ is omnipotent, and therefore able to deliver you; that he is faithful, and must deliver you, because he has promised to do so? Have you not kept your eye on his rod, and not on his hand? Have you not looked rather to the crook that struck you, than to the heart that moved that crook? Oh, recollect, that you can never find joy and peace while you are looking at the things that are seen, the second causes of your trouble; your only hope, your only refuge and joy must be to look to him who dwells within the veil. Peter sunk when he looked to outward providences, and so must you. He would never have ceased to walk the wave, never would he have begun to sink, if he had looked only to Christ, nor will you if you will look only to him.

And here let me now begin to argue with such of you as are the people of God, who are in sore trouble lest Christ should leave you to sink. Let me forbid your fears by a few words of consolation. You are now in Peter's condition; you are like Peter – *you are Christ's servant.* Christ is a good master. Will he not take care of his own? Peter, when he was in the water, was where his Master had called him to be; and you in your trouble now are not only Christ's servant, but you are also where Christ has chosen to put you. Your afflictions, remember, come neither from the east nor from the west; neither does your trouble grow out of the ground. All your suffering is sent upon you by your God. The medicine which you now drink is compounded in heaven. Every grain of this bitterness which now fills your mouth was measured by the heavenly physician.

There is not an ounce more trouble in your cup than God chose to put there. Your burden was weighed by God before you were called to bear it. The Lord who gave you the mercy has taken it away; the same God who has blessed you with joy is he that has now plowed you with grief. You are where God put you. Ask yourself this question then: Can it be possible that Christ would put his own servant into a perilous condition and then leave him there? I have heard of fiends, in fables, tempting men into the sea to drown them; but is Christ a siren? Will he entice his people onto the rocks? Will he tempt them into a place where he shall destroy them? God forbid. If Christ calls you into the fire, he will bring you out of it; and if he bids you to walk on the sea, he will enable you to tread it in safety. Doubt not, soul; if you had come there of yourself, then you might fear, but since Christ put you there, he will bring you out again. Let this be the pillar of your confidence – you are his servant, he will not leave you; you are where he put you, he cannot permit you to perish. Look away, then, from the trouble that surrounds you, to your Master, and to his hand that has planned all these things.

> If Christ calls you into the fire, he will bring you out of it.

Remember, too, who it is that has put you where you are. It is no harsh tyrant who has led you into trouble. It is no stern, unloving heart who has bidden you to pass through this difficulty to gratify a capricious whim. Ah, no; he who troubles you is *Christ*. Remember his bleeding hand; and can you think that the hand which dripped with gore can ever hang down when it should be stretched for your deliverance? Think of the eye that wept over you on the cross; and can the eye that wept for you be blind when you are in grief? Think of the heart that was opened for you; and shall the heart that did bleed its life away to rescue you from death be hard and unemotional when you are overwhelmed in sorrow? It is Christ who stands on yonder billow in the midst of the tempest with you. He is suffering as well as you are. Peter is not the only one walking on the sea; his master is there with him too. And so is Jesus with you today – with you in your troubles, suffering *with* you as he suffered *for* you. Shall he leave you? He that bought you, he who is married to you, he that has led you thus far, has helped you up to this time, he who loves you better than he loves himself, shall he forsake you? O turn your eyes from the rough billow. Listen no longer to the howling tempest, but turn your eyes to him, your loving Lord, your faithful friend, and fix your trust on him, who even now in the midst of the tempest, cries, *"It is I; do not be afraid."*

One other reflection will I offer to such of you as are now in sore trouble on account of worldly matters, and it is this – *Christ has helped you up to this time.* Should not this console you? Ah, Peter, why could you fear that you would sink? It was miraculous enough that you did not sink at first. What power is it that has held you up till now? Certainly not your own. You would have fallen at once to the bottom of the sea, O man, if God had not been your helper. If Jesus had not made you buoyant, Peter, you would soon have been a floating carcass. He who helped you then to walk so long as you could walk, surely he is able to help you all the way until he shall grasp your hand in paradise to glorify you with himself. Let any Christian look back to his past life, and he will be astonished that he is what he is and where he is. The whole Christian life is a series of miracles, wonders linked into wonders, in one perpetual chain. Marvel, believer, that you have been upheld till now; and cannot he that has kept you to this day preserve you to the end? What is yonder roaring wave that threatens to overwhelm you – what is it? Why, you have endured greater waves than these in the past. What is yonder howling blast? Why, he has saved you when the wind was howling worse than that. He that helped you in six troubles will not forsake you in this. He who has delivered you out of the paw of the lion and out of the paw of the bear, he will not, he cannot, forsake you now.

In all this, I have labored to turn your eyes from what you are seeing to that which you cannot see, but in which you must believe. Oh! if I might but be successful, though feeble be my words, yet mighty should be the consolation which should flow therefrom.

A minister of Christ, who was always in the habit of visiting those whom he knew to be noted for devotion, in order that he might learn from them, called upon an aged Christian who had been distinguished for his holiness. To his great surprise, however, when he sat down by his bedside, the aged man said, "Ah! I have lost my way. I did think at one time that I was a child of God, but now I find that I have been a stumbling block to others. For these forty years I have deceived the church and deceived myself, and now I discover that I am a lost soul." The minister very wisely said to him, "Ah! then I suppose you like the song of the drunkard, and you are very fond of the amusements of the world, and delight in profanity and sin?" "Ah! no," said he, "I cannot bear them; I could not endure to sin against God." "Oh," said the minister, "then it is not at all likely that God will lock you up in hell with men that you cannot bear here. If now you hate sin, depend on it that God will not shut you up forever with sinners. But, my brother," continued the minister, "tell me what has brought you into such a distressed state of mind?" "O sir," said he, "it was looking away from the God of providence to myself. I had managed to save about one hundred pounds, and I have been lying here ill now this last six months, and I was thinking that my one hundred pounds would soon be spent, and then what should I do? I think I shall have to go to the workhouse, I have no friend to take care of me, and I have been thinking about that one hundred pounds of mine. I knew it would soon be gone, and then, then, how could the Lord provide for me? I never had either doubt or fear till I began to think about worldly matters. The time was when I could leave all that with God. If I had not had one hundred pounds, I should have felt quite sure he would provide for me; but I begin to think now that I cannot provide for myself. The moment I think of that, my heart is darkened." The minister then led him away from all trust in an arm of flesh, and told him his dependence for bread and water was not on his one hundred pounds, but on the God who is the possessor of heaven and earth – that as for his bread being given him and his water being sure, God would take care of that, for in so doing he would only be fulfilling his promise. The poor man was enabled in the matter of providence to cast himself entirely upon God, and then his doubts and fears subsided, and once more he began to walk the sea of trouble and did not sink.

O believer, if you take your business into your own hands, you will soon be in trouble. The old Puritan said, "He that carves for himself will soon cut his fingers," and I believe it. There never was a man who began to take his own matters out of God's hand that was not glad enough to take them back again. He that runs before the cloud runs a fool's errand. If we leave all our matters, secular as well as spiritual, in the hand of God, we shall lack no good thing; and what is better still, we shall have no care, no trouble, no thought; we shall cast all our burden upon him for he cares for us. There is no need for two to care: for God to care and the creature too. If the Creator cares for us, then the creature may sing all day long with joy and gladness:

> Mortals cease from toil and sorrow,
>   God provideth for the morrow.

But now, in the second part of the discourse, I have to speak of spiritual things. To the Christian, these are the causes of more trouble than all his worldly trials. In the matters of the soul and of eternity many doubts will arise. I shall, however, divide them into two sorts – doubts of our present acceptance, and doubts of our final perseverance.

Many there are of God's people who are much vexed and troubled with doubts about their present acceptance. "Oh," say they, "there was a time when I knew I was a child of God; I was sure that I was Christ's. My heart would fly up to heaven at a word; I looked to Christ hanging on the cross, I fixed all my trust on him, and a sweet, calm, and blessed rest filled my spirit.

> What peaceful hours I then enjoyed;
> How sweet their memory still!
> But they have left an aching void,
> The world can never fill.

And now," says this doubting one, "now I am afraid I never knew the Lord; I think that I have deceived myself, and that I have been a hypocrite. Oh, that I could but know that I am Christ's, I would give all I had in the world, if he would but let me know that he is my beloved, and that I am his."

Now, soul, I will deal with you as I have been just now expounding on Peter. Your doubts arise from looking to second causes and not to Christ. Let us see if this is not the truth. Why do you doubt? Your answer is, "I doubt because I feel my sin so much. Oh, what sins have I committed! When first I came to Christ I *thought* I was the chief of sinners; but now I *know* I am. Day after day I have added to my guilt; and since my pretended conversion," says this doubting one, "I have been a bigger sinner than ever I was before. I have sinned against light and against knowledge, against grace, and mercy, and favor. Oh, never was there such a sinner under God's heaven out of hell as I am." But, soul, is not this looking to second causes? It is true, you are the chief of sinners; take that for granted, and let us not dispute it. Your sins are as evil as you say they are, and a great deal more so. Depend on it, you are worse than you think yourself to be. You think you are bad enough, but you are not so bad in your own estimation as you really are. Your sins seem to you to be like roaring billows, but in God's sight they are like towering mountains without summit. You seem to yourself to be black – black as the tents of Kedar; in God's eyes you are blacker still. Set that down, to begin with, that the waves are big, and that the winds are howling; I will not dispute that. I ask you, What have you to do with that? Does not the Word of God command you to look to Christ? Great as your sins are, Christ is greater than them all. They are black, but his blood can wash you whiter than snow. I know your sins deserve damnation, but Christ's merits deserve salvation. It is true, the pit of hell is your lawful portion, but heaven itself is your gracious portion. What! Is Christ less powerful than your sin? That cannot be! To suppose *that* would be to make the creature mightier than the Creator. What! Is your guilt more prevalent with God than Christ's righteousness? Can you think so little of Christ as to imagine that your sins can overwhelm and conquer him? O man, your sins are like mountains, but Christ's love is like Noah's flood; it prevails twenty cubits, and the tops of the mountains are covered. It is looking at sin and not looking to the Savior that has made you doubt. You are looking to the second cause, and not to him who is greater than all.

"No, but," you reply, "it is not my sin, sir, that grieves me; it is this: I feel so hardened; I do not feel my sin as I ought. Oh, if I could but weep as some weep! If I could but pray as some pray! Then I think I could be saved. If I could feel some of the terrors that good men have felt, then I think I could believe. But I feel none of these things. My heart seems like a rock of ice, hard as granite, and as cold as an iceberg. It will not melt. You may preach, but it is not affected; I may pray, but my heart seems dumb; I may read even the story of Christ's death, and yet my soul is not moved by it. Oh, surely I cannot be saved!" Ah, this is *looking to second causes* again! Have you forgotten that Word which says, *God is greater than our heart*? Have you forgotten that? O child of God! Shame on you that you do look for comfort where comfort never can be found. Look to yourself for peace! Why, there never can be any in this land of war. Look to your own heart for joy! There can be none there either, in this barren wilderness of sin. Turn, turn your eye to Christ. He can cleanse your heart; he can create life, and light, and truth in the inward parts; he can wash you till you shall be whiter than snow, and cleanse your soul and revive it, and make it live, and feel, and move, so that it shall hear his simplest words, and obey his whispered mandate. O look not now at the second cause; look at the great first cause; otherwise I shall put to you again the question, *"You of little faith, why did you doubt?"*

"Still," says another, "I could believe, notwithstanding my sin and my hardness of heart; but, do you know that recently I have lost communion with Christ to such an extent that I cannot help thinking that I must be a castaway? Oh sir, there were times when Christ used to visit me, and bring me such sweet love tokens. I was like the little ewe lamb in the parable; I did drink out of his cup, and feed from his table, and lie in his bosom. Often did he take me to his banqueting house, and his banner over me was love. What feastings I then had! I would bask in the sunlight of his countenance. It was summer with my soul. But now it is winter, and the sun is gone, and the banqueting house is closed. No fruits are on the table; no wines are in the bottles of the promise; I come to the sanctuary, but I find no comfort; I turn to the Bible, but I find no solace; I fall on my knees, but even the stream of prayer seems to be a dry brook." Ah soul, are you not still looking to second causes? These are the most precious of all secondary things, but yet you must not look to them, but to Christ. Remember, it is not your communing that saves you, but Christ's dying; it is not Christ's comfortable visit to your soul that ensures your salvation, but it is Christ's own visit to the house of mourning and to the garden of Gethsemane. I would have you keep your comforts as long as you can, but when they die, believe on your God still. Jonah had a plant once, and when that plant died he began to mourn. Well might someone have said to him, "Jonah! You have lost your gourd, but you have not lost your God." And so might we say to you: you have not lost his love; you have lost the light of his countenance, but you have not lost the love of his heart. You have lost his sweet and gracious communion, but he is the same still, and he would have you believe his faithfulness and trust him in the dark, and rely upon him in the stormy wind and tempest. Look to none of these outward things, but look only to Christ – Christ bleeding, Christ dying, Christ dead, Christ buried, Christ risen, Christ ascended, Christ interceding. This is the thing you are to look to – Christ, and him only. And looking there, you shall be comforted. But look to anything else, and you shall begin to sink. Like Peter, the waves shall fail you, and you shall have to cry, "Lord, save me, or I perish."

But again, to conclude: others of God's people are afraid that they shall never be able to persevere and hold out to the end. "Oh!" says one, "I know I shall yet fall away and perish, for look! Look what an evil heart of unbelief I have; I cannot live one day without sin. My heart is so treacherous, it is like a bombshell; let but a spark of temptation fall upon it and it will blow up to my eternal destruction. With such a tinderbox heart as I have, how can I hope to escape, while I walk in the midst of a shower of sparks?" "Oh!" says one, "I feel my nature to be so utterly vile and depraved that I cannot hope to persevere. If I hold on a week or a month it will be a great work, but to hold on all my life until I die – oh! this is impossible." Looking to second causes again, are you not? Will you please remember that if you look to creature strength it is utterly impossible that you should persevere in grace, even for ten minutes, much less for ten years! If your perseverance depends upon yourself, you are a lost man. You may write that down for a certainty.

If you have one jot or one tittle to do with your own perseverance in divine grace, you will never see God's face at last; your grace will die out; your life will be extinguished, and you must perish, if your salvation depends upon yourself. But remember, you have already been kept these months, and these years; what has done that? Why, divine grace! And the divine grace that has held you on for one year can hold you on for a century, no, for an eternity, if it were necessary. He that has begun can carry on, and must carry on too, otherwise he would be false to his promise and would deny himself.

"Ah! but," you say, "sir, I cannot tell with what temptations I am surrounded. I am in a workshop where everybody laughs at me; I am called nicknames because I follow the cause of Christ. I have been able up to this time to put up with their rebukes and their jests, but now they are adopting another plan. They try to tempt me away from the house of God, and entice me to the theater, and to worldly amusements, and I feel that, placed as I am, I never can hold on. As well might a spark hope to live in the midst of an ocean as for grace to live in my heart." Ah! but soul, who has made it to live up to this time? What is it that has helped you up till now to say no to every temptation? Why, the Lord your Redeemer. You could not have done it so long if it had not been for him; and he that has helped you to stand so long will never put you to shame. Why, if you be a child of God, and you should fall away and perish, what dishonor would be brought on Christ! "Aha!" the devil would say, "here is a child of God, and God has turned him out of his family, and I have got him in hell at last." Is this what God does with his children – loves them one day, and hates them the next; tells them he forgives them, and yet punishes them; accepts them in Christ, and yet sends them into hell? Can that be? Shall it be? Never, not while God is God. "Aha!" again, says Satan, "believers have eternal life given to them. Here is one that had eternal life, and this eternal life has died out. It was not eternal. The promise was a lie. It was temporary life, it was not eternal life. Aha! I have found a flaw in Christ's promise; he gave them only temporary life, and called it eternal." And again, the archfiend would say, if it were possible for one child of God to perish, "Aha! I have one of the jewels of Christ's crown here," and he would hold it up, and defy Christ to his very face, and laugh him to scorn. "This is a jewel that you did purchase with your own blood. Here is one that you did come into the world to save, and yet you could not save him. You did buy him, and pay for him, and yet I have got him. He was a jewel of your crown, and yet here he is, in the hand of the black prince, your enemy. Aha! king with a damaged crown! you have lost one of your jewels." Can it be so? No, never, and therefore everyone that believes is as sure of heaven as if he were there. If you cast yourself simply on Christ, neither death nor hell shall ever destroy you.

Remember what good old Mr. Berridge said when he was met by a friend one morning. "How do you do, Mr. Berridge?" "Pretty well, I thank you," said he, "and as sure of heaven as if I were there; for I have a solid confidence in Christ." What a happy man such a man must be, who knows and feels that to be true! And yet, if you do not feel it, if you are the children of God, I put to you this question: "Why do you doubt?" Is there not good reason to believe? *"You of little faith, why did you doubt?"* If you have believed in Christ, saved you are, and saved you shall be, if you have committed yourself to his hands. *I know whom I have believed and I am convinced that He is able to guard what I have entrusted to Him until that day.*

"Yes," says one, "this is not the fear that troubles me; my only doubt is whether I am a child of God or not." I finish, therefore, by going over the old ground. Soul, if you would know whether you are a child of God, look not to yourself, but look to Christ. You who are here today, who desire to be saved but yet fear you never can be, never look to yourselves for any grounds of acceptance before God. Not self, but Jesus; not heart, but Christ; not man, but man's Creator. O sinner, think not that you are to bring anything to Christ to recommend you. Come to him just as you are. He wants no good works of yours – no good feelings either. Come, just as you are. All that you can want to fit you for heaven, he has bought for you, and he will give you; all these freely you shall have for the asking. Only come, and he will not cast you away. But do you say, "Oh, I cannot believe that Christ is able to save such a sinner as I am." I reply, *"You of little faith, why did you doubt?"* He has already saved sinners as great as you are; only try him, only try him.

> Come to him just as you are. He wants no good works of yours.

> Venture on him, venture wholly;
> Let no other trust intrude.

Try him, try him; and if you find him false, then tell it everywhere that Christ was untrue. But that shall never be. Go to him; tell him you are a wretched undone soul without his sovereign grace; ask him to have mercy on you. Tell him you are determined, if you do perish, that you will perish at the foot of his cross. Go and cling to him, as he hangs bleeding there; look him in the face, and say, "Jesus, I have no other refuge. If you refuse me, I am lost; but I will never go from you. I will clasp you in life, and clasp you in death, as the only rock of my soul's salvation." Depend upon it. You shall not be sent away empty; you must, you shall be accepted, if you will simply believe. Oh, may God enable you, by the divine influence of his Holy Spirit, to believe; and then we shall not have to put the question, *"You of little faith, why did you doubt?"* I pray God now to apply these words to your comfort. They have been very simple and very unsightly words; but nevertheless, they will suit simple, unsightly hearts. If God shall bless them, to him be the glory!

Chapter 5

The History of Little Faith

Immediately Jesus stretched out His hand and took hold of him, and said to him, "You of little faith, why did you doubt?" (Matthew 14:31)

There is only one word in the original for the phrase, *"You of little faith."* The Lord Jesus virtually addresses Peter by the name of "Little-faith," in one word. I do not suppose that Peter had ever before dreamed of that name as applicable to himself. Possibly he had thought in his heart that his faith was strong even to assurance. When so lately he had seen his Master feed the multitudes with a few loaves and fish, and had helped to gather up twelve baskets of fragments, he felt that his faith was equal to anything. He who could feed so many with so little, could do any kind of wonder; and how could Peter, brave, honest Peter, ever think of doubting his Lord? O brethren, we do not know ourselves! We imagine that we are rich and increased in goods, and, lo! in the time of trial we discover that we are naked, and poor, and miserable. Those who are strong in faith to their own thinking may soon be brought into circumstances where their confidence will be grievously shaken. All is not gold that glitters, neither is all faith that speaks bravely. Peter is strong in faith on board the ship, strong in faith even as he walks on the waters; but that unexpected gust of wind, which came howling down from the mountains, took him aback, staggered him, and caused his faith to reel. Then the waters yielded under his feet, and as he began to sink he discovered his own weakness and had his discovery confirmed by the verdict of his Lord, who surnamed him *Little-faith*. Let no man think of himself beyond his own experience. Experience is the true gauge; and he who boasts of an untested faith is puffed up with pride. Stretch not your arm beyond your sleeve, lest it be frostbitten. He who glories in himself deceives himself. It is not an easy thing to endure the humiliation which must follow upon the collapse of untested confidence. Rest assured, brethren, that between here and heaven we shall need every ounce of faith that we have; and that whenever we feel too sure of our own strength, we are making sure of that which is frailty itself. Self-confidence is but the froth on the top of the cup; it is not the pure juice of the vine of truth. When a man begins to be secure in himself he will invite temptation, he will rashly venture upon needless experiments, and in the end he will need to cry in plaintive accents, *"Lord, save me!"* Learn, then, on the threshold of the text, that we are not as strong as we think we are, and that when we are most brave and daring, we may not be quite so far removed from fear and trembling as we imagine. Alas! that unbelief should mar even Peter's faith. Let him who thinks that he can walk on the waves take heed lest he sink beneath them.

In Peter's character there was a singular mixture of the strong and the weak: he rose to excellence and sank to littleness. Yet why should I speak of this as singular? For we ourselves are made of much the same materials: in us also are mingled the iron and the clay. The best of men are men at the best. Since the old nature remains, though the new nature is born in us, there is in our soul a conflict between holiness and sin, faith and unbelief, strength and weakness. We walk on the waters like our Lord, and immediately we sink like doubting Peter. The Christian man is entirely often a mystery to himself, and, therefore, it is no wonder that he is a mystery to other people. Note how Peter speaks. He cries, *"Lord, if it is You"* – a speech which, if it be not worthy of rebuke, is by no means praiseworthy, after his Lord had said, *"It is I."* Hear him again: *"Command me to come to You on the water."* Here is courage almost blazing into rashness; and yet there is a measure of obedient deference, for he will not attempt to come unless he is bidden to do so. He will risk his life if he has but his Master's permit. What diverse qualities meet in the same man! He proposes a rash venture, and yet is prudent enough to ask his Master's permission.

See him walking on the waves, and admire the strength of his faith! Could *you* do this? Immediately see him sinking because a fierce blast has blown in his face. Do you marvel at his unbelief? Would you have done better? He that knows himself knows that doubt dogs the heels of confidence. The Canaanite of distrust is still in the land, and shows himself ever and immediately at unexpected turns. Where the fairest flowers of faith, and hope, and joy do bloom, the deadliest serpents of mistrust and suspicion may yet be lurking. Abraham, that father of believers, still sinned twice by distrust when he did not acknowledge Sarah as his wife.

Peter's mixture of unbelief was not to be justified, nor may it be used as an excuse for ourselves. We shall speak of it as a matter of fact, but not as an example; for it was an improper and unreasonable thing. Peter could not answer the Lord's question, *"Why did you doubt?"* His doubting was without grounds or reason. If he believes at all, why does he doubt? The unbelief which makes faith little is to be confessed as a sin, and mourned over as such; it would be wrong to regard it as a mere infirmity, and invent excuses for it. The truth is that the Christian has no cause for doubting his Lord. The whole course of the Lord's dealing is calculated to inspire confidence. He has done nothing to create a suspicion of his love, or truth, or power. If we never doubt till we have cause for doubting, our life will be rich with faith. It is concerning little faith, and its faults and its unreasonableness, that I have to speak at this time. May God grant that all the Little-faith family may be helped to stronger confidence. May the Holy Spirit bless the word, and enable many a Ruth to pick up those handfuls that are let fall on purpose for the feeble folk who glean in these fields.

Our first topic will be Little-faith's history. It is sketched in the story of Peter. We are each one apt to act over again the part which Peter played in this narrative.

Little-faith is a true disciple, though a faulty one. Not the littleness of the faith, but the faith itself is the gift of God. None but God could make a grain of mustard seed; none but God can give even the least particle of living faith. Faith in the Lord Jesus Christ, however feeble it may be, is a fruit of the Spirit of God, and a token of the new birth. I may say of Peter on this occasion what the Lord Jesus said of him at another time: *"Blessed are you, Simon Barjona, because flesh and blood did not reveal this to you, but My Father who is in heaven."* Even the faith which can get no further than to touch the hem of Christ's garment is the work of the Spirit of God. Even that faith which cries, *"I do believe; help my unbelief"* is, as to its existence, though not as to its infirmity, the creation of the Most High. Therefore let us note that Little-faith is born in the new Jerusalem and is an Israelite indeed; therefore, it has about it that immortal life of which our risen Lord has said, *"Because I live, you will live also."*

Very early in its life *Little-faith has great longings.* See it in Peter's case. He is on board ship with his brethren while Jesus is yonder upon the waters; and Peter is so earnest to come at his Lord and be with him, that he is ready to plunge into the sea to reach him. Why could he not wait as the others did? His immediate duty was in the ship with his brethren; but his vehement desires carried him above commonplace toiling and rowing. Strong faith exhibits patience where Little-faith is in a hurry. It was well to have longings for Jesus, but it would have been wiser to have waited while the Lord came walking over the sea to the ship. The quiet, self-possessed Christian has deep longings for his Lord; but he has the assured conviction that his Lord will come to him if he continues faithful to his present duty, and therefore he waits upon the Lord. Little-faith, like Martha, runs to meet Jesus; but Strong-faith, like Mary, sits still in the house. Little-faith is feverish for immediate joy. Little-faith wants to be in heaven tomorrow. Little-faith would convert the world before the sun went down, and she grows faint because her zeal has not fulfilled her wish. Little-faith must pluck the promises while they are green; she is not content to wait till they become ripe and mellow. Yet I love her longings, and I wish to God that all men had them! However mistaken pressing desires for spiritual joy may be, they are things that come not into unrenewed hearts. Those blessed longings after Christ which some of you feel, which make you cry, *"Oh that I knew where I might find Him!"* – you may thank God for them. Those who have greater faith know that they have found their Lord; they know that he is as the sun which cannot be hidden; they feel his warmth, and rejoice in his light; yet the keen hunger after Christ which goes with Little-faith is an admirable thing, and the Lord himself has blessed it. I rejoice in the blossom of the apple tree; it is not so valuable as the fruit, but it is exceedingly beautiful; and, even so, the eager longings of a trembling heart after the Lord Jesus are full of loveliness and fragrance, and are by no means to be despised. It is the nature of Little-faith that it should be of a thirsty and eager temperament, and hasty to make a dash for present fellowship with Christ.

Little-faith was daring. Early in her life she had intense longings, and they grew so that Little-faith was willing to venture everything to have her longings fulfilled. *"If it is You, command me to come to You on the water"* – thus does Little-faith cry to her Lord. These are big words, but they come out of a trembling heart. Men often venture all the more because their focus is so small. Souls who are little in faith are often put upon desperate measures to gain hope. O beloved, are there not some of you who would give your eyes and ears, and your very lives, to see Christ, and to taste of his love? You have come up to the tabernacle this morning feeling that if Christ bid you to plunge into the sea to find him, you would think nothing of it. You feel like Rutherford when he said he could swim through seven hells to get at Christ, and think them nothing if he might but lie at his feet.

> **Souls who are little in faith are often put upon desperate measures to gain hope.**

Those vehement and burning desires within your spirit for your Lord and Master are sharp but exceedingly blessed things. You need not repress them, even though they urge you to venture everything for Christ's sake. Love's ventures for Christ will end in great profit. What shall it damage a man if he loses the whole world and gains his Savior? What loss could there be to a man though he himself sank in the sea, so long as his Lord stood there to stretch forth his hand and snatch him from destruction? Little-faith can yet be a true hero when the Lord says to her, *"Come."* It is not the sea she fears; her concern is lest the Lord should frown upon her.

At times Little-faith accomplishes great wonders. Peter, when his Master said, *"Come,"* went down upon the waters and walked the waves with ease. The Lord puts forth his strength even when we reveal our own weakness of faith. Peter took one step, and then another, upon the rolling wave, wondering all the while how it could ever be. Has not your little-faith done this? I remember the first step of faith I took, how I wondered at it, and wondered at myself. Have not you also been amazed at yourselves? Do you remember when you believed that God had saved you, seeing you had faith in Christ? Then, though you knew it to be true, you could hardly tell whether you should laugh for joy or cry for fear, when you thought upon the possibility of your being saved in Christ Jesus. You dared to believe that you were adopted into the family of God, and started back as your heart said, "How can he put me among the children?" Do you recollect reading the doctrine of election in Holy Scripture, and at last saying, "Surely, I am one of the chosen. The Lord has loved me with an everlasting love; therefore with loving-kindness has he drawn me." Was it not a piece of daring to you? Walking on the water could not have been more venturesome. You stood upright when tempted, you held on, though sorely surrounded by the Enemy; you walked towards Jesus, though the way seemed to be on the sea; a high exhilaration uplifted your spirit, you rose out of yourself; but yet down deep within there was a dormant fear, a half-developed understanding that your confidence was too good to last, that your joy was presumptuous. In your very heart you were afraid of sinking, and it was no wonder that by and by your fear became matter-of-fact.

But now comes in another bit of our history: *Little-faith is too apt to look away from the Lord.* Peter, as he walked on those billows, took his eye off his Master, and just then a tremendous hurricane rushed boisterously in his face, and poor Peter was alarmed. He had thought of the fickleness of the waves, but he had overlooked the fury of the wind. When he spoke to the Lord, he said, *"If it is You, command me to come to You on the water";* and so his faith had reckoned with the water, but it had not reckoned upon the force of the wind. That mysterious and subtle agent took him by surprise. He had forgotten that he had both winds and waves to contend with, and now the wind comes upon him as a new trial. As the blast came full in Peter's face, it chilled him to the marrow, and chilled his heart too. He heard the wind, but forgot the voice which said, *"It is I; do not be afraid."* This is the danger of Little-faith. Little-faith, at the outset, is scarcely comprehensive enough; it does not take a full view of all the possible dangers and difficulties; and so, when that which it has omitted comes to the front, it is very apt to be sorely troubled. Little-faith, your hope lies in keeping your little self wholly dependent upon your great Lord. If you begin to measure circumstances, it will go harshly with you, poor trembling creature that you are! What have you and I to do with measuring? There is one that measures with a span the whole world, and weighs the mountains in scales, and the hills in a balance. With unmeasured faith let us leave ourselves in the hands of our immeasurable God; so shall our souls be kept in perfect peace, stayed on him. I walk on the waves; yet not I, but Jesus. Therefore, I will not look to the winds, but to Jesus; neither will I think of sinking, but see him standing and hope in him.

Now, the moment he took his eye off his Master and thought of the wind, *Little-faith began to sink.* You see him going down; he is ready to perish; the proud waters prevail against him; he has no power whatever to help himself. I should suppose that Peter, being a fisherman, could swim. Why did he not strike out? Mark this, when a man begins to live by faith, if his faith fails him, even his natural ability fails with his faith. He that could swim with no faith originally, will not swim when once by faith he has begun to walk on the waters. Should he fail in his walking, he cannot fall back on his swimming. *Beginning to sink* is a terrible condition. Poor Little-faith, it never reckoned on this! Deep experiences are all the more dreadful because they are unlooked for. When Peter left the shipboard, and slid down the side of the ship, and touched the sea, his first miraculous footsteps so elated him that he hardly thought it possible that he would before long be on the verge of drowning; but now down he goes, like lead in the mighty waters. The billows open wide their great mouths to swallow up poor Little-faith, and down he goes. Is that the condition of any child of God here today? I must confess it has sometimes been mine. There was a step, and scarcely a step, between me and death. That which bore me up appeared to give way, and the waters came in even unto my soul.

Let me not finish this history of Little-faith without saying that

Little-faith knew how to pray. Though Peter did not know how to come to Christ on the waters, he knew how to come to him by prayer. Though his faith was not *what* it ought to be, it was *where* it ought to be; for his cry was to his Lord alone. He did not appeal to his brethren in the vessel, but only to his dear Master who stood so firmly on the rolling wave. He did not cry, "John, save me!" but *"Lord, save me!"* It was a short prayer, but it was a comprehensive one. It expressed his need of salvation; it proved his faith in the Lord's will to save him; it acknowledged Jesus to be his Lord, and it tacitly admitted that the Lord could save him, and no one else. In his prayer Peter leaves all other hope, and looks wholly and solely to Jesus, crying, *"Lord, save me!"* His faith quotes what the Lord had done for others in healing, feeding, and saving them; and now he cries, *"Lord, save **me**!"* (emphasis added). He asks Jesus to act as his name implies he would do: he practically says, "Savior, save me." He appeals to his authority: "You are my Lord, and you did bid me to come; therefore, as Lord, save your own servant. Save me." His short cry is full of force. Let us imitate both its shortness and its fullness. Whenever faith is weak, let prayer be strong. When you cannot do anything else but cry, then cry with might and muscle. If it is less the cry of faith, let it be all the more the cry of agony. *Beginning to sink, he cried out, "Lord, save me!"* Little children are good at crying, if at nothing else, and so is Little-faith. When Jacob was greatly afraid, he became bold enough to wrestle at Jabbok. Even Little-faith has prayer for its vital breath, its native air. Where there is life, there is breath; and where there is faith, there is prayer. O soul, are you sinking? Then cry, *"Lord, save me!"*

Now, in this little picture, have any of you recognized yourselves? Do you long for Christ? Would you venture all things for his dear sake? Do you trust him? Have you enjoyed happy moments when by faith you have accomplished things impossible to mere sense? Have you sometimes believed, and in that belief found a support for your spirit that made you more than a conqueror? Then, if at this moment there should be a collapse, and your faith should waver, pray unto the Lord. *He* stands fast if you do not. It is your wisdom to cry mightily in this your time of need, and as surely as the Lord lives, he will come to your rescue. Among all the carcasses that shall be washed up on the Dead Sea shore there shall never be found the corpse of Little-faith.

Though Little-faith has often said, "I shall one day fall by the hand of the Enemy," no weapon has yet been forged that can strike its heart or break its bones. He that believes even with a little and a trembling believing, is safe beneath the guardian care of the eternal God. *He will cover you with His pinions, and under His wings you may seek refuge; His faithfulness is a shield and bulwark.*

At the end Little-faith will grow to full assurance, and will come up into the vessel, yes, unto heaven with Christ. Little-faith shall find its way across the Jordan, and stand in its lot in the end of the days. And perhaps among the most rapturous song that shall ever salute the Redeemer's ear will be the song of those who were weak and trembling when they were here below, and yet were kept unto the end. Therefore, have confidence!

I come now to the second topic of my discourse, which is an interesting one – Little-faith acknowledged by the Lord. In my text you will observe that the Savior did not say, "You of no faith," or "You of pretended faith," but *"You of little faith."* There are times when we would give all that we have if we could only have our Master's assurance that we have even a little faith. If he does but acknowledge that it is faith, then the root of the matter is in us. I would rather have great faith than little faith; but I would rather have little faith than have great presumption, and mistake it for holy confidence. It ought to have comforted Peter, even as it did rebuke him, to hear his Lord, who could not make a mistake, acknowledge that he had faith.

> Note that little faith is faith, and *little faith is true faith*.

In following up on this subject, note that little faith is faith, and *little faith is true faith*. A grain of mustard seed has life in it as surely as the tree beneath whose spreading boughs the birds of the air find shelter. A spark is as truly fire as the conflagration which burned down a city. Little faith is not such powerful faith as great faith, but it is quite as true faith. O soul, if you have a ray of light, it came from the sun; if you have a pulse of life, it comes from the heart; if you have any measure of faith, it is the work of the Spirit of God. A pearl is a pearl, though it be no bigger than a pin's head. God's signature is as valid when he writes it small as when he uses capitals.

In Peter's case, *little faith was faith with a very solid reason at the back of it.* O child of God, little as your faith may be, yet if you believe in Christ you have faith most proper and justifiable; in fact, so strong is the ground of your little faith that the Savior even asks you, *"Why did you doubt?"* This is as much as to say, "You have every reason for your faith, but what reason have you for doubting?" Oh, dear heart, if you do come to Christ and cast yourself on him, you are doing the best and the rightest thing that you can do, and none can question your conduct. Alas, if you do even swoon away upon the dear bosom of the eternal love, none shall tear you off, none shall separate you – even in your feebleness – from Christ. He has said that the one who comes to him he will certainly not cast out; who, then, can dismiss you from his presence? You are not presumptuous; you are not going beyond what is permitted you when you do trust yourself and your all on Christ your Lord. Do it again, and do it again more thoroughly, and you shall never be ashamed of having done it; no, it shall be your glory that you dare to trust your Lord. His promise shall never be outdone by your faith. Open your mouth wide, and he will fill it. Ask for more faith, and he will give more faith, and fulfill to you greater promises; go from faith to faith, and you shall receive blessing upon blessing. There is no limit to your Lord's love; be free with it; there is no reason why you should hesitate. Christ acknowledged little faith to be faith with a solid reason at its back when he said, *"Why did you doubt?"*

Our Lord Jesus acknowledged little-faith because, little as it was, *it risked all for him.* Peter had thrown himself into the sea to come to his Master, and the Lord recognized that fact. He who risks all for Jesus and on Jesus shall not find it to be a losing speculation. Though you dare not say that you have strong faith, yet you give up the world's pleasures, and its sinful gains, and its pleasing smiles, for Christ. You would not deny him for all the treasures of Egypt. Well, then, our Lord will acknowledge you as his, and render you harmless in the end. That little faith, which is real faith, knows nothing of the timidity which haunts the heart of the hypocrite. Little-faith fears lest it should not be accepted at the last, but it is not afraid of being persecuted for Christ's sake. No, let me but know that I am his and he is mine; I will go through fire, and through water, to be with him.

Little-faith, in the case of Peter, *was coming to Jesus all the while.*

Peter, when he left the ship, left it to come to Jesus, and for that purpose only. The first step he took upon the sea was towards Jesus, and every other step was towards Jesus; and when he began to sink he sank that way, leaning towards his Master, and crying as he went down, *"Lord, save me!"* Now, the Lord Jesus always acknowledges a faith which comes towards him, however lame it may be. If you have a faith which looks to yourself, a curse rests upon it. If you have a faith which looks to priests, it is superstition. If you have a faith which looks to ceremonies, creeds, prayers, and feelings, it will fail you when you most need help. But if you have a faith whose eyes are to Jesus, whose longings are for Jesus, whose hopes are all centered in Jesus, whose steps all tend to Jesus, then you have a faith upon which Jesus sets his seal, and though he calls it *little*, yet he calls it *faith*. Be sure that that which the Lord himself acknowledges to be faith is faith, even though for the present time it leaves you dammed with the salt water from which you are newly plucked.

Once more, the Master acknowledges this faith; for, *before long, Little-faith came to walk with Jesus on the sea.* I think I have seen a picture of Peter sinking and Christ stooping to save him, but I wish that some eminent artist would paint the two walking together in peace, Peter and his Lord. What joy to think that Little-faith, once drawn from the deep, stands on those foaming waves side by side with the great saving Lord! Now is Peter conformed to his Lord. Now is the servant clothed with the might of his Master. We have formerly seen the Son of God walking in the fire with the three faithful young men, and now we see the opposite of the medal – a saint walking on the water with the Son of Man. Is it not a splendid, reassuring truth that Little-faith can grow to act like Christ? The day shall yet come when the Lord shall have so strengthened Little-faith that the things that the Lord does Little-faith shall do also, and the word shall be fulfilled: *"Greater works than these he will do; because I go to the Father."* You tell me that you cannot rejoice today; but Jesus will see you again, and your heart shall rejoice. You cannot go forth to Christian service, for you are lame through spiritual weakness; but the day comes when the lame man shall leap as a deer. The Healer of his people will lay his hand upon you and make you *strong in the Lord and in the strength of His might.* You have a greater consciousness today of your inability in yourself than you have of your ability in the Lord; but it shall not always be so. The time will come when in rapt fellowship with him, by the strength of his grace, you shall be in this world even as he is, and that glorious life which in the person of Christ walked on the sea as though it were a sea of glass, that same life shall be in you, so that you shall overcome the world, the flesh, and the devil.

I feel very glad to have even a little faith. I am truly sorry that it is so little when I know that my Lord deserves all possible confidence; but yet I am glad that it is given to me to believe on his name, for it has brought me near him, and will bring me yet nearer, and will by and by bring me to be with him where he is, and to behold his glory.

Thus I have shown you that our Lord acknowledged little faith. He did not break the bruised reed, nor disown the infant faith; but he called it faith, answered its prayer, and made it to stand with him in fellowship of power.

In the third place, I want you to notice Little-faith's deliverance. Little-faith began to sink, but it was only a beginning. The sinking did not end in Peter's drowning, but in his Lord's saving. The text says, *beginning to sink*; and truly that is the whole matter. None of God's people shall go beyond *beginning to sink*. We may be *ready to perish*, but we shall not actually perish. Our steps may be *almost gone*, but *almost* is not quite. A man may be near death, and yet live; he may begin to sink, and yet be saved. Friend, it may be that for some time you have been *beginning to sink*, but you have not sunk yet. Not yet are you consumed, not yet is the Lord's mercy gone forever, not yet has he forgotten to be gracious. Oftentimes *beginning to sink* with us is with Christ beginning to stretch out his hand. The beginning of a clear sense of our own weakness is often the beginning of the display of the power of God.

> The beginning of a clear sense of our own weakness is often the beginning of the display of the power of God.

Little-faith received its deliverance *wholly from the Lord.* As I have already said, it was not Peter's swimming that got him out of his trouble, nor was it any revival of Peter's faith which did it, but the Lord came to the rescue, and proved his power to help at a dead lift. So shall it be with you, O trembling heart. In the hour of your extremity God shall appear for you. The Lord will provide. Out of weakness you shall be made strong, for he has said, *"I will never desert you, nor will I ever forsake you."*

It was of the Lord, and therefore it was *immediate*. Will you kindly note that word in the text: *Immediately Jesus stretched out His hand*. Before he rebuked Peter for his little faith, he delivered him from his peril. O Little-faith, you have but to cry, and the Lord will help you. Do not delay your crying, and he will not delay his helping. The Lord may let the matter proceed some considerable distance till we think it is all over with us; but in the nick of time he will appear for our deliverance. At that dark moment when we read our own death warrant amid the roar of the tempest, the prompt relief of the Lord of love will arrive. No wings of cherubim can be more swift than the Lord's right hand when he means to draw his people from great waters.

It is added, *Immediately **Jesus stretched out His hand*** (emphasis added). It was an instructive action on the part of Jesus that stretching out of his hand, as if he was arousing himself to the utmost energy, and reaching beyond himself to rescue his servant. A stretched-out hand denotes the exercise of all the power of the person thus acting. In the case of God's people, it has often been necessary that he should bring them forth with a high hand and with an outstretched arm. Peter had his exodus from the water as Israel had from Egypt. Who is to know the might of God's arm if he does not stretch it out? And why should it be stretched out unless there is a need for it? It is so that our perils produce the necessity for God to stretch out his hand, and thus they turn out to be comfortable means of grace to us. Our necessities are the doors through which the Lord's great bounty comes to us. If Little-faith did not lift up its cry of dismay, the Lord's hand would not be lifted up for its rescue.

It is added, he *took hold of him*. Thus the Lord came into personal contact with his servant. See, he holds him up. The whole weight of Peter is on Christ. If Peter sinks, Jesus must sink too, for he will not let go of his hold. For the time being Peter and Christ are joined; they have only one standing, and that standing is all in Christ. O Little-faith, you do feel a closer union to Christ in your hour of danger than ever before. It comes to this, that when Jesus intercedes to save Little-faith, he bends all his strength to the deed, and takes hold of the sinking one with a grip so fast and firm that the two must sink or stand together. All the weight of Peter was on Jesus; all the security of Jesus was bestowed on Peter. Little-faith holds Jesus while Jesus upholds Little-faith. A half-hoping, half-despairing soul lays hold on Jesus with an iron grip, and on such a poor feeble one the hold of Jesus is equally tight and strong. He will never let the sinking sinner die when once that prayer has been uttered, *"Lord, save me!"* I hardly know of a more conscious union between a man and Christ than that which is accomplished when in sinking times the grip of the crucified hand is felt as our sole rescue from death. "Hallelujah, who shall part Christ's own bride from Christ's own heart?" Who is he that shall separate the most timid and trembling of all the believing company from that eternal hand which is sworn to deliver? *"I give eternal life to them,"* says he, *"and they will never perish"*; nor shall they though the heavens and the earth should pass away. The Lord must and will stretch out his hand and catch the sinking one, and grant him the same standing as himself.

I close with Little-faith rebuked. That comes last. After the poor soul is quite rescued, and set on a sure footing, then comes the loving chiding. *"You of little faith, why did you doubt?"* This is such a gentle rebuke that it almost seems to me that the Master might say as much as this to us when we enter paradise with him. It might not be unkind even there to say, *"Why did you doubt?"* When you and I have come up from our dying beds, and left all pain, and poverty, and sorrow far behind, we shall find ourselves in the golden-streeted city, and the Well-Beloved with us, and we shall look back on all the way whereby he led us; and then he may lovingly whisper in our ear, *"Why did you doubt?"* Look back on your pilgrim way. There is the Slough of Despond dried up; there is Giant Despair's head on a pole; there is Apollyon bound with chains; there is the river whose chilly stream so often frightened you, glittering in the eternal light. *"Why did you doubt?"* You doubted nothing. You made mountains out of molehills. Where everything was working for you, you said with trembling Jacob, *"All these things are against me."* Will not our Lord produce a rapture within our spirit while he brings to mind his unchanging love, his immutable truth, his immovable faithfulness? We shall eternally wonder at our own doubts. What if our Lord should say, "Did you not come up from the wilderness leaning upon me as your beloved? Did I ever fail you? Did I ever give you a cross word? Did I ever leave you or forsake you? *Why did you doubt?*" Then we shall sweetly chide ourselves to think we ever had a moment's distrust of our dear Lord, the Bridegroom of our souls, in whom our faith ought to have been as unchanging as the day.

Notice, dear friends, with regard to this question, *"Why did you doubt?"* that it is an *inconsistent* thing for a believing man to doubt his God, or distrust the power of the Lord Jesus. You do believe, and if you believe, why doubt? If faith, why *little* faith? If you doubt, why believe? And if you believe, why doubt? Oil and water will not mix. Oh, how should faith and unbelief unite? Yet they are often found together in deadly warfare. "Oh," said a dear sister in Christ to me the other day, "I cannot doubt my God." Yet she also expressed a fear lest she should be wrong at the last day. This was an odd mixture in one who knew so well the glorious gospel; but then we are all odd in some way or other. In any case, it is not good that we believe and yet disbelieve. Shall a fountain send forth both sweet water and bitter? Begone you doubts! Oh, that they would go at my bidding! What business have you here at the festival of faith? Begone, you vixens, that devour the bread of the Lord's Table, and defile our dainty things! What right have you to enter the holy abodes of faith?

While doubts are so inconsistent, are they not also most *dishonoring*? Why should we doubt our Lord? Shall it go forth to the world that we cannot trust Christ? Shall it be said that those who are saved by him, nevertheless, say it is hard work to believe him? Hard to believe him who has proven his love by the agony and bloody sweat? My Lord, I will sooner doubt my brother, and doubt my father, and doubt my wife than doubt you! My Lord, I will doubt my eyes, and doubt my ears, and doubt the beating of my heart sooner than doubt you! I will doubt the laws of nature, I will doubt everything that seems certain, I will doubt the conclusions of mathematics; but you, oh why, why, should I doubt you? No, let us hold on to the love of Jesus and cling to him, even though he should frown and chasten. Be it ours to trust a scourging God! Yes, say, *"Though He slay me, I will hope in Him."*

Once again, how *inexcusable* is this doubting among you who do believe! The only excuses worth mentioning are these. Some excuse themselves because they desire to be humble. "I dare not think that these good things are true for me. I know that I am altogether unworthy of them, and I am afraid of being proud if I take them to myself." Do you not know, dear friend, that the biggest pride in all the world is doubting God? And it is the sweetest humility to trust in God as a child trusts its father. It is the lowliest action of the heart to say, "These things are good, exceedingly good, and I am most unworthy; but then the Lord has said that he gives these gracious gifts to the unworthy; and, if he has said it, God forbid that I should question him." Who am I that I should venture to raise a doubt about the sincerity of the Lord? I must, I will, cease from all such proud questionings and cunning doubtings and be even as a newborn babe, drinking in the unadulterated milk of the Word.

> The biggest pride in all the world is doubting God.

I am persuaded that unbelief is sometimes occasioned by ignorance. I pray you, do not let such ignorance remain in you. Be diligent in searching Holy Scripture. If you do not know the Lord, nor know his providence, nor know the doctrine of the final perseverance of the saints, nor know the covenant of grace, why, then you may be staggered; but learn those things so that you may be established.

I have no doubt that unbelief is caused not only by ignorance, but also by forgetfulness. We forget the Lord's past mercies. If the Lord has plucked you like a brand out of the fire, can he not pluck you out of the sea? He that delivered you from the deadly power of sin, can he not deliver you from every temptation? In fact, the Lord has done more for us already than he ever will have to do for us in the future; for he will never have to die again upon the bloody tree, and he will never have to offer himself again as an atonement for our sin. Nine hundred and ninety-nine parts out of a thousand are ours already. We have only to shut our eyes and open them in heaven, and the rest will be ours. Today is our salvation nearer than when we believed. We are almost home! Within sight of the white cliffs of the better land! Shall we tremble now? Shall we not begin to rejoice with joy unspeakable? Does not little-faith begin to mount into assurance?

You that have not believed in Jesus, I have tried to show the way of salvation by faith in Christ. You that have believed but tremblingly, I have pointed out to you much that ought to comfort you. And to you who can believe with full assurance, I would say, Guard that full assurance with great care; it is heaven below, it is the beginning of heaven above. The Lord, the Holy Spirit, be with you all, for Jesus' sake. Amen.

Chapter 6

Hope in Hopeless Cases

"Bring him here to Me." (Matthew 17:17)

Our real text will be the entire narrative, but as it seems necessary to select some one sentence, we have chosen that before us as the true hinge of the story.

The kingdom of our Lord Jesus Christ, while on earth, was so extensive as to touch the confines both of heaven and hell. We see him at one moment discoursing with Moses and Elijah in his glory, as though at heaven's gates, and lo, a few hours later, we see him confronting a foul spirit, as though defying the infernal pit. There is a long journey from patriarchs to demons, from prophets to dumb devils; yet mercy prompts him and power supports him, so that he is equally glorious in either place. What a glorious Lord he was even while in his humiliation! How glorious is he now! How far his goodness reaches! Truly he has dominion from sea to sea; to the extremes of human condition his empire reaches. Our Lord and Master hears with joy the shout of a believer who has vanquished his foe, and, at the same hour, he bows his ear to the despairing wail of a sinner who has given up all confidence in self, and desires to be saved by him. At one moment he is accepting the crown which the warrior brings him from the well-fought fight, and at another moment he is healing the broken in heart and binding up their wounds. There is a notable difference between the dying scene of the triumphant believer as he enters into rest, and the first weeping repentance of a Saul of Tarsus as he seeks mercy from the Savior whom he has persecuted; and yet the Lord's heart and eye are with both. Our Lord's transfiguration did not disqualify him for casting out the devils, nor did it make him feel too sublime and spiritual to grapple with human ills, and so at this hour the glories of heaven do not take him off from the miseries of earth, nor do they make him forget the cries and tears of the feeble ones who are seeking him in this valley of tears.

The case of the deaf and dumb lunatic, which we read in your hearing, and to which I call your particular attention today, is a very remarkable one. All sin is the evidence that the soul is under the dominion of Satan. All unconverted persons are really possessed of the devil in a certain sense: he has established his throne within their hearts, and there he reigns and rules therefrom all the parts of their body. *The spirit that is now working in the sons of disobedience* is the name which Paul gives to the Prince of Darkness. But these possessions are not alike in every case, and the casting out of Satan, though always effected by the same Lord, is not always brought about in the same fashion. We bless God, many of us, that when we lived in sin, we were not given over to a furious delirium of it – there was method in our madness. We claim no credit for this, but we do thank God for it, that we were not whirled along like rolling things before the tempest, but were restrained and kept within the bounds of outward propriety. We are also grateful that when, being aroused and alarmed we fell under the iron rod of Satan, we were not all brought into that utter despair, that horror of great darkness, that inward torment and agony, which some are made to endure. And when Jesus came to save us, although we were much hindered by Satan, yet there was none of the foaming of pride, and wallowing of obstinate lust, and tearing of raging desperation of which we have read in memorable instances, but the Lord opened our hearts gently with his golden key, entered into the chamber of our spirits, and took possession. For the most part, the conquests which Jesus achieves in the souls of his people, though worked by the same power, are more quietly accomplished than in the case before us. For this let thanks be rendered to the God of grace. Yet every now and then there are these strange, out-of-the-way cases, persons in whom Satan seems to run riot and to exert the utmost force of his malice, and in whom the Lord Jesus displays the exceeding greatness of his power, when in almighty love he dethrones the tyrant and casts him out never to return again. If there should be only one such person here today, I shall be justified in looking after him, for what man is there among you who, having a hundred sheep, if one of them should go astray, does not leave the ninety-nine in the wilderness and go after that which is gone astray? I ask for prayers for such as have, in years gone by, been brought to Jesus and are now rejoicing in him, that we may today find out the far-off wanderers, and may, by the Holy Spirit's anointing, liberate those that are bound with fetters of iron, that they may become today the Lord's freed ones, for if the Son shall make them free, they shall be free indeed.

I shall, by my Lord's help, first enlarge upon the *deplorable case;* then we shall meditate upon the *one resource;* and then we shall conclude by admiring the *sure result.*

First, let us look, so far as time permits, into the details of the deplorable case before us.

We understand the physical miracles of Christ to be types of his spiritual works. The wonders which he worked in the natural world have their analogies in the spiritual world; the outward and natural is the symbol of the inward and spiritual. Now the lunatic who was brought by his father for healing is not so distinctly representative of a case of gross sin, though the spirit is called a foul one, and Satan is everywhere defiling people, but it is an instance of the great horror, disturbance of mind, and raving despair caused by the Evil One in some minds to their torment and jeopardy. You will observe concerning it, that *the disease appeared every now and then in overwhelming attacks of mania, in which the man was utterly beyond his own control.* The epileptic fit threw the poor victim in all directions. So have we seen melancholy persons in whom despondency, mistrust, unbelief, and despair have raged at times with unconquerable fury; they have not so much entertained these evil guests as been victims to them. As Mark puts it, *The spirit threw him into a convulsion,* so have such forlorn ones been captured and thrown by Giant Despair. The fairies have scourged them onward over dry places, seeking rest and finding none. They refused to be comforted, and like sick men their souls despised all manner of meat. They displayed no power to struggle with their melancholy – resistance did not suggest itself to them; they were taken off their feet and carried clean out of themselves in a rapture of woe. Such cases are not at all uncommon. Satan, knowing that his time is short, and perceiving that Jesus is hastening to the rescue, lashes his poor slave with excess of malice, if by any means he may utterly destroy his victim before the deliverer arrives.

The poor patient before us was filled at such times with *a terrible anguish*, an anguish which he expressed by foaming at the mouth, by wallowing upon the ground, and by crying out. At such times in his dreadful falls he bruised himself, and his delirium led him to dash himself against anything which stood before him, thus causing to himself new injuries. None can tell but those who have felt the same, what are the pains of conviction of sin when aggravated by the suggestions of the Enemy. Some of us have passed through this in our measure, and can declare that it is hell upon earth. We have felt the weight of the hand of an angry God. We know what it is to read the Bible and not find a single promise in it that would suit our case, but rather to see every page of it glowing with threatenings, as though curses like lightning blazed from it. Even the choicest passages have appeared to rise up against us as though they said, "Do not intrude here. These comforts are not for you; you have nothing to do with such things as these." We have bruised ourselves against doctrines, and precepts, and promises, and even the cross itself. We have prayed, and our very prayer has increased our misery, even against the mercy seat we have fallen, judging our prayers to be but babbling sounds obnoxious to the Lord. We have gone up with the assembly of God's people, and the preacher seemed to frown upon us, and to rub salt into our wounds, and aggravate our case. Even the chapter, and the hymns, and the prayers appeared to be in league against us, and we went home to our seclusion more despondent than before. I hope none of you are passing through such a state of mind as this, for it is of all things, next to hell itself, one of the most dreadful, and in such a plight men have cried out with Job, *"Therefore I will not restrain my mouth; I will speak in the anguish of my spirit, I will complain in the bitterness of my soul. Am I the sea, or the sea monster, that You set a guard over me? If I say, 'My bed will comfort me, my couch will ease my complaint,' then You frighten me with dreams and terrify me by visions; so that my soul would choose suffocation, death rather than my pains. I waste away; I will not live forever. Leave me alone, for my days are but a breath."* Thanks be unto God, the issues out of this slavery are often such as make angels sing for joy, but while the black night endures, it is a horror of darkness indeed. Put a martyr upon the rack, or even fasten him with an iron chain to the stake, and let the flames kindle around him, and if his Lord shall smile upon him, his anguish will be nothing compared with the torture of a spirit scorched and burned with an inward sense of the wrath of God. Such a man can join in the lament of Jeremiah, and cry, *In dark places He has made me dwell, like those who have long been dead. He has walled me in so that I cannot go out; He has made my chain heavy. Even when I cry out and call for help, He shuts out my prayer.* Or, *The spirit of a man can endure his sickness, but as for a broken spirit who can bear it?* To groan over unforgiven sin, to dread its well-deserved punishment, to fear the everlasting burnings, these are things which make men suffer with an emphasis, and make them think life to be a burden.

We learn from the narrative that the evil spirit, at the times when it took full possession of the boy, *sought his destruction* by hurling him in different directions. *"He often falls into the fire and often into the water."* So it is with deeply distressed souls. One day they seem to be all on fire with earnestness and zeal, with impatience and anxiety, but the next day they sink into a horrible coldness and apathy of soul from which it appears to be utterly impossible to arouse them. All sensitive yesterday, all insensible today. They are uncertain; you know not where to find them. If you deal with them as with a spirit that is in danger from the fire of irritableness, you have lost your efforts, for in the next few minutes they will be in danger from the water of indifference. They fly to extremes. They are like the souls fabled to be in purgatory, of whom legends say that they suffer by turns in an oven and in cells of ice. You would suppose from the way in which they speak today that they felt themselves to be the blackest of sinners, but in a short time they deny that they feel any sort of repentance for sin. You would imagine, to hear them talk at one time, that they would never cease to pray till they found the Savior, but by and by they tell you that they cannot pray at all, and that it is but a mockery for them to bend the knee. They are more fickle than the weather; their color comes and goes like that of the chameleon; they are all fits and starts, convulsions and contortions. He would be more than human who could reckon upon them for a month, for they vary more often than the moon. Their malady laughs us to scorn, their trouble baffles all our consoling efforts; only Jesus Christ himself can deal with them. It is well that we can add that he has a peculiar art in dealing with desperate diseases, and finds his delight in healing those whom all others have left for lost.

To add to the difficulties of this deplorable case, this child was *deaf*, so our Lord tells us in Mark, *"You deaf and mute spirit, I command you, come out of him."* There was therefore no way of reasoning with him at all; not a sound could pass through that sealed ear. With other men you might speak, and a soft word might calm the agitations of their mind; but no word, however gentle, could reach this poor tormented spirit, to whom sound and sense alike were impenetrable. And are there not such still, to whom words are wasted breath? You may quote promises, you may supply encouragements, you may explain doctrines, but it is all nothing; they end where they began: like squirrels in revolving cages, they are never the ones who move forward. Oh, the twistings and turnings, the complexities and the windings of poor tormented minds! It is easy enough certainly to tell them to believe in Jesus, but if they understand you, it is in such a dark manner that you have need to explain it again, and that explanation you will have to explain still further. To cast themselves simply upon the blood of sprinkling, and to rest upon the finished work of Jesus, is of all things most plain; the very child's ABC cannot be plainer, and yet for all that, it is not plain to them. They will appear to comprehend you, and then start off on a tangent. They will appear to be convinced, and for a time to give up their doubts and fears, but meet them half an hour afterwards, and you will find you have been speaking to a wall, addressing yourself to the deaf.

Oh, lamentable case! The Lord of mercy look on such, for hopeless is man's help. Glory be to God, he has laid help upon one who is mighty, who can make the deaf to hear, causing his voice to ring with sweet encouragements in the deathlike stillness of the dungeons of despair.

Next to this it appears that the afflicted one was *mute,* that is to say, incapable of articulate speech by reason of the demoniacal possession. Since he cried out when the devil left him, it would seem to have been a case in which all the instruments of speech were present, but articulation had not been learned. There was utterance of an incoherent sort; the noise-making apparatus was there, but nothing intelligible came forth except the most heartrending cries of pain. Such mute ones abound; they cannot explain their own condition. If they talk to you it is incoherent talk. They contradict themselves every five sentences – you know that they are speaking what they believe to be true, but if you did not know that, you might think that they were telling you falsehoods which confound each other. Their experience is a string of contradictions, and their utterance is even more complicated than their experience. It is very hard and difficult to talk with them for long, it wears out one's patience; and if it wears out the patience of the hearer, how burdensome must it be to the unhappy speaker! They pray, but they dare not call it prayer; it is rather the chattering of a crane or a swallow. They talk with God about what is in their poor silly hearts, but ah! it is such a confusion and mixture that when it is done, they wonder whether they have prayed or not. It is the cry, the bitter anguishing cry of pain, but it is untranslatable into words; it is an awful groan, an unutterable yearning and longing of the Spirit, but they scarcely know themselves what it means.

You are weary with the details of this sorrowful case, but I have not yet concluded the tale of woe. If any of you have never experienced the like, thank God for it, but at the same time pity and pray for those who are passing through this state of mind, and invoke now silently the hope of the great Healer, that he would come and deal with them, for their plight is past the art of man.

The father told Jesus that his son was *pining away.* How could it be otherwise, with one borne down by such a mass of disorders, so perpetually tormented that the natural rest of sleep was constantly broken? It was not likely that the strength would long be maintained in a system so racked and torn; and, mark you, despair of mind is an exceedingly weakening thing to the soul. I have known it to even weaken the body, till the worn-out sufferer has said with David, *My vitality was drained away as with the fever heat of summer.* To feel the guilt of sin, to fear the coming punishment, to have a dreadful cry in one's ears of the *wrath to come,* to fear death and to expect it every moment, above all to disbelieve God, and write bitter things against him, this is a thing to make the bones rot, and the heart wither. Read John Bunyan's *Grace Abounding,* and behold a picture there, drawn to the life of a soul that was left as a wasteland in the desert, so that it could not see when good came to it. You see a mind tossed up and down on ten thousand waves of unbelief, never resting at any time, but perpetually disturbed and distracted with surmises, suspicions, and forebodings. If these attacks continued always, and were not sometimes intermitted, if there were not little pauses, as it were, between the fits of unbelief, surely man would utterly fail and go to his long home, a prey to his own cruel unbelief.

> To disbelieve God is a thing to make the heart wither.

The worst point in the case was, *all this had continued for years.* Jesus asked how long he had been in this case, and the father replied, "From childhood." Sometimes God permits, for purposes which we do not understand, the deep distress of a tempted soul to last for years; I cannot tell for how many years, but certainly some have had to battle with unbelief on the very confines of the grave, and only at evening has it been light to them. When they thought they would die in the dark, the Holy Spirit has appeared to them, and they have been cheered and comforted. The Puritans were accustomed to quoting the remarkable experience of Mrs. Honeywood as an instance of the singular way in which the Lord delivers his chosen. She, for year after year, was in bondage to melancholy and despair, but she was set at liberty by the gracious providence of God in an almost miraculous way. She picked up a slender Venice glass, and saying, "I am as surely damned as that glass is dashed to pieces," she hurled it down upon the floor, when, to her surprise, and the surprise of all, I know not by what means, the glass was not so much as even chipped or cracked. That circumstance first gave her a ray of light, and she afterwards cast herself upon the Lord Jesus. Sometimes extraordinary light has been given to extraordinary darkness, God has brought up the prisoner out of the innermost ward where his feet had been held fast in the stocks, and after years of bondage, he has at last given perfect and delightful liberty.

One thing more about this case. *The disciples had failed* to cast the devil out. On other occasions they had been successful – they said to their Master, *"Even the demons are subject to us."* But this time they were utterly foiled. They did their best; they appeared to have had some faith, or they would not have attempted the task, but their faith was not at all equal to the emergency. Scribes and Pharisees gathered around them and began to mock them, and if there had been power in all the company of the apostles to have worked the deed, they would gladly have done it; but there they stood, defeated and dismayed – the poor patient before them racked and tormented, and they unable to give him the slightest ease. Ah! it becomes a painful case when an anxious soul has gone to the house of God for years and yet has found no consolation; when the troubled spirit has sought help from ministers, from Christian men and women; when prayers have been offered and not answered, and tears have been shed and have been unhelpful; when books which have been comforting to others have been studied without result; when teachings which have converted thousands fail to create a good impression; and yet there are such instances in which all human agency is put to defeat, and when it seems as impossible to comfort the poor troubled one as to calm the waves of the sea, or hush the voice of the thunder cloud. Hearts are to be met with still, in which the evil spirit and the Holy Spirit are brought into distinct conflict, in which the evil spirit displays all his viciousness, and brings the soul to the uttermost pitch of distress, in which I trust that the Holy Spirit will display his saving power and lead the soul out of its prison to praise the name of the Lord.

I thought I heard from some ungodly person a kind of whisper to himself: "I thank God I know nothing about these things." Pause before you thank God for this, for as evil as this is and to be deplored, it would be better if you had all this than remain altogether without spiritual sensibility. It would be better to go to heaven burnt and branded, scourged and scarred every step of the road, than to slide gently down to hell as many of you are doing – sleeping sweetly while devils carry you along the road to hell. It is a little thing, after all, to be for a season tormented and troubled by disturbances within if it shall ultimately, by God's intercession, end in joy and peace in believing. But it is beyond measure a dreadful thing to have "Peace, peace" sung in one's ears where there is no peace, and then forever to discover one's self a castaway in the pit from which there shall be no escape. Instead of being thankful, I would rather ask you to tremble. Yours is that terribly prophetic calm which the traveler frequently perceives upon the Alpine summit. Everything is still. The birds suspend their notes, fly low, and cower down with fear. The hum of bees among the flowers is hushed. A horrible stillness rules the hour, as if death had silenced all things by stretching over them his awful scepter. Do you not perceive what is surely at hand? The thunder is preparing; the lightning will soon cast abroad its mighty fires. Earth will rock; granite peaks will be dissolved; all nature will shake beneath the fury of the storm. Yours is that solemn calm today, O sinner. Rejoice not in it, for the tempest is coming, the whirlwind and the tribulation which shall sweep you away and utterly destroy you. Better to be molested by the devil now than be tormented by him forever.

I have thus brought before you a very sorrowful subject; but now, secondly, may the Holy Spirit help us while I remind you of the one resource.

The disciples were baffled. The Master, however, remained undefeated, and cried, *"Bring him to Me!"* We ought to use the resources as far as the resources will go. We are bound, further, to make the resources more effectual than they ordinarily are. Prayer and fasting are prescribed by our Lord as the means of stringing up ourselves to greater power than we should otherwise possess. There are conversions which will never be brought about by the agency of ordinary Christians. We have need to pray more, and by self-denial to keep our bodies more completely under control, and so to enjoy closer communion with God before we shall be able to handle the more distressing cases. The church of God would be far stronger to wrestle with this ungodly age if she were more given to prayer and fasting. There is a mighty effectualness in these two gospel ordinances. The first links us to heaven, the second separates us from earth. Prayer takes us into the banqueting house of God; fasting overturns the overflowing tables of earth. Prayer gives us to feed on the bread of heaven, and fasting delivers the soul from being encumbered with the fullness of bread which perishes. When Christians bring themselves up to the uttermost possibilities of spiritual vigor, then they will be able, by God's Spirit working in them, to cast out devils which today, without the prayer and fasting, laugh them to scorn. But for all that, to the most advanced Christian, there will still remain those mountainous difficulties which must be directly brought to the Master's personal agency for help. Still he tenderly commands us, "Bring them unto me."

To make the text appear practical, let me beg you to remember that *Jesus Christ is still alive.* Simple as that truth is, you need to be reminded of it. We very often estimate the power of the church by looking to her ministers, her ordinances, and her members; but the power of the church does not lie here, it lies in the Holy Spirit, and in an ever-living Savior. Jesus Christ died, it is true, but he lives, and we may as truly come to him today as did that anxious father in the days of our Lord's earthly sojourn. Miracles have ceased, it is said; so natural miracles have, but spiritual miracles have not. We have not the power to work either the one or the other. Christ has the power to work any kind of wonder, and he is still willing and able at this present hour to work spiritual miracles in the midst of his church. I do delight to think of my Lord as a living Christ to whom I can speak and tell him of every case that occurs in my ministry; a living Helper to whom I may bring every difficulty that occurs in my own soul, and in the souls of others. O think not that he is dead and buried! Seek him not among the dead! Jesus lives, and, living, is as able to meet with these cases of distress and sorrow as when he was here below.

Remember, too, that *Jesus lives in the place of authority.* When he was here he had power over devils, but yonder he has greater power still; for here on earth he veiled the splendor of his Godhead, but yonder his glory beams resplendent, and all hell confesses the majesty of his power. There is no demon, however forceful, who will not tremble if Jesus does but speak, or even so much as look at him. Today Jesus is the Master of hearts and consciences; he by his secret power can work upon every one of our minds; he can depress us or he can exalt us; he can cast down or he can lift up. There cannot be a case which shall be hard to him. We have but to bring it to him. He lives – and he lives in the place of power, and he can achieve the desire of our hearts.

Moreover, *Jesus lives in the place of observation, and he graciously intercedes still.* I know we are tempted to think of him as of one who is far away, who does not behold the sorrows of his church; but I tell you, brethren, Christ's honor is as much concerned at this moment in the defeat or victory of his servants as it was when he came down from the mountaintop. From the battlements of heaven Jesus looks today upon the work of his ministers, and if he sees them foiled, he is jealous for the honor of his gospel, and is as ready to intercede and win the victory now as he was then. We have but to look up to our Lord. He sleeps not as Baal did of old. He is not callous to our woes, nor indifferent to our griefs. Blessed Master, you are able to help, and strong to deliver! We have but to bring the matter which distresses us before you, and you will deal with it now according to your compassion.

We should also recollect, for our warning, that *Jesus Christ expects us to treat him as a living, powerful, interceding one, and to confide in him as such.* We do not know what we miss through lack of faith; we conceive that certain persons are in a hopeless condition, and thus we dishonor Christ and injure them. We leave some cases alone, and give them up instead of presenting them constantly to him; we limit the Holy One of Israel; we grieve his spirit and vex his holy mind. But if, as children trust their father, we would trust in Jesus unstaggeringly with an Abrahamic faith, believing that what he has promised he is able also to perform, then should we see even such cases as that before us soon brought into the light of day: the oil of joy given instead of mourning, and the garment of praise for the spirit of heaviness.

Now, I earnestly urge parents and relatives, and any who have children or friends in distress of mind to make a point of taking their dear ones to Jesus. Do not doubt him – you vex him if you do; do not hesitate to come and tell him today the position of your beloved one. Hasten to him, lay the sick one before him, and even if while in prayer the case should become worse instead of better, still do not hesitate, for you are dealing with the infinite Son of God, and you need not fear, you must not doubt. God grant us grace in all things in our daily troubles, and especially in soul affairs, to bring all matters to the Lord Jesus.

Lastly, and with brevity, the sure result.

When the child, or the man, or whichever he may have been, was brought before our Lord, the case looked thoroughly hopeless. He was deaf and dumb; how could the Master deal with him? Besides that, he was foaming and wallowing; what opening did there seem to be for the divine power? I cannot wonder that his father said, *"If You can do anything, take pity on us and help us!"* In most other instances the voice of Jesus calmed the spirit; but that voice could not reach the mind, for the ear was sealed. Never was there before the Savior a more thoroughly far-gone case, to all appearances hopeless; and yet the cure was divinely certain, for Jesus, without hesitating for a moment, said to the unclean spirit, *"You deaf and mute spirit, I command you, come out of him."* Christ has power to charge devils with authority. They dare not disobey. *"And do not enter him again,"* said the Savior. Where Jesus heals, he heals forever. Once bring the soul out of prison, it shall not go back again. If he says, "I forgive," the sin is forgiven; if he speaks peace, the peace shall be like a river that never ceases, running until it melts away into the ocean of eternal love. The cure was hopeless in itself, yet absolutely certain when Jesus put forth his healing hand. O you who are broken down and desponding today, there is nothing that *you* can do or that *I* can do; but there is nothing which he cannot do. Only go yourself today to him, and with a word he will give you peace, a peace that shall never be broken again, but shall last till you enter into eternal rest.

Nevertheless, the word of Christ, though sure to win its way, was stoutly opposed. The devil had great wrath, for he knew that his time was short. He began to tear and put out all his devilish force upon the poor child; and the poor creature, foaming and wallowing, fell down as if he were dead, under a terrible provocation. So often will it happen that at first the voice of Christ will make the spirit more troubled than before, not because Jesus troubles us, but because Satan revolts against him. A poor tempted creature may even lie down in despair as if dead, and those around may cry, "He is dead," but even then shall come the healing hand of tenderness and love, at whose touch the spirit shall survive. Ah, soul! If you should judge yourself to be as one dead, if your last hope should expire, if there should seem now to be nothing before you but a fearful expectation of judgment and of fiery indignation, it is then that Jesus will intercede. Learn the lesson that you cannot be gone too far from Christ. Believe that your extremities are only extremities to you and not to him. The highest sin and the deepest despair together cannot baffle the power of Jesus. If you were between the very jaws of hell, Christ could snatch you forth. If your sins had brought you even to the gates of hell, so that the flames flashed into your face, if then you looked to Jesus, he could save you. If you are brought to him when you are at death's door, yet still eternal mercy will receive you.

How is it that Satan has the brashness to make men despair? Surely it is a piece of his infernal impertinence that he dares to do it. Despair! when you have an omnipotent God to deal with you? Despair! when the precious blood of the Son of God is given for sinners? Despair! when God delights in mercy? Despair! when the silver bell rings, *"Come to Me, all who are weary and heavy-laden, and I will give you rest"*? Despair! while life lasts, while mercy's gate stands wide open; while the heralds of mercy beckon you to come, even though your sins be as scarlet, for they shall be as wool; though they be like crimson they shall be white as snow? I say again, it is infernal impertinence that has dared to suggest the idea of despair to a sinner. Christ unable to save? Never can it be. Christ outdone by Satan and by sin? Impossible. A sinner with diseases too many for the Great Physician to heal? I tell you that if all the diseases of men were met in you, and all the sins of men were heaped on you, and blasphemy and murder, and fornication and adultery, and every sin that is possible or imaginable had all been committed by you, still the precious blood of Jesus Christ, God's dear Son, cleanses us from all sin. If you will but trust my Master, and he is worthy to be trusted and deserves your confidence – if you will but trust him, he will save you even now. Ah! why delay, why raise questions, why debate, why deliberate, mistrust, and suspect? Fall into his arms – he cannot reject you, for he has himself said, *"The one who comes to Me I will certainly not cast out."* Yet, poor wretch, I do despair of converting you unless the Master does it. It is mine to tell you this, but I know you will not hear it, or, hearing it, you will reject it unless Christ shall come with power by his Spirit. O may he come today, and say to the evil spirit within you, "Come out of him, you foul spirit, and go no more into him. Let such a one be free, for I have redeemed him with my most precious blood." O pray, dear friends, that weak as my words have been today, disconnected as my thoughts have been, yet, nevertheless, God the blessed Spirit may bless them to the unfastening of bars of iron, that gates of brass may be opened, and captive ones brought forth to liberty. The Lord bless such for his name's sake. Amen.

Chapter 7

A Desperate Case – How to Meet It

> *Then the disciples came to Jesus privately and said, "Why could we not drive it out?" And He said to them, "Because of the littleness of your faith; for truly I say to you, if you have faith the size of a mustard seed, you will say to this mountain, 'Move from here to there,' and it will move; and nothing will be impossible to you. [But this kind does not go out except by prayer and fasting."]* (Matthew 17:19-21)

The narrative, of which our text forms a part, describes a scene which took place immediately after the transfiguration of our Lord. Not to divorce it therefore from its connection, let us glance at the occasion of the case, that nothing may be lost by negligence, or that perhaps we may gain something by meditation.

How great the difference between Moses and Christ! When Moses had been forty days upon the mountaintop, he underwent a kind of transfiguration, so that his face shone with exceeding brightness when he came down among the people, and he was obliged to put a veil over his face, for they could not bear to look upon his glory. Not so our Savior! He had been really transfigured with a greater glory than Moses could ever know, and yet, as he came down from the mount, whatever radiance shone upon his face, it is not written that the people could not look upon him, but rather they were amazed, and running to him, they saluted him. The glory of the law repelled, for the majesty of holiness and justice drives the awed spirits away from God. But the greater glory of Jesus attracts. Though he is holy, and just, and righteous too, yet blended with these there is so much of truth and grace that sinners run to Jesus, amazed at his goodness, attracted by the charming fascination of his love, and they salute him, become his disciples, and take him to be their Lord and Master. Some of you may just now be blinded by the dazzling brightness of the law of God. You feel its claims on your conscience, but you cannot keep it in your life. It is too high; you cannot attain to it. Not that you find fault with the law; on the contrary, it commands your profoundest esteem. Still you are in no way drawn by it to God; you are rather hardened in your heart, and you may be moving towards the consequence of desperation: "As it is impossible for me to earn salvation by the works of the law, I will continue in my sins." Ah, poor heart! Turn your eye away from Moses, with all his repelling splendor, and look to Jesus, yonder, crucified for sinful men. Behold his flowing wounds and thorn-crowned head! He is the Son of God, and therein he is greater than Moses. He bears the wrath of God, and therein he shows more of God's justice than Moses' broken tablets could ever do. Look to him, and as you feel the attraction of his love, fly to his arms and you shall be saved.

How different the spirit of Moses and Jesus! When Moses comes down from the mountain, it is to purge the camp. He seems to grasp the fiery sword; he breaks the golden calf; he strikes the idolaters. But when Jesus comes down from the mountain, he finds strife in the camp, as Moses did; he finds his own apostles defeated and beaten, just as Aaron had been defeated by the clamors of the people; but he has not a word of cursing, and instead there is a gentle rebuke – *"You unbelieving and perverted generation, how long shall I be with you? How long shall I put up with you?"* His actions are actions of mercy – not breaking in pieces, but healing; not cursing, but blessing. Love sits smiling on his brow as he touches the poor wretch who is almost dead with diabolical possession, and restores him to life and health. Go you then, to Jesus; leave the law and your own poor attempts at self-righteousness, for

> **His actions are actions of mercy – not breaking in pieces, but healing; not cursing, but blessing.**

these can do nothing but curse you. Fly to Jesus, for whoever you may be, there are pardons on his lips; there are blessings in his hands; there is love in his heart; and he will not scorn to receive even you.

How much of condescension there is in the manner of Christ! Our Lord, we have told you, had been very glorious on the mountain's top with Moses and Elijah; yet when he comes down into the midst of the crowd, he does not look down upon the cry of the poor man, nor refuse to touch him who was possessed with a devil. Observe my Master's condescension, for he stoops to attention, and yet his manner softens into pity, and presently it melts into a gracious sympathy, as if this were the only channel through which his matchless power could flow. Then remember, he is the same today as he was then.

> "Now, though he reigns exalted high,
>   His love is still as great."

He is as willing now to receive sinners as when it was said of him, *"This man receives sinners and eats with them";* just as ready to receive you, poor sinners, as when he was called *"a friend of tax collectors and sinners!"* Come to him. Bow at his feet. His love invites you still. Believe that the transfigured and glorified Jesus is still a loving Savior, willing to pardon and forgive.

Once again, what choice instruction there is in the history! After Jesus had been absent for some time, he came back. You may ask, For what purpose had he retired? Evidently he went up into the mountain to pray. It was while he was praying (and I make no doubt, fasting also) that the appearance of his face changed. By his own personal devotion, and by the Father's special revelation, he had thus come back, as it were, with great refreshment, to carry on his ministry. Therefore, we become witnesses of a remarkable power which he immediately showed forth, and of no less remarkable counsel which he pointedly spoke to his disciples when they felt their own weakness.

Thus we have before us, in our text, a peculiar case – a patient who utterly baffled the skill of all his disciples, healed at once by the great Master; and we have a reason given why the apostles themselves were not able to deliver him.

Let us look for a little while at *this very sad case;* not so singular either, I think, but that we may find the same kind round about us. Then let us notice *the scene around the case* – the father, the disciples, and the scribes. Afterwards we shall joyfully observe *the Savior's coming into the midst and deciding all the difficulty;* and, lastly, we shall pay attention to the reason he gives in private to his disciples as to why they, *before his coming, were utterly powerless to achieve the work.*

First, we have before us a very peculiar case.

It appears that the disciples had cast out devils of almost all sorts. Wherever they had gone, up to this time, this was their uniform testimony: *"Lord, even the demons are subject to us";* but now they are baffled. They seem to have encountered a devil of the worst kind. There are grades in devilry as there are in human sin. All men are evil, but all men are not alike evil. All devils are full of sin, but they are not all sinful to the same degree. Do we not read in Scripture, *"Then it goes and takes along with it seven other spirits more wicked than itself"*? It may be that there are different degrees in the wickedness of devils, and perhaps, also, in their power to fulfill their wicked impulses. We can scarcely think that all the devils are Satans. There seems to be one chief arch-spirit, one great Diabolus, who is an accuser of the brethren – one mighty Lucifer, who fell down from heaven and has become the prince of the powers of darkness. In all his hosts it is probable that there is not another like him. He stands first and chief of these fallen morning stars; the rest of the spirits may stand in different grades of wickedness, a hierarchy of hell. This poor wretch seems to have been possessed of one of the worst, most potent, violent, and vicious of these evil spirits. I believe, brethren, that here we have a picture of a certain class of individuals who are not only desperately sinful, but are also subject to extraordinary impulses which carry them to infernal lengths and depths of infamy; they are incapable of restraint, a terror to their relatives, and a misery to themselves.

All men are sinful, as I have said before, but the power of depravity in some men is much stronger than in others; at least, if it be not intrinsically stronger, it certainly has manifestations in some which we have never perceived in common among men. Let us try and pick out the case according to the narrative. How frequently, dear friends, too frequently, alas! have we seen young people who have answered to the description given here. They have had a prematureness of wickedness. When Jesus asked the father, *"How long has this been happening to him?"* the answer was *"From childhood."* I remember having once known such a child over whom outbursts of passion came, in which his face would turn black. When he was able to run around and was sent to a public school, a flint stone, a club, a brick, anything which might come next to his hand he would throw, without a moment's thought, at anyone who irritated him. His knife would be drawn from his pocket and open in an instant. The young assassin has often been prevented from stabbing others by a careful hand and watchful eye which guarded him. We have noticed this, I say, in some of the very young. They begin to lie early, and to steal soon, and the young lips even try to swear, while the anxious mother cannot understand where the child could have learned it. You have protected such a child from all contamination, and seemed to shut him in and wrap him about with holy influences; and yet, in these desperate instances, as soon as ever the child could know right from wrong, he has deliberately chosen to do wrong with a violence of self-will and recklessness of consequence altogether unusual. Some such cases we have seen. O, may God grant it may never be your lot or mine to be the parents of such children. Yet such there have been, and such men there are who have grown up now, and the youthful passions of their childhood have become developed; and you may find them with the low forehead and the dark scowling eye, if you will, in our prison houses. Or if you see them in the streets, you may hopefully wish that they may be in prison before long, for they are unsafe abroad. From childhood they seem to have been possessed with this chief of devils, and to have been carried captive by him at his will.

This lad seems also to have been afflicted with what is here called *lunacy*, which was, indeed, only a form of epilepsy. He was constantly subjected, it seems, to epileptic fits; for I think we can hardly understand lunacy to mean anything short of occasional madness. Attacks of such outrageous violence would come upon him, that there would be no enduring him. He would then dash himself into the fire, or if water were near, he would attempt self-destruction by plunging into it. We have met with persons of this kind, perfectly outrageous and beyond all command, when fits of evil came upon them. I will instance cases which I have observed.

I know a man now, he may be here today; if he is, he will recognize his own portrait. At times he is as reasonable as anyone I could wish to associate with. He enjoys listening to the Word of God. He is, in some respects, an amiable, excellent, and respectable man. But occasionally fits of drunkenness come upon him, in which he is perfectly powerless under the influence of the demon; and while it lasts, it matters not, even when he knows he is wrong, a thousand angels could not drag him from it. He is thrown into the water of self-destruction, and he will continue in it. You may urge him and reason with him, and you may think – oh, how often have some thought this who love him – he will never do that again; he is too sensible a man; he has been too well-taught; the Word of God has had such an effect upon him that he will never do it again. Yet he does. He repeats the old outbursts, and has done so for twenty or thirty years; and, if he lives, unless sovereign grace prevents it, he will die a drunkard, as sure as he is a living man, and go from his drink to damnation.

Here is another case, which I likewise draw from life. The man is kind, tender, and generous – generous to a fault. He has a home – he *had* one, I ought to say – he had a home, and he was the light of it. No one ever suspected him – that is, in his better times – of any grievous faults; but sometimes – and this has been concealed by many an indulgent friend – sometimes an attack of profaneness comes upon him, and at such seasons it matters not what the temptation may be, nor how foul the vice may be, the man runs into it. If you should meet him in the street, and talk with him, and argue with him, it would be all time and labor thrown away. No, I have known him to break up his home and cross the sea to go to another land so that he might indulge his vile passions without rebuke, or without the restraint of associating with former friends. He will come back again, brokenhearted, wondering how he could ever be such a fool; but he will go again. It is *in* him. The devil is in him, and, unless God casts it out, he will do the same again, deliberately choosing his own damnation. Though he knows it, yet so

A DESPERATE CASE – HOW TO MEET IT

possessed of the love of sin is he, that when the fit comes upon him, this diabolical epilepsy, he falls into sin with his whole might and power.

I might go on describing cases of this kind, but you will not need that I should picture anymore; it could only be to vary the different forms of sin. However, let me try one more. A lad had as good a father as ever a child could have. He was bound as an apprentice. It became whispered in a few weeks that small amounts of money were missing. The father was very grieved, so indeed was the master, and the matter was quietly hushed up. A little while after, the same thing occurred again. The contracts were canceled, and nothing more was said of it; but the father was sorely perplexed. He looked out for some other situation for the boy where he might, perhaps, recover his character. After a time it was precisely the same again. Bad companions had got hold of him, or rather, he had become a ringleader among other bad companions. Well, something else must be tried. It was tried. He has had twenty situations, and they have all been abandoned for the very same reason. And now, what do you think is his treatment of his parents? Instead of being grateful for the repeated kindness and longsuffering shown to him, he will break out sometimes into such dreadful emotions that even the lives of his parents are scarcely safe. And when he has been in his old haunts a little more than usual, he is really so terrible a being that his mother who loves him and who weeps over him would almost as soon see a fiend from hell as see him; for when he comes home, everything goes wrong. Confusion is in the house, and terror is in every heart. He acts precisely as if he were a madman. They have said, "Send him to Australia, or send him to America" – where they do send many of that sort – but if he goes there he will turn up, sooner or later, at the foot of the gallows; he is desperately set on evil, and nothing turns him aside. He tears and foams at the mouth with passion; his whole heart goes forth outrageously after anything like vice, and there appears to be not one redeeming trait in his character; or, if there is, it only seems to be subjected to the power of his lusts. He devises means to be more mighty to do mischief in the world.

What dreadful cases these are! Why am I talking of them? Dear friends, I have spoken of them because it has been laying upon my heart to encourage and comfort you who are constrained to carry a daily cross in having such relations and such children as these. It is one of the heaviest afflictions which can come upon you.

In the case before us, the child was both deaf and dumb – not, I suppose, through any organic effect, but through the epilepsy and the satanic possession. So we have often seen children – shall I look them in the face today, as I stand here? They are no children now who are positively deaf to all spiritual sounds. They have been pleaded with, but it is in vain. They know the truth, they know the whole truth, but they do not know the power of it. They are never absent from family prayer, nor in any prayer are they ever forgotten by their parents. They come to this place; they attend our classes; they go to revival services. Now and then there is something like a little emotion, but it does not come to much; they are precisely similar to the deaf adder which cannot be charmed, even if we have never charmed them so wisely. Others of the family have been converted. Nearly all the household has now been brought to Christ. Lydia has had her heart opened; God has been pleased to call young Timothy; but this one remains, and after much anxiety, much effort, and much labor, no good has been achieved. The stone seems as soft as their heart, and the ear of the deaf as much alive to rebuke as is their conscience. This, again, is a very sad case.

I meet sometimes, too, with cases of another kind – persons who are beset with very high doctrine, who have got the devil in them, puffing up their fleshly minds with a vain conceit of sound understanding, and degrading their carnal profession with a disgusting impurity of heart and life. You will talk with them; they will tell you they wish to be saved – would give their right arm to be saved, but it is not in their power. You bid them to believe in Jesus. They have no sense, they tell you, of the need of a Savior; they are not in a fit state to believe. When God's time comes, the thing will occur. They love high doctrine, they will hear nothing else but it; but then their Sunday, if there is a temptation which comes across their path, will be spent anywhere but in the worship of God; and during the week they give way to all sorts of sins. Whatever temptation comes, they go after it. The comfort they get from their religion, which they wrap about them like a cloak, is this – that no ministers speak the truth except one or two; that the truth is fatalism; that all they have to do is to be carried along like dead, inanimate logs down the stream, and that they are not at all responsible; or if they are responsible, it is merely to maintain with unflinching vigor their own crude sentiments. I have seen some of these people – good people in their way too – of whom I have thought that the conversion of drunkards was more hopeful than theirs. That damnable fatalism, which by some is put instead of the predestination of the Scriptures, has locked them up – put them in an iron cage, and so they are beyond the reach of help, going on still in their sin, rejecting the gospel of Christ, while trying to be connoisseurs of its choicest mysteries.

Now, brothers and sisters, why are such cases as these permitted? Why does the Lord allow the devil thus to fill the soul with sin?

I think it is, first, to show that there is a reality in sin. If we were all moral and outwardly respectable, we would begin to think sin was but a delusion. These daring sinners show us the reality of it.

It is to manifest the reality of divine grace; for when these are saved, then it is that we wonder, and we are compelled to say, "There is something in this. If such a hard, iron nature yet melts before the power of divine love, there must be a majesty in it."

It is to humble us too, to throw us on our back, and let us see how utterly powerless human agency is. When you cannot get in the thin end of the wedge, much less the whole wedge; when the plowshare breaks on the edge of a hard rock; when the edge of the sword turns against the armor, then it is to draw yourself out of self to God. You see, it is a deadly evil, where only omnipotence can help. Your soul says, "Lord, put out your arm! Now do it, and the glory shall be yours." This is probably the chief reason: it is in order that God may get great glory to himself. He lets the devil have it all his own way. "There," he says, "pick your own ground, fight in your own territory, maneuver in your own way, and, with a word, I will crush your power." He gives Satan great advantage, lets him entrench himself firmly in the soul from youth up, so that the victory may be splendid to the greatest degree.

We have thus before us now, for our sorrowful contemplation, the case of one whose disease mocks the physician, laughs at all human

> **If we were all moral and outwardly respectable, we would begin to think sin was but a delusion.**

endeavors, and defies the watchful care of mild and gentle treatment to mitigate its force or help its fearful symptoms.

We turn now with a passing glance to look at the scene around. The company is made up of five sorts of people.

There are the scribes – cynics, I think, to a man – "We told you so! we told you so!" they say. "Your Master pretended to give you power to cast out devils. No such thing! you cannot cast out devils. Those whom you healed were not truly possessed. Little enough was ever the matter with them. They were fanciful, and they believed in you through enthusiasm. The fools of naiveness, your incantations bewitched them, and so they got better. But you cannot cast out a devil – you cannot cast that devil out." "Now then," says one of the scribes to Andrew, "cast it out. Come, Philip, try what you can do!" And inasmuch as after all trying, the devil would not go out – "Ah! just so!" they say, "they are impostors. There is nothing in it." Just recall it, friends, to your own memories; have you not seen men of that kind? "Ah yes," they say, "the gospel converts one sort of people, such as always go to places of worship, the more intelligent and respectable of the community; but, you see, it is no good in these tough cases. These hardened ones – it cannot touch them. They are beyond its power." "Aha!" they say, "where is the boasted might of this Great Physician? He can heal your finger aches, but he does not know how to make these foul diseases fly."

Then here is the poor father, all dejected. "I brought him to you – I knew you did cast out devils, and I thought you could cast my son's devil out, and he would be healed. I am disappointed in you all. Yet I do think your Master can do it, but I am not sure that even he can. If such excellent apostles, as you are, have tried so hard and have failed, I do not think there can be any chance for me. I am full of unbelief. O, I wish I had never brought my child here at all, to make a public spectacle of him, that he might be a witness to your failures." That is the poor father. Perhaps that poor father is here today, and he is saying, "Ah, I do believe, but still I am full of unbelief. I have brought my daughter; I have brought my child under the sound of the Word; I have prayed, and wrestled with God in prayer, and my child is not saved." "I brought my husband," says one good woman, "but he is just as full of Satan as ever he was. I must give it up in despair."

And then there are the disciples, and they look pitiful indeed. "Well," they say, "we do not know how to account for it. We cannot tell you how it is. We have said the same in this case that we were used to saying in others." "Why," says one of them, "when I went abroad and just said, 'In the name of Jesus Christ I command you to come out of him,' the unclean spirit always did come out in every other case. I cannot comprehend this. I must give it up." "We all must give it up," say the apostles. For some unknown cause, this seems to be quite out of the catalog of cases which we are commissioned to cure. And so we sometimes hear dejected ministers, after preaching long at such hard shells as these, say, "Well, we cannot understand it. The gospel *is the power of God for salvation to everyone who believes.* Oh, it must be that these are foreordained unto damnation; we must give it up." That is how unbelieving ministers talk – or at least the majority of ministers in their season of misgiving and chagrin.

But then there is the general crowd. They are neither this way nor that. They say they will see fairly. "Come, clear the ring out. If Jesus Christ is not an impostor – if he is God – then certainly he can heal this poor man." Now, here is the test and the ordeal: "If that man is not healed," says the crowd, "we will not believe; but if he is, then we will believe that Jesus Christ is sent of God." O dear friends, how often we have thought of those very hard cases in this way. There are hundreds of undecided people looking on and saying, "Ah, if So-and-so were converted, then I would say there was something in it. If truly he could have a new heart and a right spirit, then I, too, would turn to God with full purpose of heart."

There was a fifth party there, and that was the devil himself. Oh, how triumphant was he! "Ah!" he seemed to say, "try your exorcism; go on with your words; preach at him; pray at me; weep over me; do what you will, you cannot get me out." There he seems to stand entrenched within the stronghold of the poor tortured heart. "Do your best, do your worst, I am not afraid of you. I have got this man, and I will keep him. I have so fixed myself in him that no power shall ever be able to heal him." So we seem to hear that vile shriek of hell over some men: "Yes," says he, "I will trust him to go into Spurgeon's tabernacle. I know that thousands there have felt the power of the Holy Spirit in making new men of them, so this is a case I can trust. There is nothing that will ever touch him. The great hammer has knocked the chains off of many others, but it cannot touch his chains; they are harder than iron. I have no fear of him"; and perhaps he is gloating in his thoughts now with the torments of the man in another world. Ah, you foul fiend! if our Master should come here today, you would sing another tune. If he should say, *"Come out of [him], you unclean spirit!"* you will go back howling to your vile den, for his voice can do what our voice never could have done. And may we not easily realize such a scene enacted in this congregation? You have the scoffers, you have the anxious parent, the ministry confessedly powerless in the matter; the crowd looking on, and the devil rejoicing that such cases are quite beyond human strength. What more can you want to animate the picture before your imagination?

But look! The Master comes.

Ah! the Master comes! Immediately the scene changes. The lieutenants and the captains who began the battle did not understand the art of war; they were rash and hasty. The right wing was broken; the left began to reel; the center almost failed. The trumpets of the adversary begin to sound a victory. Here they come – their dread artillery in front. What will become of the army now? Hold! hold! What is it that I see? A cloud of dust. Who comes galloping there? It is the commander in chief. "What are you about?" says he, "What are you about?" In a moment he sees this is not the way to fight. He comprehends the difficulties of the case in an instant. "Forward there! Forward there! Backward there!" The scale is turned. The mere presence of the commander in chief has changed the whole face of the field; and now, you adversaries, you may turn your backs and fly. It was so in Jesus' case, exactly. His lieutenants and captains – the apostles – had lost the day. He comes into the field and comprehends the state of the case. *"Bring him to Me!"* says he, and the poor wretch, foaming and tormented, is brought to him, and he says, *"You deaf and mute spirit, I command you, come out of him."* The thing is done; the victory is achieved; the undecided receive Christ as a prophet; the scoffers' mouths are shut; the trembling father rejoices, and the poor demoniac is cured.

And yet when Jesus Christ came to cure this poor child, he was in as bad a state as he well could be. No, the very presence of the Savior seemed to make it worse. As soon as ever the devil perceived that Christ had come, he began to tear his poor victim. As quaint old Fuller says – like a bad tenant whose lease is out, he hates the landlord, and so he does all the damage he can because he has got notice to quit. Often just before men are converted, they are worse than ever; there is an unusual display of their desperate wickedness, for then the devil has great wrath, now that his time is short.

The struggles of this child are appalling. The devil seemed as if he would kill him before he could be healed; and after outbursts of the most frightful kind, the poor youth lay upon the ground, pale and still as a corpse, insomuch that many said, *"He is dead!"* It is just the same with many conversions of these desperate sinners. Their convictions are so terrible, and frequently the work of the devil within them in keeping them from Christ is so furious that you would give up all hope. You say, "That man will be driven mad; those acute feelings and the intense agony of his spirit will rob him of all mental power, and then in spiritless prostration he will die in his sin." Ah! dear friends, this again is only a piece of Satan's infamy. He knew, and knew right well that Christ could set that poor young man free, and therefore he sets upon him with all his might to torment him while he may. Have I any such desperate case among my hearers today – one who has been as a son of Belial among the children of men? Is the devil tormenting you today? Do you feel tempted to commit suicide? Are you urged to some mad freak of still greater sin in order to drown your griefs and strangle your conscience? O poor soul, do no such thing, for my Master will soon stoop over you, and take you by the hand, and lift you up, and your comfort shall begin, because the unclean spirit is cast out. "Ah! he means to destroy me," says the soul under conviction. No, soul, God does not destroy those whom he convinces of sin. Men do not plow fields which they have no intention to sow. If God plows you with conviction he will sow you with gospel comfort, and you shall bring forth a harvest to his glory. As a woman at her work first plies the needle with its sharp prick, and then draws the thread after it, so

> Often just before men are converted; there is an unusual display of their desperate wickedness.

in your case the sharpness of sorrow for sin will be speedily followed by the silver thread of joy and peace in believing.

And oh, mark it! The vision just now, up there on the mountain of glory, resolved itself into "Jesus only." His peerless radiance eclipsed every other. So, too, it is "Jesus only" down here in the valley. His matchless grace can encounter no rival. Keep this forever in your mind's eye – it is the Master who did it all. His appearance on the scene removed all difficulties. In such extreme cases, there will be, and there must be, a most eminent display of God's power, and that power may be unassociated with means. Under any circumstances, it will be the Lord alone doing it, to the praise and glory of his grace.

Now we come to the last, and perhaps the most important part of the sermon. The riddle is perplexing. *"Why could we not drive it out?"* Let the Master tell us the reasons why these cases thwart our power.

The Savior said it was lack of faith – lack of faith. No man may expect to be the means of the conversion of a sinner without having faith which leads him to believe that the sinner will be converted. Such things may occur, but it is not the rule. If I can preach in faith that my hearers will be saved, they will be saved. If I have no faith, God may honor his Word, but it will be in no great degree; certainly he will not honor me. Abandoned sinners, if converted by means, are usually brought under the power of divine grace through ministers of great faith. Have you observed that there were persons who heard all the small fry of the Whitfieldian age; they had listened to this preacher and to that preacher? Under whom were they converted? Under Mr. Whitfield, because Mr. Whitfield was a man of masterly faith. He believed that the lost could be reclaimed – that the worst diseases could be healed, that the most heinous, abandoned, squandering, blasphemous sinners could be saved. He preached to them as if he expected the deaf would be charmed by the gospel melody, and the dead would be revived at the commanding call of the great Redeemer's name. At Surrey Chapel, over yonder, in Rowland Hill's day, some of the grossest unscrupulous persons and biggest scamps who ever infested London were saved. Why? Because Rowland Hill preached the gospel to big sinners, and believed the fact of big sinners being converted. The respectable people of his day said, "Oh, yes! it is only the tag, rag, and bobtail who go to hear Mr. Hill."

"Just so," said Mr. Hill, "and welcome tag, and welcome rag, and welcome bobtail; they are the very people that I want." "What is the good of such people as they are, going to hear the gospel? Why does Mr. Hill try to preach to harlots and thieves?" they said. "They are just the very people," said Mr. Hill. "I believe that these people can be saved." It was lack of faith in the others; for if a man has faith as a grain of a mustard seed, let it be ever so little, yet, if it is true, it is mighty in proportion to its power. Mr. Hill had the power of faith, and he was the means of the conversion of very great sinners. A few years ago it was utterly hopeless to try and reclaim fallen daughters of sin, but a few men had faith that it could be done, and it has been done; and I will now be bold to say that if there be a great sinner here, such as I tried to describe just now, some gross case of hellish possession, if that person is not saved, it is for the lack of faith in our case. If we have brought that person before God, and have been anxious about his salvation, and God has not heard that prayer, it is because we could not believe it possible that such a case could be saved. If God gives you the power to believe that any soul will be saved, it will be saved; there is no doubt about that.

Still, our Savior added, *"But this kind does not go out except by prayer and fasting."* What did he mean by that? I believe he meant that in these very special cases the ordinary preaching of the Word will not benefit, and ordinary prayer will not suffice. There must be an unusual faith, and to get this there must be an unusual degree of prayer; and to get that prayer up to the right point, there must be, in many cases, fasting as well. No doubt there is something special about the admonition to prayer, from the association in which it stands. One sort of Christians will use formal supplications, and the petitions they ask are founded upon a sense of form, without any glow of feeling. Another sort will wait for the Spirit to move them, and when certain impulses stimulate their minds, they rejoice in a sense of liberty. Yet I show unto you a more excellent way. There are those who watch unto prayer, wait before the Lord, seek his face, and exercise patience till they get an audience. Such disciples continue in their seclusion until they have that experience of access for which they crave.

And what is fasting for? That seems the difficult point. It is evidently supplementary to the peculiar continuance in prayer, practiced oftentimes by our Lord, and advised by him to his disciples. Not a kind of religious observance, in itself meritorious, but a habit, when associated with the exercise of prayer, that is unquestionably helpful. I am not sure whether we have not lost a very great blessing in the Christian church by giving up fasting. It was said there was superstition in it; but, as an old priest says, we had better have a spoonful of superstition than a bowl full of gluttony. Martin Luther, whose body, like some others, was of a big and bulky tendency, felt as some of us do, that in our flesh there dwells no good thing, in another sense than the apostle meant it; and he used to fast frequently. He says his flesh was accustomed to grumbling dreadfully at abstinence, but fast he would, for he found that when he was fasting, it stimulated his praying.

There is a treatise by an old Puritan called "The soul-fattening institution of fasting," and he gives us his own experience that during a fast he has felt more intense eagerness of soul in prayer than he has ever felt at any other time. Some of you, dear friends, may get to the boiling point in prayer without fasting. I do think that others cannot, and probably if we did sometimes set apart a whole day for prayer for a special object, we should at first feel ourselves dull, and lumpish, and heavy. Then let us resolve, "Well, I shall not go down to my dinner. I shall stop here. I feel anxious for a praying frame of mind, and I will keep alone"; and if when the time for the evening meal came on we should say, "I feel a little of the cravings of hunger, but I will satisfy them with some very slender nutrient – a piece of bread, or something of the kind – and I will continue in prayer," I think that very likely towards evening our prayers would become more forcible and vehement than at any other part of the day. We do not exactly recommend this for those who are weak. There are some men with little or no burden of flesh about them; but others of us of a heavy make, with sluggishness for a temptation, have to cry out because we are rather like stones on the ground than birds in the air. To such, I think, we can venture to recommend it from the words of Christ.

At any rate, I can imagine a father here setting apart a day of prayer, going on, wrestling with God without any intermission, pleading with him till, as it was said of the famous martyr of Brussels, he would so pray that he forgot everything except his prayer; and when they came to call him to a meal, he made no answer, for he had got out of all earthly things in his wrestling with the angel, so that he could not think of anything besides. Such a man taking up the case of a gross sinner, I believe, would be the means of that sinner's conversion; and the reason why some are never brought to Christ is, speaking after the manner of men, because we have not got the qualified men to deal with them, for *"this kind does not go out except by prayer and fasting."* When we have prayed, and have reached the point of true faith, then the sinner is saved by the mighty power of God, and Christ is glorified. I think I have some in this house who are ready to say, "Well, if such is the case, I will try it. I will take the Master at his word." Brother, brother, if half a dozen of us joined together, it might be better; no, *"If two of you agree about anything,"* it would be done. Let some of us put it to the test upon some big sinner, and see whether it does not come true. I think I may fairly ask you who are lovers of souls, who have eyes which do weep, and hearts which can feel, to try my Master's prescription, and see if the most unmanageable devil which ever took possession of a human heart be not driven out as the result of prayer and fasting, in the exercise of your faith. The Lord bless you in this thing, and may he bring us all to trust in Jesus by a saving faith. To him be glory, forever and ever. Amen.

Chapter 8

"If You Can"

"If You can do anything, take pity on us and help us!" And Jesus said to him, "'If You can?' All things are possible to him who believes." (Mark 9:22-23)

We are all familiar with the story of this youth, who was possessed by a dumb spirit, which caused him to fall into violent fits of epilepsy, and worked worse evils, casting him, at times, into the waters, and into the fire, to destroy him. The father intended to bring his child to Jesus, of whom he had heard so much; but our Lord being absent, he made his application to the disciples. They failed to effect a cure; but by and by the Master came from the mountaintop, and then the father addressed himself to the Lord. I want you to notice some lessons from this story before I come to the text.

The main thought which I would emphasize is that our Lord would have us clearly know, when we seek a blessing, what it is we are really seeking. If you go to Jesus Christ for anything, either for yourself, or someone else, the Savior will earnestly desire that you know what it is that you are asking of him. You know there is much blind praying: asking for mercies because you know that such and such words are proper, without having a clear and vivid idea of what the blessing is which is intended by those words. Now, our Savior loves us to pray with the understanding of, and to have a consciousness of, our need, and some perception of what it is that we want him to do. Therefore, try to get into your own heart a clear notion of what it is that you are seeking, for Christ would have you know why and for what you are pleading with him.

Therefore, when this man came with his sick child, the Savior permitted him to give a statement of the case; and, with the eagerness of love, the father entered into full particulars of the evil which had befallen his son. This was not needed by the Savior for his own information; he knew all about the dumb spirit's possession of the poor lad, and all the misery that had resulted from that possession. But the heartrending account was given, first, in order that the father might distinctly recollect the evil from which he desired his child to be saved; and, then, that those who were standing around might know what kind of miracle it was which Jesus Christ was about to work. Sometimes it will be a very healthy thing for seekers to stop a while and say to themselves, "What is it we are seeking?" Christ may say to you, *"What do you want Me to do for you?* What is it you really are asking for?" There are many that cry, *"Lord, save me!"* who perhaps have no distinct idea of what they are to be saved from, or what they are to be saved to.

In connection with this statement of the case, our Lord had permitted this poor man to make a petition to his disciples. I will not say that it was on purpose so that he might meet with a failure, but I do believe that failure was meant to teach the man a valuable lesson, and certainly it was designed to instruct the disciples, showing clearly to both that all hope lay in Jesus Christ himself. You have been seeking, dear friend. Now, how have you hoped to get saved? "Why, by heeding the means of grace," say you. Quite right, and I have not a word to say against the means of grace any more than I should have a word to say against the apostles; but the means of grace cannot save you any more than the apostles could cast the devil out of that child. It is not the means of grace, but it is Christ himself that you must get to, just as it was not the apostles, but the apostles' Master who had to work this miracle. Perhaps you have been sitting in these pews for years, expecting something to come to you by your constant and continued attendance. The Lord wants to get you thoroughly convinced that you will not be saved except by going to Jesus Christ himself. No Bible readings, no sermon hearings, and even no prayers, if they are relied upon, can save you. Your reliance must be upon the wonder-working Christ of God. If you will trust the Savior, you shall be saved at once. If you can believe now, you shall have immediate forgiveness of every sin, and instantaneous salvation by the power of the Christ of God. But it may be that you have not thought of this. You have been going round about, and now you are to be sickened of all that, so that you shall say, like the man in the narrative, *"I told Your disciples to cast it out, and they could not do it.* I have used the means of grace, I have heard your ministers, I have read good books; but neither books, nor ministers, nor services, nor all combined can cast the devil out of me. Lord, you must do it." The failure of every other hope is another thing that Christ would have us know when we come to him for a great blessing.

> Your reliance must be upon the wonder-working Christ of God.

Yet further, when the poor father had stated the case, and had confessed that he was disappointed with the disciples, the Savior caused him to see another exhibition of the mischief from which he would have his child saved. There and then, before them all, as they brought the boy to Jesus, the devil began to tear him, perhaps more violently than ever; he foamed at the mouth, and seemed, at last, to fall into such a condition that those who looked on said, "He is dead. The case is utterly hopeless." In the very presence of Christ, the evil spirit made a supreme effort to retain his hold of his victim, or to destroy the body in which he dwelt, before he left it. Now, beloved, the Lord may, in your case, if you are a seeker, permit sin to break loose in you in a possibly worse form than ever you have yet seen it, before he drives it out. It may be you will give yourself up for dead; in fact, I hope you may, for when death strikes every carnal hope, and you utterly despair of salvation in yourself, then is the very moment when the omnipotent power of divine grace comes in and manifests itself without limit. Oh, you who are driven today to utter self-despair, I am glad of it! I expect to see Christ come to you, and raise you up, and say to the evil spirit, *"Come out of him and do not enter him again."* God grant it may be so! Or, if your anxiety is about somebody else, it may be that God will permit the sin in the dear one to break out worse than ever. You have been praying for months, perhaps for years, and at last, it will seem quite hopeless. You will bring your husband or your child to Christ, and instead of seeing any change for the better, there may appear, at the time, to be even a change for the worse. Yet remember, it was then that Jesus said, *"'If You can?' All things are possible to him who believes."* It may be that he will let us see, more vividly than we have ever perceived before, the desperateness of the case, in order that we may the more clearly understand the greatness of the mercy which we are seeking at his hands.

I shall run the text, as it were, with two handles. You see, properly, it should be confined to the case of a person who is praying for others, for this was spoken to a father who was pleading for his son. But the same principle applies all around, and so I beg those who are praying for themselves to take as much of the sermon home as they can; and may God the Holy Spirit make it suitable to them! We come, then, with this introduction, to our text.

There are two "ifs" here. The poor troubled man said to Christ, *"If,"* implying some measure of doubt: *"If You can do anything, take pity on us and help us."* Then comes the other *"If,"* when Jesus said unto him, *"'If You can?' All things are possible to him who believes."*

Let us begin by saying, in the first place, that the *if* is not in Christ as to whether he can save you, or as to whether, in answer to prayer, he can save the object of your anxiety. There really is no *if* in reference to Christ, though it is quite probable that your unbelief is suggesting some doubt about his love, or power, or willingness to save.

There cannot be any *if* about Christ being able to save a sinner, or to do anything, because, first, *he is God's beloved Son.* Upon the snowy slopes of Hermon, down whose steeps he had come to confront the multitude in the plain, Christ had been transfigured, and in all his glory he had shone like the sun in the presence of his three disciples, whiter than the snow which lay around them. And out of the cloud which overshadowed them there had come forth a divine voice: *"This is My beloved Son, listen to Him!"* Now, if Jesus Christ is such a favorite of heaven, the darling of the eternal Father, will he deny him anything? I do not say that *if* as being at all doubtful about the matter. The revelation of the glory on the mount and the voice out of the opened heavens are evidence enough of his sonship. Even the devil himself could not deny that Jesus was the Son of God. In the wilderness of temptation, he indeed said, *"If You are the Son of God, command that these stones become bread";* but he knew in his heart that Christ was truly the Son of the Most High God. On many occasions, the demons, whom Christ cast out, cried aloud to him, *"You are the Son of God!"* Being God's true Son, can anything be impossible to him? Did he not say, *"All authority has been given to Me in heaven and on earth"*? When I think of the love which God bears to his dear Son, I cannot imagine him stinting Christ in power to bless. He is able to save unto the uttermost all that come unto God by him, for he is the everlasting Son of the eternal Father.

And remember, next, if that argument is not enough, that *Jesus Christ is God.* After that, can there be any "if" as to his power? What is there that God cannot do? He has made this world. He has made those millions of worlds that adorn the midnight skies; but all that God has ever made, though it be far beyond our conception, is but as a speck compared with what he could make if he pleased. He has done exceedingly great marvels, such as have astounded men; but all that God has ever done is as nothing compared with what he could do if he willed to do it, for with him all things are possible. And Jesus Christ being very God of very God means that all things are possible with him. He can save everyone present in this house now. Breathe a believing prayer to him and you will prove his power, for he will save you. His word runs very quickly; and if he does but send it forth, it will belt the world, and within the next few years, if he chooses so to work, all nations shall call Jesus blessed. But when you and I have one of God's promises to plead with him, we may know most surely that he will keep it; we never need insert an "if" as to whether he can or not. O beloved, if we were more wicked than we are, he could change us, and if our children or our friends were sunk in sin more deeply than they are, which God forbid they should be, he could still save them. *The Lord's hand is not so short that it cannot save; nor is His ear so dull that it cannot hear.* Fie on you, you doubting one! Shame on you, you trembling heart! There cannot be any "if" with the Christ of God, God's favored Son, yes, God's equal, who is girded with omnipotence.

And, in the third place, remember that *as Savior, works of grace are easy for him.* If you will but think just for a minute of what he has done in order to provide for man's salvation, I think you will see there cannot be any "if" with him. See him hanging on the accursed tree, nailed up to the gallows that he may die. His pains of body are inconceivably great; but meanwhile he is forsaken of his God, and is brought into unknown tortures of soul. That is the Son of God who is dying so; it is he whose face is the glory of heaven who is thus dying the death of a felon, *the just for the unjust, so that He might bring us to God.* I have such a conviction of the power of Christ's death that if it were revealed to me that, on the cross, he redeemed not only one world, but also as many fallen worlds as there are stars, I could well believe it. Oh, the blood of the Son of God! What merit there must be in such a sacrifice as that! Infinite Deity united to perfect manhood, and the whole life laid down that men might live! Tell me that Christ cannot save! Tell me that his blood will not wash out the most scarlet sin that ever defiled any man! I know better. There must be infinite virtue in the atoning sacrifice of Christ. There cannot be an "if" about the power of the Crucified One to forgive all who come to him, and trust in his great sacrifice.

If you question the power of his death, remember that he rose again from the dead, and upward he went into glory, and there today he sits enthroned. I think I can see him now, at the right hand of the Father, clothed with everlasting honor and divine majesty. What is he doing? Look! He lifts his hands. He pleads for sinners. Will the Father deny him anything? He makes intercession for the transgressors. Will God refuse to bless them? Oh, by the living Christ at God's right hand, pleading the merit of his own sacrifice, I would have you confident that there cannot be an "if" about his power to save any of the children of men!

Do not tell me that you are the worst sinner that ever lived. I will take it for granted that you are, and I will go further than that, and suppose you are a great deal worse than you think you are. I have sometimes had people coming to me as inquirers, and, sitting in a chair opposite me, they have begun by telling me about their dreadful sins. I have generally said to them, "You need not tell me that. I have not the slightest doubt that you are a thousand times worse than you tell me, or than you think you are. You are only fit to be cast into hell"; and then they say, "Ah! it is so, it is so." Right glad am I to hear them consent to the verdict, for that is the sort of people that Jesus Christ came to save. Do you think that he came to redeem some little miserable morsel of a sinner who never did anything very much that was wrong? Well, very likely he did; but he came to be a great Savior for great sinners. Suppose that, someday, you come and with glowing enthusiasm tell me there is a great doctor in London. I should probably say, "What does he do?" "He has a large number of patients," you answer. "But what does he do?" I say again. At length you give the astonishing reply, "He cures bad fingers." Well, I do not see much in that. But suppose, on the contrary, that in answer to my question, "What does this great physician do that you are so enthusiastic about?" you are able to give a true report, and say, "He has restored a great many persons who were given up by everybody else. He can cure the very worst diseases; in fact, they say that if a man were almost dead, he could make him alive." Why, then, indeed, I would begin to sing his praises too, and, if I were diseased, I would go to him for a cure. I am more confident about the power of Christ to heal; for to him I went when my sin was past all human remedy, and he made me every bit whole. There is no language strong enough to tell of his power to save and bless. If you believe that my Master can only save a small sinner who has only a little imperceptible sin about him, I tell you that you do not know him. He is a great Savior for great sinners; and however grossly guilty you may have been, lament it, mourn over it, but remember that Christ is able to save even the very chief of sinners. He is able to save them now, just now, where they are standing or sitting, and to send them out of this house as new creatures in him.

> He is a great Savior for great sinners.

Thus you see that the "if" is not in Christ. But now, secondly, where is the "if"? The "if" is in our lack of faith. Jesus said to the man, "'*If You can?*' *All things are possible to him who believes.*" But why is faith lacking?

The answer is, first, that it is *a reasonable demand,* and that it is most unreasonable to expect Christ to do anything for us if we will not believe in him. The very least thing that a great surgeon could expect of a patient would be confidence in his skill. Do not marvel, therefore, that Jesus Christ does expect you to believe in him, and *"if you will not believe, you surely shall not last."* If you refuse Christ your confidence, you cannot wonder if he refuses you his salvation: *"If You can."* It seems almost as if the Lord in astonishment echoed this poor father's words, starting back in wonder that he should be so misunderstood, that any human being should come to him, who created all things, and yet doubt his power. The poor leper, who came to him after the Sermon on the Mount, had a different way of expressing his misgiving. He said, *"If You are willing,"* doubting not Christ's power to heal, but his willingness to do so. I know not which is worse, but I am sure that both are unreasonable; for if either the willingness or ability is absent, Christ cannot be a Savior for sinful men. But, as we often sing,

> He is able,
> He is willing; doubt no more.

Faith is lacking, in the next place, because it is *for God's glory*. It would not be for Christ's glory to bless those that do not believe in him. Shall he reward unbelief? Will you have it said that Christ came to this earth, and that he lived and died for the salvation of sinners, and that, after that, though a man would not believe in him, he still gave him pardon and mercy? No, there shall never be such a thing as a pardoned unbeliever, a saved man who does not believe in Christ. That would be to the dishonor of Christ, and would make him to be rather the patron of sin than the Savior from sin. Faith is required, then, so that God may have the glory of man's salvation.

> **We are led farthest away from God when we doubt the love which he has sealed with the blood of his own heart.**

This faith is also *for our own good*. Our Lord meant to bless that poor man by healing his child, but he meant to bless him doubly by healing him of his unbelief, for it is indeed a horrible weakness for a man to lack faith in his Creator. It is an appalling disease of spirit for a man to be doubtful of his God. I have looked down the list of crimes, and though there are some that are truly abominable, yet when I have looked into the very foulest transgression, I have not seen anything so vile as the sin of a man who doubts the love and power of Christ who died that men might live. This is the masterpiece of hell's temptation. We are led farthest away from God when we doubt the love which he has sealed with the blood of his own heart. It is therefore for our own good that we should believe. Here and always God's glory and our good are closely joined. To glorify God will be to enjoy him forever.

Faith, then, is a reasonable, glorious, and blessed thing, and in the sinner's case *it is absolutely necessary to salvation.* We must believe in Jesus Christ if we would be saved. But can't we be saved without believing? No. What will become of us if we do not believe in Jesus Christ? Well, I will make no "ifs" nor "ands" about that. *"He who has disbelieved shall be condemned."* I do not care to beat about the bush, or seek for any more refined version of the text; let it stand there in its own terrible simplicity: *"He who has believed and has been baptized shall be saved; but he who has disbelieved shall be condemned."* If you do not believe in Jesus Christ, you will be condemned, whatever that means; and it means something truly terrible, to be condemned by God and driven from his presence because we do not believe in him. There is no help for it, for there is no other salvation, and there is no other door of hope except through faith in the appointed Savior of mankind, as John Newton, that great sinner saved by marvelous grace, says,

> The worst of all diseases
>   Is light, compared with sin;
> On every part it seizes,
>   But rages most within.
>
> 'Tis palsy, poison, fever,
>   And madness, all combined:
> And none but a believer
>   The least relief can find.

There is where the "if" is, then; it is in our lack of faith.

But now, in the third place, let me ask, What puts the "if" there? Why is it that we cannot believe? If some unprejudiced person, who before had been totally unacquainted with the Bible, read it for the first time, and was asked, "Is it a hard thing that God asks of men in order for their salvation that they should believe in Jesus Christ whom he has sent?" any unsophisticated mind would reply, "No, that must be the easiest thing in the world, for God cannot lie." Such a verdict would be absolutely true, for the gift of his Son, whom he loved as he loved himself, proves the honesty of God, and leaves no room for doubt as to the certainty and the heartiness of his willingness to bless the sons of men. God could not be false, and could not go so far with the falsehood as to give his own Son to die; that is altogether inconceivable. It seems of necessity, then, that God is true in declaring that he will save those who trust in his Son; and it looks, at first sight, as if it would be the simplest thing in all the world to trust in Jesus Christ, and so indeed it is. But why is it that there are any "ifs" about it? Why is it needful that Christ should say, "If you can believe"?

The reason is because *we are alienated in heart from God.* If we were right with God, faith would be a matter of necessity. But we do not love God. By nature we even hate him, and that is why we do not trust him. It would be a very wretched thing to meet with a young man who, if you were speaking to him in praise of his father, should say, "I do not believe in my father." If you continued, "But your father is a man of the highest integrity," would it not be sad to hear him reply, "I cannot trust him"? "Oh, but your father is kindness itself," you might add; and if the lad said, "Yes, I hear what you say, but I do not believe it, I cannot trust him," you would know that there was some dreadful family feud, or some most unhappy circumstance that had twisted that youth's mind so that he did not love his father and therefore did not believe in him. Supposing his father to be a man of undoubted repute and integrity, the last thing that you would expect to happen would be that his own son would say, "I cannot believe him." Now, concerning God, who among us will so blaspheme as to say that he was ever false? Yet men do say it, and do not seem at all startled at what they have said. Though it is written, *The one who does not believe God has made Him a liar,* men will still calmly tell us, as if it were an amiable weakness rather than a sin, "Sir, I cannot believe in Christ; I cannot believe in God." It is, then, because you are alienated from him, because you do not love him. Lament this; confess it before God; and when your heart is renewed by his grace, then faith will come as a matter of course.

Another reason for this "if" is that *we are idolaters by nature.* "No, no," say you, "we are not idolaters." I say we are idolaters by nature – all of us; for what is an idolater but one who wants to have an idol, or a something which he can see and trust in, and which shall represent to him the invisible? The Roman Catholic becomes an idolater as he puts before him the crucifix, or some precious relic of the saints. But you may become an idolater too, without seeming to be so superstitious. You are such indeed, if in earthly provisions, for instance, you cannot trust God. If before you trust him you need to have your income regularly guaranteed; it is not God you then trust, it is the money. So with your soul. You could trust God, you say, if an angel were to come from heaven to speak, or if you heard a voice in the night. So, then, it is not God that you would trust, but an angel, or a voice. You want something to see and something to hear. It is ingrained in human nature thus to seek a sign, but what is that but idolatry? Oh, that we would get rid of this and say, "God is invisible. I am not to expect to see him; I am to trust him. I am to believe that he who made the heavens and the earth, and who gave his Son to die will save me; and lo, I put my trust in his dear Son, once and for all!"

> If before you trust him you need to have your income regularly guaranteed; it is not God you then trust, it is the money.

Another reason why this "if" comes in is *because we measure God by ourselves.* We cannot think that God can forgive us because we find it so hard to forgive our fellow creatures. We cannot conceive that God will do it freely, from no motive but that of pure grace, because we are so greedy. We want to be paid for what we do, and unless we can see some chance of reward, somewhere or other, we are very slow to make anything like a sacrifice. So we think that God is altogether such as we are, whereas you remember it is written, *"For as the heavens are higher than the earth, so are My ways higher than your ways and My thoughts than your thoughts."* We measure God by our fellow men. We say, "Such and such a one is very good, but he would never forgive after this fashion. He would give generously, but he certainly would not give after the style that God is spoken of as giving." Thus, as the Ethiopians are said to make their angels with black faces, we imagine God to be like ourselves or other men, and therefore find it difficult to believe in him. Dismiss from your thoughts all such ideas of God. You might sooner hold the ocean in the hollow of your hand, or span the heavens with your fingers, than, unaided by grace, get an idea of the greatness and glory of God by all your searching. Never forget that he is as great in mercy as in any other of his attributes. He delights to forgive. It is the joy of his heart to press to his bosom his prodigal children. Nothing gives such intense satisfaction to the heart of God as the manifestation of his boundless grace. I wish you could believe this. But it is because we thus limit the Holy One of Israel that we find the simple matter of faith so difficult. Because of this there stands that great, ugly, black, stiff "if." "If you can believe."

In conclusion, let me ask another question, and seek to answer it. How can this "if" be removed? Are there any in this house who are longing to be saved, and who have been putting an "if" upon Christ, and saying, "Lord, if you can"? First, let them know that the "if" lies with themselves; and then let us join hands and see if we cannot turn this "if" out. Come, brother, let me help you. If this "if" has been too strong for you, I would ask God's Spirit to bless a few words to you so that this "if" may be got rid of. With reference to that other "if" which came from the lips of the leper, and to which I have already referred, I heard of a little girl whose mother found her one day with a carving knife and the family Bible. "What are you doing?" she asked her child, in some anxiety for the safety of both the child and the book. "O mother," she said, "I was reading about that man who came to Jesus and said, *'If You are willing, You can make me clean,'* and I thought he ought not to have said 'if' to Jesus, so please, mother, I am scraping it out." A very good thing to do with all our "ifs." How shall we go to work with this one? Well, we had better imitate this man with his epileptic child possessed of a devil.

First of all, *you must confess the faith that you have.* This man said, "I do believe." There is something in that. If you cannot go as far as you would like to, go as far as you can. What do you believe about Jesus Christ? Come, poor, dear, trembling heart, and run over in your mind now what you do believe about him. I think I could have said, before I really did trust Christ, "Lord Jesus, I believe you are the Son of God." I believed that; I never doubted it. "And I believe that you are sent to be the Savior of men." I do not know that I ever doubted that. Some of you from your childhood have believed that too; your mother taught you that; and when you read the Scriptures, you were sure of it. Well, now, just turn that over. "Lord, I believe you are the Son of God. I believe you are God. I believe you are able to save. I believe your precious blood takes away the sin of all who trust you. I believe that whosoever trusts in you has everlasting life. I believe that you have sent your gospel into the world, saying, *'He who has believed and has been baptized shall be saved.'* Lord, I believe all this." That is a matter to be very thankful for; and yet, do you know, that it is a matter that will condemn you unless you go farther, because if you believe as much as that, you ought to believe more? I can understand the atheist or deist not trusting Christ. I can understand the Socinian not trusting Christ; but if you are sound in your doctrinal beliefs, I cannot think of an excuse for you why you should not trust Christ. If a man says to me, "I believe you, sir, to be a thief; I cannot trust you," that is perfectly consistent, is it not? But if he says, "Sir, I believe you are an upright man who would not on any account do a doubtful thing, and yet I cannot trust you," I am not anxious to answer such a man as that, for out of his own mouth he condemns himself. So, some of you go so far that if you do not go farther you will condemn yourselves. Surely, in all reason, if a man can say to Christ, "I believe that you are the Christ that came into the world; I believe that you are the Son of God; I believe that you were raised again from the dead; I believe that you sit at the right hand of God, pleading for sinners," that man must also add, "Therefore I trust you." It is the natural inference to be drawn from it. God help you, then, to confess such faith as you have!

The next way to knock this "if" over is to *appeal to Christ to be helped against it.* "[Lord,] I do believe," said this poor man; "*help my unbelief.*" He cried out of the depths of his soul, "O Lord, help me against my unbelief!" So, poor heart, you have been trying to believe! Did you ever try this man's plan of believing that Christ could make him believe? That is odd, is it not? You see, he must have had faith in Christ, or else he would not have said, *"Help my unbelief."* Let us imitate him, and cry with Cowper –

> Heal us, Emmanuel, here we are,
>   Waiting to feel thy touch:
> Deep-wounded souls to thee repair,
>   And, Savior, we are such.

> Our faith is feeble, we confess,
>   We faintly trust thy word;
> But wilt thou pity us the less?
>   Be that far from thee, Lord!
>
> Remember him who once applied
>   With trembling for relief;
> "Lord, I believe," with tears he cried,
>   "Oh, help my unbelief!"

Oftentimes there is a great deal more faith in a poor sinner's heart than he thinks there is. He really is trusting the Savior and does not know he is doing so. He is saved, and yet is afraid to think it can be possible. Long after I knew the Savior, and believed in him, at times I used to be staggered with the thought that it was too good to be true. The tempter would say, "It cannot be that you really are forgiven, that you are Christ's own, that you are washed in his blood, and saved forever!" Well, it does almost seem to be too good to be true; but then, nothing is too good to be true when you are dealing with a king. If it be a king who is about to act, we say that the grander and kinglier a thing it is, the more likely is it to be done. But rise higher than kings. If it is excellent, if it is infinite, if it is altogether inconceivable but for its having been revealed, then it is the more likely to be true; for it is more like God. Oh then, I pray you, bring your unbelief before Christ, and let it die in his presence! Unbelief does not like the cross. If you look up to the dying Savior, to the risen Christ of God, unbelief dies. God help you, then, to say, "[Lord,] I do believe; help my unbelief."

> **If you look up to the dying Savior, to the risen Christ of God, unbelief dies.**

One other thing you must do if you are to follow the example of this father: *Bring the case to Christ.* This poor man brought his child to Christ. It was a hard tug, and he asked others to help him. Do you not see how the suffering child was tossed about, sometimes this way, sometimes that way? You may have seen some poor man or woman who is subject to fits, and noticed in what a way such people are convulsed. But this poor child was much worse; he was foaming at the mouth, raving, tearing, and full of the fiend. The father is trying to help his boy: sometimes he holds him by the waist, then the child tears away; then another helps to grasp one hand, while the father gets hold of the other. He drags him to Christ, pulling him almost piecemeal to Christ; but he gets him there at last. *"Bring him to Me!"* said Christ; and what better could the father do, or can you do, than obey the command and bring your loved one? So he did, and he laid him down at Jesus' feet. Where else is so fitting a place for the sick or devil-possessed as at the feet of the Savior? *To whom shall we go* if we turn away from his tender heart? When the boy in the harvest field cried out in pain, his father said, *"Carry him to his mother."* Where else could he be so soothed and helped, and where else but in Christ can you or your children hope for blessing?

That is what I want you to do with your friends; get them somehow to Jesus Christ by mighty, vehement, determined prayer. And when you have prayed for them, try to get them to hear the gospel. I like to preach to people who have never heard the gospel before; it is grand work. There are some of you upon whom I fear that I shall never make an impression; you have been hammered upon so long that I am afraid you have become gospel hardened. Take a person out to look at the stars – some countryman who has always been able to see. Perhaps he does not make any remark, or he simply says, "Oh, I have gone across the moor many a night! I don't see anything particular in the stars." But here is an old man brought from the ophthalmic hospital. He has been blind for many years; in fact, he forgets whether he ever could see. By a skillful operation the film is taken from his eyes. Take him out at night, and the first things he sees are the stars. He says, "What a sight! How glorious! How divine!" Those are the kind of people to whom it is a joy to preach; for when the Lord gives sight to those who were blind, and they see for the first time, how glad they are to see him! Persons who do not often have flowers are charmed with the sight of them and find much delight in their fragrance. Yet I have heard of a flower girl who sold violets in the street and had to take those that remained home to her poor miserable room every night, till she said that she hated the smell of violets; she could not bear them, having gotten so accustomed to them. "That is strange," says one; yet that is how some of our gospel hearers speak. They say that we preach too long, and they begin to criticize our sermons. I dread above anything that your nostrils should become so familiar with the sweet smell of the rose of Sharon and the lily of the valleys that their fragrance should become nauseous to you. How sad it would be that any of you should get so familiar with the gospel that at last you would say, "What a weariness it is!" May this never be the case; and lest it should, come now and bring your case before Christ! It is no use to bring it before me and let me preach to you. It is no use to bring it before the mere means of grace. Turn to the Lord Jesus who is beside you, and tell him all the case. Say to him that you renounce all other hope and trust yourself in his hands. Believe in him this moment, lest by chance the very gospel itself should be *an aroma from death to death* to you. If you trust in Christ, you must have life. O Spirit of God, help many to come this very hour and trust in the Crucified One, for Jesus' sake! Amen.

Chapter 9

Faith Omnipotent

And Jesus said to him, "'If You can?' All things are possible to him who believes." (Mark 9:23)

I must take your minds back to the scene in the midst of which Christ uttered these memorable words. Christ had been upon the mountaintop, transfigured in the presence of his three disciples. During his absence, the disciples remaining had been put in a quandary. They found themselves, for lack of faith, unable to work a miracle. And the Pharisees triumphed. Christ came down just at that very moment and turned the scale. We find a parallel case in the story of Moses, when with his servant Joshua he went up to the mountain and beheld the glory of the Lord. While he and Joshua were absent below, evil lifted up its head, and those who would walk by sight prevailed over the poor weak faith of Aaron, so that he made for them a golden calf; and lo, as Moses returned, he saw the people given up to the worship of this image which they could see with their eyes and handle with their hands. Faith had left the field routed because the champion was not there, and sinful sight was for the moment triumphant. Moses dashes boldly into the midst of the people, and instantly they are put to confusion; some tremble, and the most brazen of them are made to hang their heads. He lays hold upon their molten calf, grinds it to powder, and makes them drink it. Now, our Lord with his Joshuas – Peter, and James, and John, the three-elect out of the elect – had been on the mountain of transfiguration. The rest, like Aaron, found themselves attacked by those who wanted to see signs and wonders. But being unable to furnish these signs and wonders due to their lack of faith, the Pharisees pushed their advantage, and the hosts of God seemed to fly before them. But suddenly, like a great King, Christ stands in their midst. The Pharisees are uncomfortable, a miracle is performed, faith triumphs, and the doubters are shamed. Like some mighty general who, having been absent from the field of battle, finds that his lieutenants have rashly engaged in action and have been defeated – the left wing is broken, the right has fled, and the center begins to fail – he lifts his flag in the midst of his troops, and bids them rally around him. They gather; they dash upon the all-but-triumphant foemen, and soon they turn the balance of victory and make the late victors turn their disgraceful backs to flight. Brethren, here is a lesson at the very outset. What we want for conquest is the shout of a king in the midst of us. The presence of Christ is victory to his church; the absence of the Lord Jesus entails disgraceful defeat. O armies of the living God, count not your numbers, rely not upon your strength, reckon not upon the ability of your ministers, boast not in human might; nor on the other hand be dismayed because you are few, nor tremble because you are feeble. If he be with you, more are those that are for you than all those that are against you. If Christ be in your midst, there are horses of fire and chariots of fire round about you.

> **The presence of Christ is victory to his church; the absence of the Lord Jesus entails disgraceful defeat.**

> When he makes bare his arm,
>   Who can his cause withstand?
> When he his people's cause defends,
>   Who? who shall stay his hand?

Lift up your eyes, then, to the hills, from where Jesus comes who is your help, and entreat him never to forsake his people, but to dwell with them, and walk among them forevermore.

The matter about which the dispute had arisen was this: a certain man had a demoniac son, who was afflicted with a mute spirit which threw him into convulsions and ravings of the most hideous kind. The father, having seen the futility of the endeavors of the disciples, had little or no faith in Christ, and therefore when he was bidden to bring his son to him, he said to Jesus, *"If You can do anything, take pity on us and help us!"* Now there was an *"if"* in the question, but the poor trembling father had put the *"if"* in the wrong place. Jesus Christ, therefore, without telling him to retract the *"if,"* just puts it in its legitimate position. "No, truly," he seemed to say, "there should be no 'if' about my power, nor about my willingness; the 'if' lies somewhere else. *'If You can?' All things are possible to him who believes."* The man received faith, offering at the same time a humble prayer for an increase of faith, and instantly Christ spoke the word, and the devil was cast out with an injunction never to return. Brethren, you and I see that there is an *"if"* somewhere, but we are perpetually blundering by putting it in the wrong place. *If* Christ can convert heathens? No, no, *if* the church can believe he can. *If* Christ can make the ministry successful? No, *if* you can believe he can. *If* Christ can give me the pardon of sin, *if* he can give me high enjoyments, *if* he can lift me above doubts and fears? Not so, brethren, not so; you have misplaced your *if*. It is *if* you can believe; for if you can, even as all things are possible to Christ, so shall all things be possible to you. Faith stands in God's power and in God's majesty. It wears the royal apparel and rides on the king's horse, for it is the grace which the king delights to honor. Girding itself with the glorious might of the all-working Spirit, it becomes, in the omnipotence of God, mighty to do, to dare, and to suffer. *"All things,"* without limit, *"are possible to him who believes."*

I shall dwell upon *some of the achievements of faith,* and then notice *where faith's great power lies.* God help us to speak on both of these points with divine power.

First, some of the achievements of faith.

Time would fail me if I should attempt to rehearse the record of those who have earned a good report through faith. It is not necessary that my humble tongue should recapitulate what Paul, with inspired lips, has uttered in the ears of the church. Turn to the eleventh chapter of Hebrews and see there a mighty triumphal arch which God the Holy Spirit has raised in commemoration of the splendid triumphs which faith has achieved. Behold this tower of David, built for an armory, on which there hang a thousand bucklers, all shields of mighty men. With joy the church recounts her honorable ones, for the Lord utters his voice before his army, for his camp is very great. But it is not necessary that I remind you of these ancient things; I will rather speak of some of the things which faith can perform today, even today.

First, we will consider faith in *its relationship to guilt.* Here we may say, in your hearing, if you can believe, guilt can be removed. Perfect pardon and complete justification are possible to the vilest sinner if he can believe in Christ. Behold, my brethren, faith going forth to conflict with sin. Mark for a moment its determined struggles, but see it coming back, like David, with Goliath's head in his hand – a mighty conqueror through the strength of its God. Faith in dealing with sin *does not forget the greatness of it.* Our sin is tremendous; it is not possible for us to overestimate its guilt. The sinner, under the most awful convictions, never exaggerated the evil of sin, it is a dreadful and a bitter thing; but faith deals thus with it. "What if my sin be great? I have a great Savior; surely he is able to take my sin, even if it were a hundred times as great as it is, and to cast it all into the depths of the sea. I know that I have greatly revolted, and have sinned with many aggravations against my God; but I believe in his great mercy, and I know that he is able to blot out my sins like a cloud, and my transgressions like a thick cloud." Faith does not lessen sin in the estimate of a sinner; but it exalts Christ, so that the sinner firmly and fully believes that if his sin could be multiplied by all the number of the elect, yet he who is mighty to save could roll all the burden away and make him free. The greatness of sin is no barrier to its removal, if you can believe.

> The greatness of sin is no barrier to its removal, if you can believe.

Many, also, are troubled with a consciousness of *the deserved punishment of sin.* They are made to look into hell; they seem to hear the wailings as they ascend from the place of torment. Such awful passages as these are in their troubled mind: *Topheth has long been ready, . . . a pyre of fire and plenty of wood;* "*These will go away into eternal punishment*"; *[where their worm does not die, and the fire is not quenched.]* But faith says, "Yes; but despite all this, the agonies of Christ were so great that they are a suitable and full atonement by which all these torments can be, by God's mercy, fully removed from those who trust in Jesus, and they can even mount to the upper skies." To know the deserved punishment of sin, and yet believe that Christ can pardon – this is faith's work. Not to make out sin to be a slight mistake, or a small and trivial offense, but to confess that the full weight of God's eternal arm can be none too heavy to fall upon the man who has dared to insult his Maker's laws, and despite all this to believe that the atonement made by blood upon the cross was enough, and more than enough, to atone for all. This is the victory of faith – to know that the blood of Jesus Christ, God's dear Son, cleanses us from all sin.

Multitudes, also, I know, are very much vexed by remembering *what guilt has done* in them. "I am," says such a one, "so hard-hearted, I have so little repentance, I am so prayerless, I have nothing good in me; I am everything that is vile; there is not a commendable thing in me to move the pity of God." Now, faith comes in and says, "It is even so; but, despite all this, I do believe the naked promise of God; I come to Jesus as I am, having nothing in myself, but possessing all things in him." Nor will faith let the hardness of the heart, or the stubbornness of the will, be any argument why the soul should not rest on Christ, but believing all that could be laid to its charge, and sorrowfully repenting of it all, still faith says, "It is written, *'The one who comes to Me I will certainly not cast out.'* I come, and Jesus cannot, will not, cast me out." When I feel my soul softened, when I feel the motions of the living fire within me, then to believe that Christ can save me is no great faith; but when I feel no spiritual life, when my heart is as hard as a lower millstone, and I see myself as corrupt as a dunghill, then to believe in him who justifies the ungodly, then to take the mercy which Christ gives to the very chief of sinners – this is a masterpiece of faith, and herein faith makes all things possible to him that believes.

> In hope against all human hope,
>   Self desperate, I believe
> Thy quickening word shall raise me up,
>   Thou shalt the Spirit give.

> The thing surpasses all my thought,
>   But faithful is my Lord;
> Through unbelief I stagger not,
>   For God hath spoke the word.
>
> Faith, mighty faith, the promise sees,
>   And looks to that alone,
> Laughs at impossibilities,
>   And cries, "It shall be done."

Sinners also are greatly troubled when they are awakened concerning *the future*. "You will sin again," says Satan, "just as you have done. All claims to a new life will be notable failures; you will go like the dog to his vomit, and return like the pig, that was washed, to her wallowing in the mire." The revived mind clearly perceives that this would inevitably be the result, if the work were to be performed by human strength; but faith denies the slander by looking to the Lord alone. Though in me, that is, in my flesh, there dwells no good thing, yet he is able to save unto the uttermost them that come unto God by him. Faith clutches that promise: *"I give eternal life to [My sheep], and they will never perish; and no one will snatch them out of My hand"*; and she looks upon the future with the same eye of faith with which she looks back upon the pardoned past, and rests herself upon the faithfulness and power of God to save. At times these old sins will rush in upon the believer's mind with a terrific force. Gathering dreadful strength from the justice of God, our eyes are tormented with the vision of an angry God, with his sword drawn, ready to strike us for our offenses. Glorious is that faith which can fling itself into the arms of God, even when the sword is in his hand, and will not believe that God can strike the sinner who relies upon the blood of Jesus. Mighty is that faith which, looking at justice, stern and severe, trembles not, but cries, "You are merciful and just to forgive me my sins, for I have confessed them. Christ has made full atonement, and you will not twice demand the debt. He paid it once, and you cannot lay anything to my charge." Triumphant is that faith which marches right up to heaven, and stands before the blazing throne of the great and holy God, and yet can cry, *Who will bring a charge against God's elect? God is the one who justifies; who is the one who condemns? Christ Jesus is He who died, yes, rather who was raised;* and this even when sin rolls like a black flood, and the remembrance of the past has lashed the soul to tempest.

When we really know the blessed merit of Jesus' blood, when we fully understand the excessive mercy of God, and when we come to know the overflowing love of the Father towards his beloved children, then we shall not look upon sin as being less sin than before, but we shall no longer fear its penalizing consequences, being confidently assured in our soul that none of these sins can destroy us; that not the whole of them together can for a moment shake our standing in him, nor by any means put us in any danger of eternal wrath, since we are covered with the righteousness of Christ and washed in his blood. Brethren, our sins, when pardoned, should increase our delight in God, since they afford us evidences of his exceedingly abundant grace and love. Amalie Sieveking, a notable Christian heroine, one of the most zealous workers of modern times, writes this: "The sense of my own powerlessness but brings me nearer to him whose strength is made perfect in weakness. I give myself up to his guidance, in cheerful trust that he will finish the work which he has begun, and help the poor stumbling child again and again to rise, ay, should it stumble a hundred times a day – And this is the point I want you to notice – sometimes I feel as though I must lay bare to others the whole accumulated amount of my guilt, that they may with me admire the riches of divine longsuffering." This is how faith learns to deal with sin – to make it a foil to show the brightness of mercy – the setting in which the diamond of divine love flashes with supreme luster. The faithful heart always remembers its sin with shame; but still it remembers God's pardoning love with gratitude, and the sorrow helps to increase the thankfulness. The lower we sink by reason of the fall, the higher our love for God rises when we reflect on how his strong hand has taken us *up out of the pit of destruction, out of the miry clay, and He set my feet upon a rock making my footsteps firm.* Oh! I wish that some of you who are full of sin would believe that Christ can save you. *"All things are possible to him who believes."* What if you are the blackest

> Brethren, our sins, when pardoned, should increase our delight in God.

sinner out of hell, and you think the devil himself white compared with yourself? Yet if you can trust Christ today, then *all things are possible to him who believes.* Whiter than the newly fallen snow shall you be in an instant, if you can now rest your soul upon Jesus, who is able to save.

Let us now observe faith in the midst of *those constant attacks of which the heir of heaven is the subject.* Here faith again does all things. My brethren, no sooner is a Christian born, than there is a great stir about him, even as concerning Christ himself, Herod was seeking the young child so that he might destroy him. We all know how constantly the world attacks us, more especially if we will be separate from it, and will keep our garments white, and will not indulge in the common pleasures, nor be guided by the ordinary, general truths of society. Then the world howls at us like a pack of wolves. What then? Why, faith finds here but an easy task, for it learns to glory in tribulations, delightfully remembering the beatitude of Jesus on the mount – *"Blessed are you when people insult you and persecute you, and falsely say all kinds of evil against you because of Me. Rejoice and be glad, for your reward in heaven is great; for in the same way they persecuted the prophets who were before you."* This is an everyday conquest with the Christian, to laugh at Satan's threats. *This is the victory that has overcome the world—our faith.* The world attacks us also with its smiles, and unhappy is the man who has no faith, for soon the allurements of the world will overcome him. But he who is full of faith, when the world offers him silver, replies, "No, I am rich in gold," and if the world would give him treasure, he would say, "I have a better portion than you can offer me. Will you tempt a king with farthings, or a prince with a beggar's broken provisions of food? I am heir of all things in Christ; this world is mine, and heaven is mine too." So he laughs to scorn all the smiles of the wicked, just as he did in the case of their frowns.

Alas, brethren, we are equally attacked by *the flesh.* The lusts within are not dead; they are powerful still, and we know it to our cost. But here, too, faith overcomes; for while faith recognizes the power of the flesh and the lusts thereof, it so lays hold upon Christ, so that it is lifted up into heavenly places, and is able to tread its corruptions under foot. Faith says to the believer, "Be assured that notwithstanding all the plague of your own heart, and all the dreadfulness of your nature, yet you shall as surely conquer as Christ has conquered, and you shall one day be as pure and spotless as even Christ himself before the Father's throne." Up and at your lusts, believer! There is no sin which will not yield to faith. There is no necessity that we should always be sinning as we have been; we *can* overcome our lusts. You *can* drive out these Canaanites; though they dwell in cities walled to heaven, and have chariots of iron, you shall put your feet upon their necks and utterly destroy them. Little by little you may assuredly drive them out, but only by faith; not by works, not by trust in your own moral resolutions, but by trust in the sprinkled blood of Jesus can you overcome all temptation and subdue your sin.

> With my sling and stone I go,
>   To fight the Philistine,
> God hath said it shall be so,
>   And I shall conquer sin;
> On his promise I rely,
>   Trust in an Almighty Lord,
> Sure to win the victory,
>   For he hath spoke the word.
>
> In the strength of God I rise,
>   I run to meet the foe,
> Faith the word of power applies
>   And lays the giant low.
> Faith in Jesus' conquering name,
>   Slings the sin-destroying stone,
> Points the word's unerring aim,
>   And brings the monster down.

So it is with *the devil*. The devil comes out against us, but we are more than a match for him when our faith is firm. Upon the shield of our faith we catch his arrows, and by the sword of our faith we strike him to the very core. There is no temptation that ever can attack a believer but that faith can certainly supply an antidote. If I believe in Jesus I have his promise that I shall overcome, and I shall overcome, because

I believe that promise. Even if I should get beneath the devil's foot, and he should lift his sword to strike me, if I could say, "Rejoice not over me, O my enemy, for when I fall I shall still rise again," I should rise, and victory would be mine. Faith overcomes even hell itself and its crowned monarch; for defense, it is a full suit of armor, and for attack, it is our battle-ax and weapon of war.

As for the *trials of this life*, it is marvelous what feathers these are to faith, for she perceives that troubles come from God. Chrysostom has a gloss upon that passage in Job, where Job says, *"The Lord has taken away."* He did not say the Chaldeans did it, nor the Sabeans, though they certainly were the instruments; but *the* **Lord** *has taken away* (emphasis added). The believer seeing God's hand in everything that happens to him feels pleased with all alike. As providence is in his Father's hand, he knows that it is always guided by love, by wisdom, and by grace; and so he thinks his worst days to be as good as his best. His foul days are fair; his dark days are bright; in full confidence he believes that all things work together for his good, and he leaves the working of them entirely with his God. Oh beloved, it is only lack of faith that makes this world such a place of sorrow to God's people; but when we get faith, faith laughs at every tribulation, no matter whatsoever source it may come from.

Thus I have shown you that *"all things are possible to him who believes."* Rise up, O hosts of hell, and shoot your arrows! You heavens, prepare your tempests! O earth, cast forth your floods; and you, O flesh, come forth with all your blasphemy and wickedness. Faith walks unharmed amidst all your fury as more than a conqueror through him that has loved her.

We turn your attention to another point: *the obtaining of eminence in grace.* Many professed Christians are always doubting and fearing, and they think that this is the necessary state of believers. By no means, brother! *"All things are possible to him who believes";* and it is possible for you to get into a state in which a doubt or a fear shall be but as a bird of passage flitting across your soul, but never lingering there. When you read in biographies of the high and sweet communions enjoyed by favored saints, you sigh, "Alas, these are not for me." Oh climber! if you have but faith, you shall stand upon the very pinnacle of the temple, for *"all things are possible to him who believes."* I know you read about what some great men have done for Jesus; what they have enjoyed about him; how much they have been like him; how they have been able to endure for his sake; and you say, "Ah! as for me, I am but a worm; I can never attain to this." There is nothing which one saint was that you may not be. There is no height of grace, no attainment of spirituality, no position of assurance, no post of duty which is not open to you if you have but the power to believe. Get up, get up from your dunghills; lay aside your sackcloth and your ashes. It is not good that you should grovel in the dust, oh children of a king. Ascend! The golden throne of assurance is waiting for you! The crown of confidence in Jesus is ready to decorate your brow. Wrap yourself in scarlet and fine linen, and dine sumptuously every day; for if you believe, you may eat the fat of kidneys of wheat; all your land shall flow with oil, and wine, and milk, and honey; your soul shall be as a watered garden; and your spirit shall be satiated as with marrow and fatness. *"All things are possible to him who believes."*

And yet a fourth point: the power of faith in reference to *prayer*. Here *"all things are possible to him who believes."* In prayer we are sometimes staggered by reason of the *great* things we are about to ask; but faith looks at the great promise, the great God, and his great love, and thinks that even a great thing is but a crumb from the Master's table. Then again, we are often driven back by a sense of unworthiness; but faith looks at *Christ's* worthiness, and believes that his worthiness is quite sufficient to put our unworthiness altogether out of court. Then we are apt to think of God's delays; but then, faith thinks that God cannot deny though he may delay, so she hangs on till the promise is fulfilled. Though the vision delays, she waits for it till it comes, for she is sure that it *will* come. And, oh! it is a splendid thing to see faith wait upon God in prayer, and renounce all carnal means, depending simply and wholly upon the naked promise, and believing that God can do his own work and perform his own word. Brethren, no man ought to doubt in these modern times but that God *will* answer prayer, and that faith with prayer can do anything.

We have often heard of George Müller of Bristol. There stands, in the form of those magnificent orphan houses full of orphans, supported without committees, without secretaries, supported only by that man's prayer and faith, there stands, in solid brick and mortar, a testimony to the fact that God hears prayer. But do you know that Mr. Müller's case is but one among many? Remember the work of Francke at Halle. Look at the Rough House just outside of Hamburg, where Dr. Wichern, commencing with a few reprobate boys of Hamburg, only waiting upon God's help and goodness, has now a whole village full of boys and girls, reclaimed and saved, and is sending out on the right hand and on the left brethren to occupy posts of usefulness in every land. Remember the brother Gossner, of Berlin, and how mightily God has helped him to send out not less than two hundred missionaries, throughout the length and breadth of the earth preaching Christ, while he has for their support nothing but the bare promise of God, and the faith which has learned to reach the hand of God, and take from it all it needs. And need I remind you of a story we told you last Friday night – the story of Pastor Harms, in Hermannsburg, where, by the power of that man's faith in preaching the Word, he has seen the barren wilderness made to blossom like the rose, till his church has become a very model of what a church of God ought to be, a living and working body from which he sends out missionaries to the coast of Africa, having nothing for their supply but the offerings or the people drawn from them by the exercise of prayer and faith. I was reading a memorable passage in his life where he says he was wanting to send his missionaries out to the Gallas tribe in Africa, but could not find any means. So he says,

Then I knocked diligently on the dear God in prayer; and since the praying man dare not sit with his hands in his lap, I sought among the shipping agents, but came to no speed; and I turned to Bishop Gobat in Jerusalem, but had no answer; and then I wrote to the missionary Krapf in Mornbaz, but the letter was lost. Then one of the sailors who remained said, "Why not build a ship, and you can send out as many and as often as you will." The proposal was good, but, the money! That was a time of great conflict, and I wrestled with God. For no one encouraged me, but the reverse; and even the truest friends and brethren hinted that I was not quite in my senses. When Duke George of Saxony lay on his deathbed, and was yet in doubt to whom he should flee with his soul, whether to the Lord Christ and his dear merits, or to the pope and his good works, there spoke a trusty courtier to him: "Your Grace, *Straightforward makes the best runner!*" That word has lain fast in my soul. I had knocked at men's doors and found them shut; and yet the plan was manifestly good and for the glory of God. What was to be done? *Straightforward makes the best runner.* I prayed fervently to the Lord, laid the matter in his hand, and, as I rose up at midnight from my knees, I said, with a voice that almost startled me in the quiet room: *Forward now, in God's name!* From that moment there never came a thought of doubt into my mind.

Friends! The churches of Christ have no need of the modern machinery which has supplanted the simplicity of faith. I truly believe if the Lord swept the committees, secretaries, and missionary societies out of the universe, we should be better without them if our churches would but trust God, send out their own men, raise the money to support them, and believe that God would bless them. I hope the church will soon say, like David in Saul's clanking armor, *"I cannot go with these, for I have not tested them,"* and with only her sling and her stone, confident in her God, I the church will confront her foe. We can do all things, if we can but trust Christ. *"All things are possible to him who believes"*; but nothing is possible to your schemes and to your systems. God will sweep them away, and happy shall be that man who shall lead the caravan in their utter destruction. Go up against her, take away her shields, for they are not the Lord's; he did not ordain them, nor will he stand by them. Act in faith, O you people of God, and prove the power of prayer, for *"all things are possible to him who believes."*

There is another point upon which I have already entrenched, and that is, in the service of God, *"all things are possible to him who believes."* I know the devil will say to you, "Why, you have no gift." And what if you don't? If you have the gift of faith, you may do something, and fulfill your mission. Perhaps you are a minister; you have been laboring in a village with very little success. Brother, may it not be that you did not believe that God would give you success? For if you had believed it, you would have had it. You are not hampered by God, but hampered by your own bowels. I know what it is to go to my chamber and feel ashamed of many a sermon I have preached, and moan and groan over it; and

I have known what it is to discover, within a month, that the sermon has been far more useful in conversion than those which I thought had something about them which might render them effective. The fact is, God wants not our power, but our weakness; not our greatness, but our nothingness. Oh, brother, if God has called you to a work that is ten times harder than you have strength to perform, go and do it in *his* strength, and *"all things are possible to him who believes."*

I wish that this age would breed a few extravagant men. We are getting so dull, so cold, so commonplace – we all run in the same cartful, imitating one another; in the sight of one of the heroes of old, we little men do walk under their huge legs, and look around to find ourselves dishonorable graves; and all this is because we have left off faith. Let a man believe that God has called him to a mission; let him say, "Forward, in God's name!" and that man will tell upon his times, and carve his name in the rock of ages, and leave memorials behind him which angels shall gaze upon when the names of emperors and kings have been swept into oblivion. Men and brethren in this church – many and many a time have I stirred you up to faith, and there are some few of you who begin to know what faith means; but oh, I fear there are many of you still that have not come to the fullness of the meaning of faith. To live in a region of miracles, to be called fanatics, to see God's hand as visibly as you see your own, to recognize him as greater than second causes, to find him as one whose arm you can move, whose power you can command, to stand in an extraordinary position, far above the place where reason can put you – to know that you are a distinguished, separated, specially favored child of God. Oh! this is heaven begun below. Believe me, I often marvel how people can think that the present attainments of the church are all the church can expect. I look upon decent tradespeople, respectable ministers, and amiable women, and so forth, doing something, but doing very, very little – and I am apt to say, "What! What! Is this all Christ shed his blood for – to make us do this? Is this all the Holy Spirit does, to make a man get through a decent sermon on a Sunday? Is this all? Is this God's work? I see God's work in nature, and there are towering Alps, and roaring seas, and waterfalls

> God wants not our power, but our weakness; not our greatness, but our nothingness.

lashed to fury; but I look on God's work in the church – little, little, little everywhere. Littleness is stamped upon the brow of today; we do not do and dare. And I am inclined to think that until we see some great and daring deed attempted, and some great and marvelous thing done for Christ, we shall not see the glory of the Lord revealed so that all flesh shall see it together. What are we doing here, all of us cooped up in this little island, all of us living in England? *The whole world lies in the power of the evil one.* How is it our hearts beat not for the heathen? We must stay at home; we have calls. But is not the call of God louder still, if we had but faith? But we are so carnal – we live so much on the *things that are visible,* that we cannot do a rash, brave, or graceless act for the Master. God help us to do it! Then shall the church arise and put on her beautiful garments; and woe to you, Ashkelon, when Israel's God is in the camp! Woe to you, Gaza, for your gates shall be carried on our shoulders when once we believe we are strong enough to bear them to the top of the hill, posts and bars and all! *"All things are possible,"* in the service of God, *"to him who believes."*

Finally, when we shall come to die, sickness shall cause us no anxiety, the solemn mysteries of the last article shall give us no alarm, the grave shall be no place of gloom, judgment shall know no terrors, and eternity shall have no horrors; for to him that believes, all things are possible, and death and death's shade give way before faith. Heaven yields to faith; hell trembles at it; earth is powerless before it, and lies in the hand of the faithful man, like clay upon the potter's wheel, to be molded as he wills.

I come to my last point, and may God bless it. Where lies, then, the secret strength of faith? It lies in the food it feeds on; for faith studies *what the promise is* – an emanation of divine grace, an overflowing of the great heart of God; and faith says, "My God could not have given this promise, except from love and grace; therefore it is quite certain that this promise will be fulfilled." Then faith thinks, *"Who gave* this promise?" It considers not so much its greatness, as "Who is the author of it?" She remembers that it is God who cannot lie – God omnipotent, God immutable; and therefore she concludes that the promise must be fulfilled, and forward she goes in this firm conviction. Then she remembers, also, *why* the promise was given – namely, for God's glory, and she feels perfectly sure that God's glory is safe, that he will never stain his own ornamental plate, nor mar the luster of his own crown; and therefore she concludes that the promise must and will stand.

Then faith also considers the amazing *work of Christ* as being a clear proof of the Father's intention to fulfill his word. *He who did not spare His own Son, but delivered Him over for us all, how will He not also with Him also freely give us all things?* Then faith looks back upon *the past,* for her battles have strengthened her, and her victories have given her courage. She remembers that God never has failed her; no, that he never did once fail any of his children. She recollects times of great peril, when deliverance came – hours of awful need, when as her day her strength was; and she says, "No, I never will be led to think that he can now renounce himself, and change his character, and leave his servant." Faith, moreover, feels that she cannot believe a hard thing of her dear God. Is it wrong to use that expression? I must use it, for he *is* dear to me! I think this is one of the things I have repented of above all other sins I have committed – the sin of ever doubting him who loves me so well that he would sooner die than I should perish, and he did die that I might live. What! that God so dear to my soul – do I doubt him? I would not spread a report that my father was a liar, or that my mother would renounce herself. No, blessed parents, you would not be unkind to me; and, my blessed God, my faith knows that you *cannot* be unkind; your love will *make* you faithful even if your faithfulness were not enough of itself. If our God *can* leave us, then indeed I am mistaken in his character. If I can *dare* something for God, and he can leave me, then I have misread Scripture. I do not believe, young warrior, if God shall prompt you to dash into the thick of the battle, that he will leave you, as Joab did Uriah, to fall by the arrows of the enemy. Only dare it, and God will be greater than your daring. But we refuse to be honorable. A little hardship, a little difficulty, a little danger, and we shrink back to our lowly sloth. Oh, that we would rise to the glory of believing!

Dearly beloved, I have tried thus to stir up your souls, but I am very conscious that we cannot have this faith in Christ except as we have more of his Holy Spirit. But then we have the promise – *"If you then, being evil, know how to give good gifts to your children, how much more will your heavenly Father give the Holy Spirit to those who ask him?"* Ask for more faith. This church is enough of itself for the conversion of the whole world, if God will give us faith enough. If the little band at Jerusalem were all that was needed, a band of more than two thousand faithful men and women might be enough, if we had faith. And look at all the churches around; would their success be as little as it is if they had more faith? All things are possible, and yet we do nothing! Everything is within our reach, and yet we are poor! Heaven itself is on our side, and yet we are defeated! Shameful unbelief! be put to death forever! Glorious faith! live in our souls! I hope that both sinner and saint will believe in the mercy and goodness and truth of God as revealed in Christ, and that we will take this home with us for today's meal – *"All things are possible to him who believes."*

> Faith treads on the world and on hell;
>   It vanquishes death and despair;
> And, O! let us wonder to tell,
>   It overcomes heaven by prayer,
>
> Bids sins of a crimson-like dye
>   Be spotless as snow and as white;
> And raises the sinner on high
>   To dwell with the angels of light.

Chapter 10

All Things Are Possible

Jesus said unto him, If thou canst believe, all things are possible to him that believeth (Mark 9:23 AKJV)

I believe that our own Authorized Version conveys to the mind of the reader the sense intended by the Gospel writer; it is, however, exceedingly probable that in exact words the Revised Version is nearer to the original. It runs thus – *And Jesus said to him, "If You can! All things are possible to him who believes."* Our own version better expresses the sense to the general reader, and the main object of a translation is to give the meaning. The father of the lunatic child had said to our Lord, *"If You can do anything, take pity on us and help us"*; and our divine Master virtually replies, "The 'if You can' lies not with me, but with you. It is not if *I* can, but if *you* can." Thus you see the word *believe* is implied if not actually expressed. Jesus would certainly go as far as ever the man's faith could go; but as the rule of the kingdom is *"It shall be done to you according to your faith,"* the man's unbelief would hamper the Lord in his working. If the pleader could be rid of unbelief, Jesus would get rid of the devil from his child. The difficulty of casting out the demon lay mainly in the lack of faith in the father. Let it, then, be understood as the teaching of this text, that the difficulties in the way of souls that would be saved do not lie with Jesus Christ, but with themselves. They need never ask the question, "Can Jesus forgive?" or "Can he renew?"

There is a prior question – Can you believe that he can forgive and that he can renew? If God's grace enables you to say, "I can and do believe that Jesus can work in me according to the full measure of my need," then all difficulty has vanished. Your faith is the shadow of the coming blessing, the token of the Lord's favor towards you. When your faith believes in Christ's omnipotence, he is omnipotent to you, for *"all things are possible to him who believes."*

I long at this time to get at some here who cannot get to Christ. I wish to God that by his Spirit I may deal with their difficulties so as to remove them once and for all, so that they may come just as they are, and put their trust in Jesus, and find eternal life this day.

The first subject we shall speak about is the vital question – What is believing? After all these hundreds of years of gospel preaching, is this question necessary? I believe it is so necessary that if faith were explained in every sermon, it would not be too often spoken of. It is a good rule that every tract ought to contain the gospel; and it ought to be put in the plainest way, for still, despite all the gospel-teaching which is around us, nothing is so little known or so little understood as faith in the Lord Jesus Christ. I am also bound to admit that many explanations of faith are no explanations, but that they tend to make the subject darker than it was before; and I am fearful lest my own explanation should be of the same order. Certainly, I will do my best to avoid such a catastrophe, for I will speak very plainly.

> Your faith is the shadow of the coming blessing, the token of the Lord's favor towards you.

Let us take the man before us as an example, and from him let us see what faith is. This man evidently believed that Jesus was a healer, for he says, *"I brought You my son."* He would not have brought his son to Jesus if he had not felt some measure of confidence in him. *It is a good beginning of faith to know that if I am saved it must be through Jesus Christ alone.* It is well to be aware that the salvation of the soul must come from the work of Jesus, and from no one else, since no other name is given among men whereby we must be saved. This man had also some slight faith in Christ's willingness to help him. It may not have been very strong, but still it was there, or else he would not have laid the stress of his prayer upon the Lord's power. He did not say, "If

You will, You can," but *"If You can do anything, take pity on us and help us!"* Looking up into that blessed face so full of singular tenderness, the man felt that he might say, "Have pity on us." From some persons we could not ask for pity or fellow-feeling, because they do not appear to have any; they wear a harsh look, and a chill air surrounds them. But the Savior was not so. The man felt that Jesus was full of pity, and his appeal was that this pity would show itself to him and his son. *It is a good beginning to saving faith if you believe that Jesus is willing to save you.* I trust that many of you have advanced as far as this.

What is it really and savingly to believe in Jesus? The pleading father had not yet reached that point of faith which would secure the miracle; more was needed, but what was it? *He needed to believe in Christ's power in reference to his own case.* The point in which his faith failed was our Lord's power as to the special case now before him, for he said, *"If You can do anything."* Before you condemn the anxious father for his doubt, let me remind you that his son was in a very evil and difficult situation, and our Lord had just caused him to remember and review the sad features of the case. The father had sorrowfully set forth in detail the fact that *"whenever it seizes him, it slams him to the ground and he foams at the mouth, and grinds his teeth and stiffens out"*; and then he had further told the Lord that the youth had suffered from this ever since he was a child. Then he had gone still more into detail, saying, *"It has often thrown him both into the fire and into the water to destroy him."* After that painful detail he added his pitiful *"If You can."* Do you wonder at it? Jesus seems to tell him, "If you can believe in the teeth of all this, then you shall see the salvation of God." It is very easy to say, "I believe" when you have no sense of your sin and no consciousness of your danger. It is the easiest thing in the world to say, "Yes, Christ can save me" when you do not really believe that you need saving. Faith, where there is no present sense of need, is but the image of faith, and not the grace which saves the soul. This is the question: *Can you, my dear hearer, at this moment trust Jesus to save you, though you feel that you are full of sin?* Can you say, "Lord, I am possessed with the spirit of evil; I am under bondage to him, and have been so since I was a child. I have been driven to one sin and so cast into the fire, and then I have been hurled into the opposite sin and so thrown into the water. I have been torn with passion, and torn with evil desires; I have sinned against light and knowledge, I have sinned against love and mercy; I have sinned in thought, and word, and deed; I have sinned grievously and continually, and yet I believe that you can pardon me, and that you can make me a new creature. Wicked as I am, I believe that you can drive sin from the throne of my heart and cause me to love you and to serve you all my days." If you can believe in Jesus after this fashion, he will save you; yes, he has saved you. If you, as an undeserving sinner, can so honor the mercy of God as to believe that through Christ Jesus he can blot out your sin, it shall be done unto you. Only remember that this confidence must not come to you because of your forgetfulness of your sin, but rather while you are conscious of it and humbled on its account. If I persuade myself that I am merely a sinner in name, then I shall only find Jesus to be a savior in name. If I am not such a sinner as to deny that I am a sinner, but pay the Lord the compliment of saying, "Oh yes, I am a sinner; we are all sinners," then I am a sham sinner, and I shall become a sham believer, and the true Savior will have nothing to do with me. Jesus came to save that which is really and truly lost. The downright sinner, who dares not deny his guilt, is the object of the Lord's saving search. In the teeth of your conscious guilt, can you believe that Jesus can wash you and renew you? Then you have one main element of the faith which saves.

> If I persuade myself that I am merely a sinner in name, then I shall only find Jesus to be a savior in name.

Yet, mark you, if this man could by any possibility have believed in Christ's power to save his son and yet had refused to bring him to Jesus for healing, he would have missed one of the essentials of true faith. For, listen. *If you would get to the very heart and bowels of faith, you have it here: it is to trust the Lord.* Trust! trust! that is the word. To believe that Christ is able to save you is an essential thing, but to put yourself into his hands that he may save you is the saving act. Believe Christ's word to be true, then appropriate that word unto yourself as spoken to you. Believe that it is true to you, and rest in the truth of it – that is saving faith. To see Christ as such a Savior as you need, able and willing to save you, is a right good sight, but you must also take this Savior to be yours. Say heartily, "Into that hand which was nailed to the cross I commit my guilty soul, hoping and believing that Jesus will forgive all my trespasses, and cause me to love all that is true and holy hereafter and forever."

> Thou canst, thou wilt (I dare not doubt),
> The indwelling demons chase;
> I trust thy power to cast them out,
> I trust thy pardoning grace.

He who trusts in Jesus is saved. I did not say, "He *shall be* saved," but he *is* saved. *"He who believes has eternal life." Through Him everyone who believes is freed from all things, from which you could not be freed through the Law of Moses.*

Will you be pleased to notice about this man's faith that *it was not perfect faith*? Though it obtained for him the healing of his son, it was weak faith, and for its weakness he was blamable; but the faultiness of his faith was not the destruction of his faith. A feeble faith can receive a mighty Savior, even as a beggar with a paralyzed hand can receive a golden gift. An heir to an estate has as good a title to it when he is a child as he will have when he is grown up, and even so little faith possesses the inheritance, though as yet it be a babe. The anxious father had to cry, "Lord, *help my unbelief*," but that unbelief, confessed and lamented, did not shut him out of the blessing. The unbelief which lingers around our faith is a thing to be gotten rid of by the help of Christ, but still it will not destroy the virtue of the faith which we possess. So, dear friend, if your faith in Jesus Christ amounts to this – that you believe him able to save, and you do therefore trust him – you are a saved man, even though you may be staggered with a host of fears, and troubled with a multitude of sins. Your faith has saved you, go in peace; for that faith of yours shall grow from a mustard seed into a far-spreading tree. I wish that you could take Jesus up into your arms as Simeon did, for then would you say with full assurance, *"My eyes have seen Your salvation."* But if you cannot do so much as that, at least stretch out your finger and touch the hem of the Lord's garment; for if you do but touch his clothes you shall be made whole. The faintest contact with the ever-blessed Christ will open up a way by which saving power will flow out of him into you. Oh, how blessed it is to think that God has ordained this plain way of faith for poor sinners! It is of faith that it might be of grace, to the end that the promise might be sure to all the chosen seed.

This faith in the Lord Jesus ought to be to each one of us the easiest thing in all the world. If we were what we ought to be, it would never occur to us to doubt our Lord Jesus; and our shameful unbelief in him is the most conclusive evidence of our need of him, for we must have become grievously wrong in heart to be forced to admit that we find it difficult to believe in Jesus. What an insult to him! What a crime on our part! Remember the whole story of grace and blush for your wicked unbelief. God, the ever-blessed, whom we had offended, sent his dear Son to be made in the likeness of sinful flesh, and he dwelt here among us as our brother, friend, and helper. In the fullness of time he took upon himself our sin and sorrow, and went up to the cross with the awful load of our guilt. Though still the well-beloved Son of the Father, he suffered even unto death in the room and place of his people, and God's record concerning him is that he has set him forth as the propitiation for sin. God has accepted his atonement, will not sinners accept it? This is the Savior; God has ordained him as such. Will not the sinner agree that Jesus should save him? If not, why not? If we were not fallen to the uttermost degree of depravity we should cry out with delight, "Lord, we believe. Blessed be the dear name of Jesus, our Substitute, we can and do trust him. We are quite sure that if the Lord God has made Jesus to be his salvation to the ends of the earth, then he must be a perfect salvation; therefore, we accept him with joy and delight." But this is the curse of our nature, the innate vice of our hearts, that we cannot believe our God, thus making him a liar. Oh, the horror of suspecting his truth whom angels adore with veiled faces! Oh, the daring presumption of questioning the promise of a faithful God! It is horrible, horrible, horrible to the last degree to mistrust the almighty Father, to doubt his bleeding Son! There ought to be no room for an "if" when we know that in the Lord Jesus all fullness dwells. I am not at this moment speaking to those who reject the Word of God, and deny the deity of Christ. I can understand their position, and will deal with them at another time; but I am now speaking to you who accept this Bible as God's word, and unquestioningly believe that Jesus

Christ is divine. To you I say that your refusal to put your trust in him is without excuse; at least, I cannot find an excuse for you. Remember those strong words of the Lord Jesus – *"If I speak truth, why do you not believe Me?"* If you believe Jesus to be the Son of God and the Savior of men, why do you not trust your own soul with him? Why not at this moment confide in him whom you admit to be worthy of your trust?

I have tried thus to explain the nature of faith. I will now, in the second place, deal with the startling question, How is it that faith can be difficult? It certainly is difficult to some. It cannot be so in itself, yet many in trouble of heart find it to be so, and those that labor to bring them to Christ find themselves hard put to it.

Why? First, *it is difficult to get the very idea of faith into some men's minds* – not only difficult for them to believe, but even to know what it is to believe. I have met with persons who have attended a place of worship regularly for twenty or thirty years, and yet they have never made the discovery that faith is a childlike trust in Jesus. I, as a lad, was taught this blessed secret by the Spirit of God; but it was at the first a great wonder to me that I should have attended evangelical ministries for years, and yet should not have known what was meant by believing in Christ. That simple truth broke in upon my mind like a new revelation. I had read the Bible; there was no part of it with which I was not acquainted, and yet even from that blessed book I had not learned what believing in Christ meant. Is not this unusual? It is remarkable, and yet it is a general fact. We try by illustrations, by anecdotes, and by parables to drill the notion of faith into men, but we cannot even get it into their heads, much less into their hearts. Martin Luther complained that he thought he must take the Bible and bang it about his hearers' heads because he could not get them to see its clear teaching as to justification by faith. This idea of believing is alien to men's minds, and it can only dwell there by forcing its way against the tendency of human nature. Again, I say, that this is a sad proof of human depravity, since in itself it is no difficult idea; it is the simplest thought that can be uttered or accepted. Trust your salvation with Christ, and Christ will save you, is a lesson which a child may learn. Still, the unregenerate do not think so. They muddle it all up and stick to their belief that faith is something to be felt, or seen, or done, or suffered. To trust their God, to rely upon the atonement of his Son – this is not to their mind, and so their foolish heart is darkened, and they cannot see the way which lies straight before them.

When we get that thought into our hearers' heads, then there comes the next difficulty: *to make them believe that faith can save them.* It seems so difficult to believe this *because the way is so easy.* They say, What! Am I, after thirty, forty, fifty years of sin to be delivered from all the punishment of my transgressions by simply trusting in the Lord Jesus Christ? If you were to tell them that they must go to a desert and live there as hermits on berries and cold water for the rest of their natural lives, they would believe the message. If they were bidden to scourge themselves with whips of wire, they could expect some good result from such suffering, but not from mere believing. If they were to look at the idea of appeasing God by their personal suffering, it would soon become impossible to believe; yet for a time they incline to it rather than to the doctrine of salvation by trust in the great Substitute. Hideous imaginings, despairings, and dreads are also looked upon hopefully by many; they hope that by deep feelings they may arrive at forgiveness, and may force their way to heaven by the gates of hell. But to trust Christ, and to believe the promise of God, is a thing too simple for them; they fear that safety is not to be found so soon! Ah! poor soul, if the prophet had bid you to do some great thing, would you not have done it? How much rather then when he says to you, "Believe and live"?

I wish you would change your opinion as to what faith really is, for it is by no means so insignificant a matter as you suppose. Simple as it is, there lies within it great excellence and value. Faith in God is the divinest exercise of the mind. To believe in God and his Christ is to be reconciled to God and restored from enmity. We are in unison of heart with those we trust. To believe your God is to worship him; the essence of worship is faith. For a poor sinner to trust the Lord gives him more honor than the cherubim can bring him with their loftiest notes of praise. In the teeth of all my sin and sinfulness, with a thorough sense of my guilt, I believe that the blood of Jesus has saved me – is not this true praise? To confess scarlet sins, and yet to say, *"Wash me, and I shall*

> To believe your God is to worship him; the essence of worship is faith.

be whiter than snow" gives unto the Lord great glory for his mercy and his power. Yet the doctrine of "believe and live" startles poor sinners because it is too easy!

When they get over the idea of its extreme ease, they say to themselves, "This news is certainly too good to be true. Do I really understand you, sir, that if I trust the Lord Jesus now I am at once delivered from sin and am made a new creature in Christ?" Yes, you understand my teaching if that is the sense you find in my words. Yet you say it is too good to be true. Do you not see how poorly you think of your God? I know that pardoning grace is infinitely above your deservings or thoughts; but then does not the Lord say of himself, *"As the heavens are higher than the earth, so are My ways higher than your ways and My thoughts than your thoughts"*? Grace may be too good for you to expect, but it is not too good for God to bestow. Oh, that you would think better of God than you have done, and say of his amazing grace, "It is just like him!" Sing with me these words –

> Who is a pardoning God like thee?
> Or who hath grace so rich and free?

Salvation pitched in such a key as this, given freely to whosoever believes in Jesus! Why, that is like the Lord, and we will accept it as having the divine stamp and imprint upon it. He forgives like a God, and this does not stagger our faith, but confirms it.

Then, again, men are astounded by *the rapidity of justification*. Shall fifty years' sinning be forgiven in a moment? Shall an instant's believing end the guilty past, and commence a holy future? It is even so; in one instant a man begins a course of believing which introduces him into a new world. What is strange about this? Is it not God's way to do wonders in a short time? He took but a week to fit the earth for man; no, six days sufficed, and on the seventh he rested. To make the light in which we rejoice only needed the Lord to say, *"Let there be light."* In the case before us our Lord only said to the demon, *"I command you, come out of him, and do not enter him again,"* and the deed was done. If we had all time at our disposal, we could not work such wonders; but to God there are no limits as to length or brevity of time. A thousand years are to him as one day, and one day as a thousand years. He speaks, and it is done. Think of it – salvation in a moment! The moment a sinner believes, he lives unto God, and his trespasses are forgiven. Oh sinner, why should you doubt it? Yet we cannot get the conscience-stricken one to believe it.

If we lead our friends out of this difficulty, they plunge into another. *They cannot be satisfied with the Word of God alone as the grounds for their faith.* Why do I believe that I am saved? I know that I am saved because the Word of God says, "He that believes in him has everlasting life, and I do believe in Jesus, and therefore I have everlasting life." "But," says one, "if I had that word applied to me with power, then I could and would believe it." Just so; but until then you refuse to believe the promise of God, and treat him as a liar! God must give you some pledge or bond beyond his promise, because his Word is not good enough for you, though you admit that even with a good *man* his word is his bond. But you cannot trust your God. "Oh, but if I had a dream." Just so. You would have more faith in a silly dream, perhaps caused by indigestion, than you have in the solemn word and written promise of God. "Oh sir, but if an angel were to speak to me, I could believe." Just so; and if God does not choose to send the angels, what then? Then he is not to be believed, but treated as a liar. What is this but saying, "Lord, you shall bow to my whims, or else I will not believe a word you say." Has it come to this? Dare you demand signs of God? Then let me ask you, Is this Book God's word? Say "No," and I can understand your conduct; but if you believe, as I know you do, that this is the very word of God, how dare you disbelieve? If all the angels in heaven were to march by me in a file, and assure me that God would keep his word, I should say, "I did not require you to tell me that, for the Lord never fails to be as good as his word." God is so true that the witness of angels would be a luxury. If my father were to make a statement, I certainly would not call in his servant to confirm it. If this book be dictated by the Holy Spirit, it is ours to believe it without demanding confirmations or applications. Let us say, "That word is true, for God has said it. Jesus Christ came into the world to save sinners. I am a sinner, and I trust him to save me. Inasmuch as the Word says, *As many as received Him, to them He gave the right to become children of God, even to those who believe in His name,* I do believe on his name, and therefore I have the power and privilege to become a child of God, and a child of God I am. God says so; that is enough for me." We cannot get men to see that the Word of the Lord is surer than all signs and wonders – they want something in addition.

If we compel them to acknowledge that the Word of God is the only and sufficient basis of faith, *they immediately begin to look at their own believing as if it were the Savior.* They cry, "My faith is so weak; my faith is so variable; my faith is so shaken," and so forth. It is as if those who were bidden to look to the brazen serpent had, instead, tried to see their own eyes. Here is a child thirsty, and there is a flowing fountain; you give the child a cup so that it may drink of the water. The child does not go to the fountain, but is so pleased with its empty cup that it tries to satisfy its thirst out of it. What a foolish child! Or suppose it should refuse to go to the fountain because the cup was of earthenware, or of tin; would not that be a strange way for a thirsty child to act? A child needs the cup to drink out of, but it cannot drink out of an empty cup. Faith is the cup, but Christ is the fountain. Faith is a secondary thing compared with Christ. We must have faith to be as the finger with which we touch the hem of the Master's garment, but the finger does not work the cure. Shall I refuse to touch because perhaps I have not washed my finger clean, or it has no gold ring upon it, or there are traces of rheumatism upon it? To attach so much importance to the finger as to refuse to touch Christ's garment with it would be insanity. Do not mind your finger; touch the garment's hem. Sinner, get yourself to Christ somehow, anyhow; for if you get to him you will live. It is not, after all, the greatness nor the perfection of your faith, but it is *his* greatness and *his* perfection which is to be depended on.

Then the next trial is that we cannot get troubled sinners *to see the difference between their faith and its fruits.* "I would believe in Christ," says one, "if I were as holy as So-and-so, who is a believer, but then you see I am a sinner." Now mark, dear friend, that the person of whom you speak in that fashion does not think himself to be one particle more deserving than you are. If you talk to that good man he will tell you that

> **Faith is the cup, but Christ is the fountain. Faith is a secondary thing compared with Christ.**

whatever holiness you can see in him is the work of grace, and that at the beginning he came to Jesus just as you must come, that is, as a sinner. Faith produces holiness; but when we come to Jesus, at the beginning we come as unholy persons, and as such he receives us. Suppose that I have a number of bulbs which I am told will produce most remarkable flowers. If I believe the statement I shall take care to have them properly planted. The gardeners are beginning to put such things into pots so that they may have hyacinths and other fair flowers in the winter and early spring. Suppose that I resolve not to plant my bulbs because I use my own eyesight, and I come to the conclusion that since I cannot see a hyacinth or even the beginnings of one in any of the bulbs, therefore there can be no use in planting them. Why, everyone would tell me that in this matter I must go by faith, and plant my hyacinth in order that I may in due time see it bloom. "That bulb will yield a beautiful blue flower," says one. I answer that it is a brown, dried-up sort of onion, and that I will throw it on the dunghill, for I can see no bud or flower in it. What a simpleton I should be if I talked so! Though I cannot *see* it, yet there is, closely compacted and quietly hidden away within that bulb, a slumbering thing of beauty which will wake up at the call of spring. Even so, if you believe in Christ, there is a holy life packed away within your faith, and it will gradually develop itself. Even within a feeble faith there are the elements of ultimate perfection. If you do truly trust Christ, your preparation for glory has begun. As the king was hidden in the oak, so is Christ hidden in true faith. Do not, however, expect to see all this at the beginning; look to the root now and the growth will follow. You are not to come to Christ because you are healed, but to get healing; your faith must be a sinner's faith before it can be a saint's faith. Trust Christ while yet you are foul, lost, and undone, and he will wash, save, and restore you.

> Your faith must be a sinner's faith before it can be a saint's faith.

Still we find the awakened ones clinging to the idea that they must be something or feel something before they can trust Jesus. We cannot get them to see that the whole of their salvation lies in Jesus Christ and in Jesus Christ alone. We cannot wean them from some sort of reliance upon their own feelings, or weepings, or prayers, or Bible readings, or some other form of working. Why, they will even look to their own faith rather than to Jesus Christ alone. Do you not know that our Lord has offered a full atonement for sin, and brought in a perfect righteousness for his people? His propitiation is to be accepted as full and complete, and his righteousness we are to wear as our own. Our whole trust must go to the perfect work of our Lord, it must not even rest on our faith. To trust in our own trusting would be absurd. A wounded man has healing ointment given to him and a piece of linen with which to bind on the ointment; now, if he were to wrap the linen around the wound and leave out the healing agent, he could not expect a cure. Faith is the linen whereon the ointment of Christ is spread, and we must not put it out of its due place and order, or we shall be making it a rival to Christ. Oh, that I could clear up some of the difficulties with which men surround themselves, so that they would consent to look out of themselves to Jesus only!

We must now speak to the last point. Oh, you that are seeking rest, dwell upon each word as it is now lovingly delivered to you. What is it that can make faith easy? The Holy Spirit alone can do that; but he does so by bringing certain truths to remembrance. Faith is rendered easy to a man by the Holy Spirit when, first of all, he sees clearly *the infallible certainty of the sacred record;* and this is the record that God gave concerning his Son, that he that believes in him has everlasting life. Is this Bible true or not? I believe in every letter of it. I accept it as God's word in the most unreserved sense, and so do you to whom I now speak. Well, if that be so, then it remains no longer difficult to believe what is plainly taught in this book. If God has spoken, then questions are ended. It may be a hard saying, it may be a dark saying; it may seem to be too good to be true; but what of that? Do we dare to question the Lord? He is not a man that he should lie, nor the Son of Man that he should repent. He has said that whosoever believes in Jesus shall not perish, but have everlasting life; and if we have so believed, eternal life is ours.

The next thing that the Spirit of God helps us to see is *the applicability of that record to ourselves.* That is to say, we read that *Christ Jesus came into the world to save sinners,* and we conclude that, as we are just such, we may look to him to save us. We read, *"Come to Me, all who are weary and heavy-laden, and I will give you rest."* We labor and are heavy-laden, and therefore we come, and he gives us rest. We read that *at the right time Christ died for the ungodly;* and knowing that we are ungodly, we take heart and come to him who justifies the guilty through his righteousness. We read again, *Let the one who wishes take the water of life without cost.* We feel that to will is present with us, and therefore we freely take the living water. We read once more, *"Go into all the world and preach the gospel to all creation";* and as we are creatures, we conclude that the gospel has something to say to us. On one or another of these accounts we see that the gospel is directed to us, and so we receive it. It is better for us that the promise should be directed to us in terms of character than that it should mention our actual names. Is your name John Brown? Well, if the gospel came in a letter to you, directed to John Brown, what might you not say if you were tempted to doubt? You would think to yourself that there are many more John Browns besides yourself, and therefore the message might not be for you. If it was directed to your address, you might then fear that another John Brown once lived at that house, before you were born, and so you would fear to appropriate the message lest it should prove to be out-of-date. Even supposing that your name was there, and the address and the date, you might be mistrustful enough to imagine that there was a mistake, or that some other person of your name had used your address for the day. If you mean to ride on the back of unbelief, then any delusion will do for a saddle. But when the promise comes to him who believes in Jesus, there can be no question that it is ours if we believe. We read, *If we confess our sins, He is faithful and righteous to forgive us our sins.* Is it not clear that if we have confessed our sins, mercy is ours? It is a blessed thing for us when the Spirit of God leads us to see that the gospel is free to all who are made willing to receive it.

Another thing that makes faith easy is when the Spirit of God shows us *the glory of Christ's person.* Our Savior is truly God, and this fact helps us to believe in him. It strikes me that the poor anxious father may have been much helped to believe in our Lord by that peculiar majesty which shone around him through his having just come down from the Mount of Transfiguration. It was a very hard case which exercised the poor man's mind, and therefore our Lord appeared to him with an unusual splendor – a splendor of which we read, *When they saw Him, they were astonished.* The sight of our Savior's face helped the trembling father to cry, *"I do believe."* Oh, if the Spirit of God will lead you to read the Scriptures till you get a clear idea of the Godhead and perfect manhood of the Lord Jesus, you will feel that everything is possible with an almighty Savior. *Is anything too difficult for the Lord?* Our Lord has gone up unto his glory, and he is able to save unto the uttermost those that come unto God by him. Oh, if you could but grasp the idea that he who asks for your trust is the Son of the Highest, who has all power in heaven and in earth, then you could not, you would not, withhold your confidence! As for myself, knowing beyond all doubt my Lord's divinity, it seems easy enough to rely upon him. I have told you before what John Hyatt said on his dying bed when his deacons said, "Mr. Hyatt, can you trust your soul with Christ now?" "One soul!" said he. "I could trust a million souls with him if I had them." Even so could I trust the Lord Jesus not only with my soul, but also with all the destinies of earth and heaven, time and eternity. Every child of God may safely say that. I could trust Jesus with all the souls that ever lived or shall live, if they were all mine. Surely, he is able to keep that which we have committed to him.

> He who asks for your trust is the Son of the Highest.

Another great help to faith is to perceive *the completeness of the divine work and sacrifice of the Lord Jesus.* He took our sin upon himself, and in his own body on the tree was made sin for us, that we might be made the righteousness of God in him. Only let your eyes behold the Son of God suffering the death-agony for guilty man, and you must believe in his power to redeem. I have thought that if men had been more sinful than they are, and if they were a million times as numerous as they are, and if every star that studs the midnight sky were a world, and all crowded full of sinners, still the sacrifice of God himself must from the glory of his nature be such a vindication of the law that it might well suffice as a reason for forgiving a rebel universe! Shall the infinitely Holy One suffer for the guilty? Shall the Eternal take upon himself humanity, and bow his head to death? Then the sacrifice must possess such boundless effectualness that none may fear that it will fall short of their need. No limit can be set to the power which lies in the divine atonement. My

God, I see that you have given your own Son to die, and surely in his precious blood there is more than sufficient reason for my faith in you.

If that does not lead you to believe, then perhaps the Spirit of God will go to work in another way. Some have been helped to believe in Jesus by *the sight of others converted, justified, and made happy.* When someone like yourself is saved, you take courage. "I have been a thief," says one.

> The dying thief rejoiced to see
> That fountain in his day;
> And there may you, though vile as he,
> Wash all your sins away.

"I have been an adulterer," says one. Alas! so was David, but he said, *Wash me, and I shall be whiter than snow.* "I have been a murderer," sobs a third. So was Manasseh, who shed innocent blood very much. "But I have been a persecutor and a blasphemer." So was Saul of Tarsus, yet he obtained mercy. "But I seem to have far more of the devil in me than anybody else." So had Mary Magdalene, out of whom Christ cast seven devils. You think you are a sinner all by yourself, but there have been others like you, and the door through which others have passed into mercy is open for you. If I had been a little rabbit in the day when Noah brought the living creatures into the ark, I do not think I would have been troubled about whether there was room for me to enter the ark; but if I had been so timid, I would have forgotten all my fears when I saw the elephant come up and his mate with him, and had seen them go tramping through the door. Then I would have known assuredly that there was room for me. Oh, you who have been kept moral and upright, and therefore are not outwardly great sinners, surely you may enter where the chief of sinners has found ready admission. The salvation of others is often a sweet encouragement to sinners to trust in Christ.

> **The salvation of others is often a sweet encouragement to sinners to trust in Christ.**

Lastly, I will tell you one thing which will make you trust him, and that is, *desperation as to all other hopes.* It is a singular thing that despair is often the mother of faith, but the mother dies when the child is born.

We were many of us led to believe in Jesus because we had nothing else to trust in. When we are driven to the last extremity, then it is we come to Jesus and take him to be our all in all. A boy was awakened in a house which had caught on fire. He could be seen from the street, poor child, and his danger was great indeed. He rushed to the window. His father stood below and called to him to drop himself into his arms, but it was a long way down, and the child was afraid. He clung to the window, but dared not drop. Do you know what made him let go his hold and fall into his father's arms? There came a burst of fire out of the window and scorched him, and then he dropped directly. I wish that some of you would get just such a touch of the fires of despair as to compel you to say,

> I can but perish if I go;
> I am resolved to try,
> For if I stay away I know
> I must forever die.

Years ago, one of our students was greatly emaciated with what seemed to be consumption. He had heard of a certain medicine which was said to be useful in such cases, but he had no faith in it. When he was growing worse and worse I said, "Brother, you are at death's door; try that man's stuff. There may be something in it. At any rate, nothing else does you any good." He took the medicine through sheer despair of all other prescriptions, and God blessed it to him so that he is alive today. He would never have tried the remedy if he had not felt that there was no other hope. Even so, it will be well for you to be driven into a corner as to your soul's estate, so that you may believe in Christ Jesus and say with his disciples in old time, *"Lord, to whom shall we go? You have words of eternal life."* Here is a closing verse for you to sing at home by yourself:

> A guilty, weak, and helpless worm,
> On Christ's kind arms I fall:
> He is my strength and righteousness,
> My Jesus and my all.

Chapter 11

Faith's Dawn and Its Clouds

Immediately the boy's father cried out and said, "I do believe; help my unbelief." (Mark 9:24)

Last Sabbath morning we expounded upon the way by which faith comes to the soul. *So faith comes from hearing.* It is our joyful persuasion that on the past Sabbath, faith actually came to many, and they were enabled to rest themselves upon the Lord Jesus Christ to their soul's salvation. Now, every good shepherd knows that he ought to look very carefully after the newborn lambs, and, therefore, it seemed to me that it would be most expedient today to search after those who have just believed in Christ, and to endeavor to strengthen and help them against the very serious trials which are likely to occur due to their present weak condition. When a man first lays hold upon Jesus he is very apt to be in distress, if his joy is not always at its full height. He is untrained in spiritual conflict, and easily dismayed; the tremor of his former conviction is upon him, and he is prone to relapse into it. The light which he has received fills him with intense delight, but it is not very clear and abiding; he sees men as trees walking, and is ready to conjure up a thousand fears. The weakness of newborn faith, therefore, calls for the compassion of all who love the souls of men. In addition to their own weakness they are liable to special dangers, for at such times Satan is frequently very active. No king will willingly lose his subjects, and the Prince of Darkness labors to bring back those who have just escaped over the confines of his dominion. If souls are never tested afterwards, they are pretty sure to be attacked on their outset from the City of Destruction to the Celestial City. Bunyan very wisely placed the Slough of Despond at the very commencement of the spiritual journey. The cowardly fiend of hell attacks the weak, because he wishes to put an end to them before they get strong enough to do mischief to his kingdom. Like Pharaoh, he wishes to destroy the little ones. He seeks, if possible, to beat out of them every comfortable hope, so that their trembling faith may utterly perish. Perhaps the text chosen for today will be suitable to many here. I trust it may, and that the Spirit of God will give us reflections upon it which shall come home comfortably to all troubled souls. *"I do believe; help my unbelief."*

In the text there are three things very clear. Here is *true faith*; here is *grievous unbelief*; here is *a battle between the two*.

Very clearly in the text there is true faith. *"I do believe,"* says the anxious father. When our Lord tells him that if he can believe, all things are possible to him, he makes no objection to it, asks for no pause, wishes to hear no more evidence, but cries at once, *"I do believe."* Now, observe that we have called this faith *true faith,* and we will prove it to have been so. First, it was faith *in the person of Christ*. It is a great mistake to imagine that to endorse sound doctrine is the same thing as possessing saving faith, for while saving faith accepts the truth of God, it mainly concerns itself with the person and work of the Lord Jesus Christ, and its essence lies in reliance upon Jesus himself. I am not saved because I believe the Scriptures, or because I believe the doctrines of grace; but I am saved if I believe Christ, or, in other words, if I trust in him. Jesus is my creed. He is the truth. In the highest sense the Lord Jesus is the Word of God. To know him is life eternal. By his knowledge he justifies many. I do not know that the father in the narrative before us had heard many sermons. I am not sure that he had very clear notions about everything that concerned the Savior's kingdom; it was not essential that he should have, in order to obtain a cure for his son. It was a very desirable thing that he should be an instructed disciple, but

> In the highest sense the Lord Jesus is the Word of God. To know him is life eternal.

in the emergency before us the main thing was that he should believe Christ to be both able and willing to cast the devil out of his son. Up to that point he did believe; and, though his faith may have been deficient in breadth as well as in depth, yet it enabled him to realize that the Messiah who stood before him was the Lord, and it led him to place all his reliance upon him. He did not believe in the disciples; he had once trusted them and failed. He did not believe in himself; he knew his own impotence to drive out the evil spirit from his child. He believed no longer in any medicines or men, for doubtless he had spent much on physicians; but he believed the man of the shining countenance who had just come down from the mountain. When he heard him say, *"'If You can?' All things are possible to him who believes,"* he at once said, *"I do believe."* Beloved hearer, I hope that you have come, at some time or other – perhaps it is since last Sabbath day – to put your trust in Jesus in the same way, believing him to be able and willing to save you. This is the faith that will effectually save you. Do you rest in him, in him your God, your brother, your Savior; in him as living among the sons of men; in him as bleeding and suffering, as a substitutionary sacrifice, in your stead; in him as risen from the dead no more to die; in him as sitting at the right hand of the Father, clothed with power to save? Do you trust him? If not, whatever you believe, and however orthodox your creed, you are short of eternal life; but, if all your trust rests in him, if you bring all your help from him, if his wounds are your only shelter, his blood your only plea, himself your only confidence, then you are a saved man, your transgressions are forgiven you for his name's sake, and you are accepted in the beloved. Rejoice with fullness of joy, for you have a right to do so, since every gladsome thing is yours.

The faith of this good man was true and saving for another reason. It was personal faith *about the matter in hand,* faith about the case which he was pleading. Have you never found it to be wonderfully easy to believe for other people? I know when I was seeking the Savior, I had no doubt about his receiving any other repentant soul. I felt certain that if the vilest sinner out of hell had come to him, he was able to save him. And though I had no faith in him on my own account, yet had I met with another distressed soul in a similar condition to myself, I believe I would have encouraged him to put his trust in Jesus, though I was afraid to do so myself. To believe for others is an easy matter, but when it comes to your own case, to believe that sins like yours can be blotted out, that you, who have so badly played the prodigal, may be received by your loving Father, that your spiritual diseases can be cured, and that the devil can be cast out of you – here is the labor, here is the difficulty. But, beloved, we must believe this or else we do not have saving faith. O my Savior, shall I trifle in faith by believing or pretending to believe that you can heal a case parallel to mine, and yet cannot heal mine? Shall I draw a line and limit you, Holy One of Israel, and say, "You can save up to me, but not so far as I have gone"? Shall I dream that your precious blood has some power, but not power enough to blot out my sins? Shall I dare, in the arrogance of my despair, to set a boundary to the merits of your plea, and to the virtue of your atoning sacrifice? God forbid. Jesus is able to save to the uttermost them that come unto God by him – he is able to save *me*. Him that cometh unto him he will in no wise cast out; I come to him, and he will not, cannot, cast me out. Do you have a personal faith, a faith about yourself, about your own sins, and your own condition before God? Do you believe that Christ can save you? Sink or swim, do you cast yourself upon him, your own proper self? He, his own self, bore our sins in his own body on the tree; and we, our own selves, must cast ourselves upon him. If we have so done, then we, like the man in the narrative, have the real faith, the faith of God's elect.

Lest any, however, should think this a very small thing, let me go on to show you that this man's faith was real, because it was *faith which triumphed over difficulties,* difficulties which typify our own, and therefore it was clearly the work of the Spirit of God, for no other will endure the trial. I shall ask you, dear hearer, whether faith has triumphed over difficulties in your case. For observe, his child was grievously tormented, and the malady was of *long standing.* When the Savior said to him, *"How long has this been happening to him?"* he said, *"From childhood."* Must it not have seemed, now that his son had grown older, a very unlikely thing that he could recover? We expect our children to outgrow some of their complaints; but here was one who, after many years, was none the better. Years had only increased but not diminished his pains. Yet in the teeth of that, the man believed that Christ could cast that long-established demon out of his son.

Dear friend, your case of sin is similar. The sins of your youth rise up before you now – are they not in your bones? The sins of your early manhood, and the sins of your riper years, and, perhaps, the sins of your decaying years – all these come up before you. Can the Ethiopian change his skin, or the leopard his spots? If so, then he that is accustomed to doing evil may learn to do well. Can I – after lying soaked in the scarlet dye till it is ingrained in my very nature – be washed and made whiter than snow? Crimes so long continued, evil habits so deeply rooted, can all these be overcome? O soul, if you have true faith, you will say, "Yes, I believe that since Christ is God he can deliver me from all evil, and forgive me from all sin. Even if I had lived as long as Methuselah, and had continued all that while in the vilest of transgressions, yet Jesus is so mighty to save that he could deliver me in a moment. His word is, *'Any sin and blasphemy shall be forgiven people.'* Looking to those dear wounds, those fountains of love and blood, I do believe, and will believe, that all my years of sin are gone as in a moment, and like thick clouds before a mighty wind are blown away never to return." Oh, this is faith, poor soul. I pray God will enable you to exercise it.

This man had for a long time considered his son's case to be *hopeless*. Well he might. In addition to the fact that the child was subject to attacks of epilepsy and to extreme fits of fury, he was deaf and mute, so that no intelligent expression of feeling could come from him. If at any time he felt stronger and better, he could not give his father a word of hope, he could not utter his gratitude for the sympathetic care that watched over him, and neither could he hear any word of consolation which his father addressed to him. The ear was closed and the tongue was bound. Painful affliction, exceedingly painful to the parent, and to be continued year after year! At last the father must have felt there was no use in making any further effort. The child must be controlled, but he could not be restored; he was a hopeless maniac. Perhaps there is someone here today who has grown hopeless of salvation; he has felt as if his case was one out of the catalog of mercy; he has written bitter things against himself, and supposed that God has sealed those bitter things and made them true. But you see the father in the presence of

Christ believed over the head of his despair, "in hope believing against hope," and I pray that you may do the same. In the presence of Christ the man's confidence came back to him. Have you, my hearer, a hope that can do the same? I never could have believed it was possible for me to be delivered from my sins till now I see that he who came to save me is my Maker; he who came to redeem me is he who bears the earth's huge pillars on his shoulders and sustains all things by the word of his power. With him nothing can be impossible. I see his pierced hands and feet, and feel that if he stooped to suffer in the sinner's stead, the merit of his sacrifice must be great beyond conception.

In Jesus the hopeless one has hope.

In Jesus the hopeless one has hope, he who had despaired otherwise now bids his heart to be of good cheer. Oh, that is true faith which will not permit itself to be any longer the slave of doubt and despondency now that it sees Jesus the Lord drawing near. It is a mighty faith which refuses to sit any longer in the valley of the shadow of death, but arises and shakes itself from the dust, and puts on its beautiful garments.

The father had another trial for his faith in the fact that he had just then *tried the disciples*. He brought his child to Christ, and Christ being absent, he asked the apostles who were in the valley what they could do. They tried their best, but having lost their Master's power, they utterly failed; and this must have been a very violent trial to the father's confidence. He knew that on other occasions Christ's power had passed through the apostles, and he had worked his miracles by them; but here was a complete cessation of their ability to heal. If Jesus did not choose to work by them on this occasion, the suggestion would arise in the man's heart, "Perhaps his own power also has become lessened." But he put the thought aside, and believed notwithstanding all. And, O soul, have you tried ministers and tried God's people, and hoped to get comfort, and have you found none? Have you gone to the ordinances and found them like dry wells? Have you resorted to the hearing of the gospel and found even it to be barrenness to your spirit? Yes, but permit no shadow of suspicion to cross your mind as to the Lord's ability or willingness to save you. Come to the feet of Jesus and still believe in him. Whatever reason may say in your soul to excite you to despondency on account of past defeats, believe firmly that his power is still invincible; his arm is not shortened that he cannot save, neither is his ear heavy that he cannot hear. It was good that you should see the failure of man so that you might glorify the grace of God. It was good that the servants should be unable so that the Master's ability might be the more conspicuous. May the Lord help you to believe that though no man can do you good, though all the pastors and bishops of the church, and all the martyrs and confessors of past ages, and all the apostles, and all the prophets, are unable to find a balm in Gilead that can meet your case, yet there is a hand, a pierced hand, which can heal your wounds and bleed a balm into your soul which shall effectually restore you. Yes, true faith believes over even such a discouragement as this.

I would have you notice also, once more, while we are upon this point, that this father believed in Christ and his power to save, though *the child was at that very moment passing through a horrible stage of pain and misery.* The spirit which possessed this poor child was accustomed to throwing him sometimes into the fire, and sometimes into the water. This is just our condition: for our spirit has sometimes been thrown into the very fire of presumption, and at another season into the floods of despair. We have alternated between the cold of melancholy and the heat of self-conceit. We have at one time cried, "I love pleasure, and after it I will go"; and at another time we have said, "My soul chooses strangling rather than life; I wish not to live always." When Satan is in a man, and he is full of despair, he goes to all extremes and rests nowhere, walking like the unclean spirit himself through dry places, seeking rest and finding none. At the moment while the father was speaking, the poor boy was on the ground wallowing in dreadful outbursts of his disorder, foaming at the mouth, and grinding his teeth. Satan had great wrath because he knew that his time was short. When the Savior spoke and commanded the devil to come out of him, the fiercest struggle of all took place; for the unclean spirit tore the child, and the most terrible cries were heard. Still the father said, *"I do believe."* Now, it may be you are yourself full of great trouble, vexed and tormented with innumerable fears of wrath to come; a little hell burns within your soul, anguish unutterable has taken hold of you, your heart is like a battlefield torn by contending hosts which rush here and there, destroying on every side. You are yourself an embodied agony; you are like David when he said, *The cords of death encompassed me . . . I found distress and sorrow.* Can you now believe? Will you now accept the word of the Most High? If you can, you will greatly glorify God, and you will bring to yourself much blessedness. Happy is that man who can not only believe when the waves softly ripple to the music of peace, but also continues to trust in him who is almighty to save when the hurricane is let loose in its fury, and the Atlantic breakers follow each other, eager to swallow up the ship of the mariner. Surely Christ Jesus is fit to be believed at all times, for, like the North Star, he abides in his faithfulness, let storms rage as they may. He is always divine, always omnipotent to help, always overflowing with loving-kindness, ready and willing to receive sinners, even the very chief of them. Sorrowful one, do not add to your sorrows by unbelief, for that is a bitterness which is unnecessary to mingle with your cup. Better far is it to say, *"Though He slay me, I will hope in Him."*

There must be power unbounded in him who stooped to die upon the cross. Come to Calvary and see! Can you look to that head crowned with thorns, and mark the ruby drops standing on his brow, and yet be doubtful of his power to save? Can you mark that sacred face, more marred than that of any man – marred with our griefs and stained with our sins, can you gaze on it and remain an unbeliever? Survey that precious body tortured in every part for our transgressions, and can you still distrust him upon whom the chastisement of our peace was laid? Can you behold those hands and feet fastened to the dishonorable wood for the guilty? Can you look upon that spectacle of woe, and know that Christ is divine, and yet harbor doubts as to his power to save you? As for myself, I am constrained to cry, "Lord, I believe, I must believe; you have yourself compelled my faith." Let all things reel beneath my feet, but the cross of my Lord stands fast. If the Son of God has died for sinners, it is certain that the believing sinner cannot die, but must be saved, since Jesus bled for him. May God grant to every one of us to stand just there where the poor father did as to his faith, and say as he did, *"I do believe."*

I am forced to leave this topic incomplete, for the time commands me to hasten on. The faith before us was earnest: it led the man to tears of repentance, it taught him to pray, and it led him to open confession. In all these points may your faith be of an equal character.

But now we must turn to the second part of the subject, for here is unbelief. *"Help my unbelief,"* said he. He had doubted the power of Christ. He had said, *"If You can do anything, take pity on us and help us"*; but yet he had faith and he had affirmed it; he had not kept it secret within himself as though he were ashamed of it. Before the scoffing scribes he had confessed, *"I do believe."* He affirmed it, too, with remarkable earnestness, for he said it with tears, as though his heart saturated his confession, running over at his eyes to moisten the words, "Lord, I do believe; do not doubt it, I lie not; I do believe in you." But then he went on to make the confession that at the same time there was an unbelief lingering in his soul. *"Help my unbelief,"* said he. Although his faith had triumphed over the considerations which I just now mentioned, which appeared enough to dampen it, if not to quench it, yet these considerations may have had some effect upon his mind: they did not prevent his believing, but they hampered his faith with many questions. Some unbelief lingered, though faith was supreme. Learn from this that a measure of doubt is consistent with saving faith, that weak faith is true faith, and that a trembling faith will save the soul. If you believe, even though you are compelled to say, *"Help my unbelief,"* yet that faith makes you whole, and you are justified before God.

> A measure of doubt is consistent with saving faith.

I thought I would, under this second topic, mention some reflections which often cause unbelief to trouble the heart which, nevertheless, has been enabled by the Holy Spirit to believe.

First, there are many true believers who at the beginning are tested with unbelief because they have now, more than ever they had before, *a sense of their past sins.* Many a man receives a far deeper sense of sin after he is forgiven than he ever had before. The light of the law is but moonlight compared with the light of the gospel, which is the light of the sun. Love makes sin to become exceedingly sinful.

> My sins, my sins, my Savior!
>   How sad on thee they fall;
> Seen through thy gentle patience,
>   I tenfold feel them all.

> I know they are forgiven,
>   But still their pain to me
> Is all the grief and anguish
>   They laid, my Lord, on thee.

The light of the promise gleaming in the soul reveals the infinite abyss of horror which lies in indwelling sin. In the light of God's countenance we discover the filthiness, the abomination, the detestable ingratitude of our past conduct. We loathe ourselves in our own sight. While we bless God that sin is pardoned, we are staggered to think it should have been such sin as it is, and the natural feeling resulting from our discovery is a fear that we cannot be pardoned. We ask ourselves, Can it be that such sins are forgiven? Possibly the memory of certain peculiarly heinous sins becomes very vivid to our conscience; we had half-forgotten them, but they spring up with dreadful energy, and cast suspicions into our mind as to whether forgiveness is possible. Oh, that we could blot out those evil days! We have said, "Cursed be the sun that it rose on such a day as that in which I so defiled myself with iniquity." Thus, under a sense of sin, though there is the belief that we are pardoned, there may also arise the unbelief against which we need the Lord to help us.

Some have been staggered, at times, by *a consciousness of their present feebleness*. "Yes," says one, "I trust the past is blotted out, but then how can I hope that I am saved? What a poor creature I am. I try to pray, but it is not worth calling it prayer. I go up to God's house vowing that I will praise his name, and I get talking on the way and forget all about it, and I am dull all through the service. Then I was tempted yesterday, and I spoke unadvisedly with my lips, or I did not defend the cause of my Lord and Master against that skeptic as I ought to have done. Only, just lately, I hoped that I had found peace with God, and yet I am behaving like this. Why, I must be a hypocrite; it cannot be that I am a saved soul. Surely if my sins were forgiven me I should act very differently from this." Now that is often the cause of unbelief. The soul still hopes in Jesus and rests in him, and she has nowhere else to go; but for all that, the old monster of unbelief gives her a desperate twitch, and she trembles while she hopes.

Some others have been made to shiver with unbelief on account of *fears for the future.* "I am afraid I shall not hold on," says one. "Why, to be a Christian you must persevere to the end. With such a heart as mine, how can I hope to be steadfast? And in such a position as mine, surrounded by so many ungodly associates, how can I hope to persevere? I see So-and-so made a profession, and he has gone back; and I know such a one who said he was a Christian, and he is a worse man than he used to be. Suppose the last end of me should be worse than the first; suppose I should put my hand to the plow and should look back and prove unworthy of the kingdom." Poor heart, it forgets that word: *"I will never desert you, nor will I ever forsake you,"* and remembers not that other word: *"I give eternal life to [My sheep], and they will never perish; and no one will snatch them out of My hand."* Rightly filled with a holy anxiety to hold on to the end, it gives way to improper unbelief, for it ought to rest confident that Jesus changes not; and, where he has begun the good work, he will carry it on and perfect it unto the day of Christ.

I have known some, again, whose unbelief has been excited by *a consideration of the freeness and greatness of the mercy bestowed.* I recollect how this staggered me once. I had believed in Jesus, and rejoiced in his salvation, but in meditating upon divine grace I was overcome with fear. What! Pardoned, justified, a child of God, an heir of heaven, a joint heir with Christ, one of God's elect, security of heaven, with a crown waiting for me at the last, and power to win that crown daily secured to me – why, it seemed altogether too good to be true. Unbelief whispered, "It cannot be." If such great grace had been shown to others I would not have marveled. If men of great abilities, of high station, and of eminent character had received such grace, I could have believed it; or even if that holy woman, who had so long been a patient sufferer, had been so blessed, it would have appeared an ordinary circumstance. But for such a sinner as I was to be thus favored appeared to be too strange a miracle of love. I do remember how the very grandeur of the divine mercy threatened to crush me down and bury me under its own mass of goodness. I could believe that the Lord would give me a little mercy, but that he should give me such mercy and such unexpected favor almost exceeded belief. And yet, what folly is there in such ideas, for were we not told beforehand that *"as the heavens are higher than the earth, so are My ways higher than your ways and My thoughts than your thoughts"*? Do we not know that we are dealing with a great God, of whom the prophet asks, *"Who is a God like You, . . . who forgives iniquity, transgression and sin"*? Do we think that God will only give according to our stinted measure? Is God to take man for his model? Remember that word: *[He] is able to do far more abundantly beyond all that we ask or think.* Instead of the greatness of the divine mercy staggering us, it ought to console us and assist us to believe, seeing that it is so in harmony with his nature. Yet, oftentimes, on this sea of love poor leaky vessels have begun to sink.

I have known, too, not a few whose unbelief has arisen through *a sacred anxiety to be right* – a most proper anxiety if not pushed beyond its sphere. The idea has been suggested to them: "Suppose I should be after all presumptuous, and should deceive myself by thinking I am saved, whereas I am not? What if I should cover the wound, when it ought to be lanced, before there can be effectual healing?" How I wish that all hypocrites would be troubled with this sort of fear. It would be a great mercy for many boastful professors if they had grace enough to doubt. I think Cowper was right when he said,

> He that never doubted of his state,
> He may, perhaps he may too late.

But yet, this anxiety may be carried too far, and the soul may slide into despondency through it. I ought to be afraid of presumption, but it cannot be presumptuous to believe God's word. I ought to be afraid of saying, *"'Peace, peace,' but there is no peace"*; but if peace comes to me through the word of Christ, I need never be suspicious of it, let it be as profound as it may. I may doubt myself; I may go further and I may despair of self, but I must not doubt the Lord. If he has said, "Trust in me, believe in me, and you shall be saved," then if I believe in him, it is no presumption to know that I am saved. If he has declared that he who believes in him is justified from all things from which he could not be justified by the law of Moses, and if I have believed in him, then I am justified from all my sins. There is far more presumption in doubting the Lord than there ever can be in trusting him. Faith is no

Faith is no more than God's due.

more than God's due; it ought never to be looked at as too daring. If I believe in Jesus I have no right to say, "I hope I am saved," for that implies a doubt of God's declaration that the believer is saved. I have no right to say, "I sometimes think I am saved." I *am* so undoubtedly if I believe in Jesus. It is no matter of opinion, but a matter of certainty. There is nothing in this world about which a man may be so sure as about his own salvation, because other things come to us by the evidence of our own fallible senses, or by the testimony of men who may be mistaken; but the fact that the believer is saved is sealed to us by the testimony of God himself, who cannot lie. When the Scripture says plainly, *"He who has believed and has been baptized shall be saved,"* I, having believed, and having been baptized, ought not to question the divine declaration, but should be as sure that, if I have believed, I am saved, as I am sure that I exist. This assurance is attainable, and should be the common condition of the believer. Yet has it often happened, I say, that an anxiety, which was commendable in its outset, has ended in a blameworthy unbelief.

Once more, I have known unbelief arise in some souls through *a most proper reverence for Christ, and a high esteem for all that belongs to him.* You remember our text a few Sabbath mornings ago told us of John, who, when he saw his Master in all his glory, fell at his feet as though dead. Ah, when the soul gets near to Jesus it perceives his perfection, and becomes conscious of its own imperfection; it sees his glory, and becomes aware of its own nothingness; it sees his love, and blushes at its own unloveliness; and then it is very, very apt to be tortured with mistrust, though it ought not so to be.

And I have even known when children of God just converted have come into the church, they have had such a high esteem for their brethren and sisters that they have feared to be numbered with them. When they have heard some earnest brother pray, they have said, "Oh, what a prayer, I shall never be like that man"; and, perhaps, they have listened to the preaching of some servant of God and said, "Ah, I cannot come up to that standard; the very existence of such a man as that condemns me." It is beautiful to see the little children loving the elder sons of the family, and admiring what they see of the father in them; but even this holy modesty may be turned into unbelief, though it ought not so to be. For, O child of God, if Christ be so lovely, you are on the way to be made like him; and if there be anything beautiful in any of his people, that same shall be given unto you, for they also are as you are, men of equal passions as yourself; and God who has done great things for them will do the same for you, for he loves you with the selfsame love.

I have thus set before you the unbelief which often will exist side by side with faith. Now, let us notice very briefly the conflict between the two.

It is observable that this poor man did not say, "Lord, I believe, but I have some doubts," and mention it as if it were a mere matter of common intelligence which did not grieve him. Oh no, he said it with tears; he made a sorrowful confession of it. It was not the mere statement of a fact, but it was the acknowledgment of a fault. With tears he said, "*I do believe,*" and then he acknowledged his unbelief. Learn then, dear hearer, always to look at unbelief in Christ in the light of a fault. Never say, "This is my infirmity," but say, "This is my sin." There has been too much in the church of God regarding unbelief as though it were a calamity commanding sympathy, rather than a fault demanding censure as well. I am not to say to myself, "I am unbelieving, and therefore I am to be pitied." No, "I am unbelieving, and therefore I must blame myself for it." Why should I disbelieve my God? How dare I doubt him who cannot lie? How can I mistrust the faithful promiser who has added to his promise his oath, and over and above his promise and his oath has given his own blood as a seal, that by two immutable things, wherein it was impossible for God to lie, we might have strong consolation? Chide yourselves, you doubters. Doubts are among the worst enemies of your souls. Do not entertain them. Do not treat them as though they were poor forlorn travelers to be hospitably entertained, but as rogues and vagabonds to be chased from your door. Fight them, slay them, and pray God to help you kill them, and bury them, and not even to leave a bone or a piece of a bone of a doubt above ground. Doubting and unbelief are to be despised and are to be confessed with tears as sins before God. We need pardon for doubting as much as for blasphemy. We ought no more to excuse doubting than lying, for doubting slanders God and makes him a liar.

Then again, having made a confession of his unbelief as you observe, the father in the narrative prayed against it, and an earnest prayer it was. It was, *"Help my unbelief."* It is very noticeable that he does not say, "Lord, I believe; help my child." No, nor does he say, "Lord, I believe; now cast the devil out of my boy." Not at all; he perceives that his own unbelief was harder to overcome than the devil, and that to heal him of his spiritual disease was a more needful work than even to heal his child of the sad malady under which he labored. This is the point to arrive at, to feel that there is no deficiency in the merit of Christ; no lack of power in his precious blood; no unwillingness in Christ's heart to save me, but all the hindrance lies in my unbelief. There is the point. O God, bring your power to bear where it is lacking. It is not because the blood will not cleanse me, it is because I will not believe; it is not because Christ's plea is not heard, but because I do not trust that plea. If I am not in the possession of full salvation, it is not because Christ is not mighty to save, but because I do not lean on him fully and entirely. O God, you see this is the center of the difficulty, so bring your power to bear on that difficulty. I ask only this. No more do I cry, "Help me here, or help me there," but "Help my unbelief." That is the Slough of Despond; I carry that in my heart, that is the weak point. "Lord, strengthen me just there." It is well when, in addition to confession, we bring up all the great guns of fervent prayer to bear upon that position which needs to be carried by storm.

> No physician can cure unbelief but Christ.

And, lastly, this man did well in looking for the help against his unbelief to the right place. He did not say, "Lord, I believe, and now I will try to overcome my unbelief." No, but rather "Lord, help," as if he felt that the Lord alone could do it. No physician can cure unbelief but Christ. He is the cure for it, and he is the physician too. If you have any unbelief, take the blood of Christ to cure it with. Think of him – God in the glory of his person, tabernacling among men, working out a perfect righteousness, dying a felon's death upon the cross in the sinner's stead. Think of him as rising from the dead, no more to die. Think of him as ascending into heaven amid the shouts of angels. Think of him as standing at the right hand of God with the keys of death and hell on his belt. Think of him as always pleading the merit of his blood before the Father's throne, and, as you consider concerning him, in the power of the Spirit, your unbelief will die, for you will say, "Lord, the thought of you has helped my unbelief; while I have been studying you, and feeding my soul on you, and making you to be as bread and wine to my soul, my unbelief has gone. I do believe in you, and I will, for you have helped my unbelief." Go, any of you who are in trouble about this matter, go where you gained your first faith, go there to get more. If you first obtained your faith at the foot of the cross, go there again to end your unbelief. View the flowing of his soul-redeeming blood, and continue viewing it till you shall by divine assurance know that he has made your peace with God. God bless you in Christ Jesus. Amen.

Chapter 12

Conflict

While he was still approaching, the demon slammed him to the ground and threw him into a convulsion. But Jesus rebuked the unclean spirit, and healed the boy and gave him back to his father. (Luke 9:42)

This child, possessed with an evil spirit, is a most fitting emblem of every ungodly and unconverted man. Though we be not possessed with devils, yet by nature we are possessed with devilish vices and lusts, which, if they do not distress and vex our bodies, will most certainly destroy our souls. Never a creature possessed with an evil spirit was in a worse plight than the man who is without God, without Christ, and without hope in the world. The casting out of the unclean spirit was moreover a thing that was impossible to man and only possible to God; and so is the conversion of an ungodly sinner a thing beyond the reach of human ability, and only to be accomplished by the might of the Most High. The dreadful screams, foamings, and convulsions caused in this unhappy child by the unclean spirit are a picture of the sins, iniquities, and vices into which ungodly men are continually and vehemently prodded, and are a type of that sad and terrible suffering which remorse will by and by bring to their conscience, and which the vengeance of God will soon cause to occupy their hearts.

The bringing of this child to the Savior by his parents teaches us a lesson, that those of us to whom the care of youth is entrusted, either as parents or teachers, should be anxious to bring our children to Jesus Christ, that he may graciously save them. The devout desire and compassion of the father for his child is but a pattern of what every parent ought to feel for his offspring. Like Abraham, he should pray, *"Oh that Ishmael might live before You!"* and not only put up the prayer, but also strive in the use of the means to bring his child to the Pool of Siloam that by chance the angel may stir the stream, and his son may step into the water and be made whole. The parent should place his offspring where the Savior walks, that he may look upon him and heal him. The coming of the child to Christ is a picture of saving faith, for faith is coming to Christ, simply believing in the power of his atonement. And lastly, the slamming to the ground and convulsions which are mentioned in my text are a picture of the comer's conflict with the Enemy of souls. *While he was still approaching, the demon slammed him to the ground and threw him into a convulsion.* Our subject will be the well-known fact that coming sinners, when they approach the Savior, are often thrown down by Satan and torn, so that they suffer exceedingly in their minds, and are nearly ready to give up in despair.

There are four points for our consideration. So that you may easily remember them I have made them alliterative: the devil's *doings, designs, discovery, and defeat.*

First, the devil's doings. When this child came to Christ to be healed, the devil threw him down into a convulsion. Now this is an illustration of what Satan does with most, if not all sinners when they come to Jesus to seek light and life through him; he throws them down and convulses them. Allow me to point out how it is that the devil causes those extraordinary pangs and agonies which accompany conversion. He has a multitude of devices, for he is cunning and crafty, and he has diverse ways of accomplishing that end.

First of all, he does this by *perverting the truth of God* for the destruction of the soul's hope and comfort. The devil is very sound in divinity. I have never yet suspected him of heterodoxy. I believe him to be one of the most orthodox individuals in creation. Other people may disbelieve the doctrines of revelation, but the devil cannot, for he knows the truth, and though he will misrepresent it often, he is so crafty that he understands that with the soul convinced of sin, his best method is not to contradict the truth, but to pervert it. Now I will mention the five great doctrines which we hold to be most prominent in Scripture, by the perversion of each of which the devil tries to keep the soul in bondage, darkness, and despair.

First, there is the great doctrine of *election* – that God has chosen to himself a number that no man can number, who shall be holy, since they are ordained to be *a people for His own possession, zealous for good deeds*. Now the devil agitates the coming soul upon that doctrine. "Oh," says he, "perhaps you are not elect. It is of no use your coming, and struggling, and striving; you may sit still and do nothing, and yet be saved, if you are to be saved. But if your name is written among the lost, all your praying, seeking, and believing cannot save you." Thus the devil begins preaching sovereignty in the sinner's ear, to make him believe that the Lord will assuredly cut him off. He asks, "How can you suppose that such a wretch as you can be elected? You deserve to be damned, and you know it. Your brother is a good moral man, but as for you, you are the chief of sinners; do you think God would choose you?" Then if the tempted one is instructed that election is not according to merit, but of God's free will, Satan opens another battery, and insinuates, "You would not feel like this if you were one of God's elect; you would not be allowed to come into all this suffering and pray so long in vain." And again he whispers, "You are not one of his," and thus attempts to throw the soul down and tear it in pieces. I would just like to have a blow at his schemes by reminding our friends that when they come to Christ they never need to puzzle themselves about the doctrine of election. No one, in teaching a child the alphabet, makes him learn Z before he has learned A; so a sinner must not expect to learn election until he knows faith. The text with which he has to do this is: *"He who has believed and has been baptized shall be saved,"* and when the Lord has enabled him to learn and believe that, he may go on to this: *Chosen according to the foreknowledge of God the Father, by the sanctifying work of the Spirit, to obey Jesus Christ and be sprinkled with His blood.* But if he cannot shake off the subject from his mind, he need not do it, for

> **The devil's best method is not to contradict the truth, but to pervert it.**

he may remember that every repentant person is elect, every believer is elect. However great the sinner, if he does but repent, that is a proof that he is elect; if he does but believe on Christ, he is as certainly elected as his faith is genuine.

I cannot tell that I am elected before I know whether I believe in God. I cannot tell a thing unless I see its effects. I cannot tell whether there is a seed in the ground unless you enable me to stir up the soil, or to wait till I see the blade shooting from under the earth; so I cannot tell whether your name is written in the Lamb's Book of Life until I see God's love manifested in you in the stretching out of your hearts towards God. I cannot disembowel the deep rocks of obscurity to find out that hidden thing, unless evidences and effects furnish me with spade and mattock. There is a newspaper in Glasgow called the *Christian News,* alias, the *Un-Christian News, or Christian Wasp,* and the editor says of me that I am not fit to preach God's Word because I do not know (can you guess what it is?) who God's elect are. He writes words to this effect – "According to his own confession, the young man does not know who God's elect are until he has asked them questions and knows their character." Well, if I did, I should be marvelously wise indeed. Who does know them apart from those signs, and marks, and evidences, in the heart and life which God always vouchsafes to his elect in due time? Shall I unlock the archives of heaven and read the rolls, or, with presumptuous hand unfold the Lamb's Book of Life to know who are God's elect? No; I leave that for the editor of the *Christian News* to do, and when he publishes a full and correct list of the elect, no doubt it will be bought up tremendously, and the printer will speedily make a fortune by it. Let not the soul be distressed about election, for all who repent and believe do so, as the effect of their election.

The next doctrine is that of *our depravity* – that all men are fallen in Adam, that they are all gone aside from the truth, and that moreover by their practice they have become full of sin; that in them dwells no good thing, and that if any good thing shall ever come there, it shall be put there by God, for there is not even the seed of goodness in the heart, much less the flower of it. The devil torments the soul with that doctrine, and he says, "See what a depraved creature you are. You know how dreadfully you have sinned against God; you have gone astray ten thousand times. See," he says, "there are your old sins still crying after you"; and he waves his wand and gives a resurrection to past iniquities which rise up like ghosts and terrify the soul. "There, look at that midnight scene; remember that deed of ingratitude? Hark! do you not hear that oath echoed back from the walls of the past? Look at your heart; can that ever be washed? Why, it is full of blackness. You know you tried to pray yesterday, and your mind wandered to your business before you were half through your prayer; and since you have been seeking God you have only been half in earnest, knocking at the door sometimes, and then afterwards giving it up. It is impossible that you should ever be forgiven; you have gone too far astray for the shepherd to find you; you are altogether filthy; your heart is deceitful above all things and desperately wicked, and you cannot be saved." Many a poor soul has had a most terrible wrenching with that doctrine. I have felt something of it myself, when I have truly thought that I must be torn in pieces by the dread remembrance of what I had been. The devil throws the sinner down and pulls him almost limb from limb, by persuading him that his guilt is heinous beyond parallel, and his iniquities are far beyond the reach of mercy, and his death warrant is signed.

> It is not the greatness of sin that can cause any man to be damned, if there be not a lack of faith.

Ah! poor soul, get up again; the devil has no right to throw you down. Your sin cannot be too great for God's mercy. It is not the greatness of sin that can cause any man to be damned, if there be not a lack of faith. If a man has faith, notwithstanding all the sins he may have ever committed, he shall be saved; but if he has but one sin without faith, that one sin shall utterly destroy him. Faith in the blood of Christ destroys the sting of sin. One drop of the Savior's precious blood could extinguish a thousand flaming worlds if God should will it, much more put out the burning fears of your poor heart. If you believe in Christ, you shall say to the mountain of your guilt, *"Be taken up and cast into the sea."*

Then, there is the doctrine of *effectual calling,* that God calls his children effectually; that it is not the power of man which brings us to God, but that it is the work of God to bring man to grace; that he calls those whom he would save with an effectual and special call which he vouchsafes only to his children. "There now," says the Evil One, "the minister said there must be an effectual call; depend upon it that yours is not such a call; it never came from God; it is only a few heated feelings. You were excited a little under the sermon, and it will all be gone directly, like the morning cloud or the early dew. You have strong desires sometimes, but at other seasons they are not half so vehement. If the Lord drew you, you would be always drawn with the same power. It will be over soon, and you will be all the worse for having been inclined to go to God under these legal convictions, and then, afterwards, running away from him." Well, beloved, tell Satan that you don't know whether it is an effectual call, but you know this, that if you perish you will go to Christ and perish only there. Tell him you know it is so effectual that you cannot help going to Christ; that whether it is to last or not you cannot say, *that* you will let him know by and by; but that you are resolved (for this is your last defense), if you perish, to perish at the cross of Christ; and so by the help of God you may by such means overcome him when he throws you down on that doctrine.

The devil will also pervert the doctrine of *final perseverance*. "Look," says Satan, "the children of God always hold on to their way; they never cease being holy. They persevere; their faith is like the path of the just, shining more and more unto the perfect day; and so would yours be if you were one of the Lord's. But you will never be able to persevere. Don't you remember – six months ago, when you were lying on a sick bed you resolved to serve God, and it all broke down? You have vowed many times that you would be a Christian, and it has not lasted two weeks. It will never do; you are too fickle; you will never keep fast hold on Christ; you will go with him a little while, but you will be sure to turn back; therefore, you cannot be one of the Lord's, for they never do turn back." So he tries to pull and tear the poor soul on that great and comforting doctrine. The same nail on which a sinner must hang his hope the devil tries to drive into the very temples of his faith, that he may die like Sisera in the tent of Jael. Oh, poor soul, tell Satan that your perseverance is not yours, but that God is the author of it; that however weak you are, you know your weakness, but that if God begins a good work he will never leave it unfinished. And repelling him thus, you may rise from that throwing down and convulsion which he has given to you.

Then there is the doctrine of *redemption*, with which the unclean spirit will assault the soul. "Oh," says Satan, "it is true Christ died, but not for you; you are a peculiar character." I remember the devil once made me believe that I was one alone, without a companion. I thought there was no one like myself. I saw that others had sinned as I had done, and had gone as far as I had, but I imagined that there was something peculiar about my sin. Thus the devil tried to set me apart as if I did not belong to the rest of mankind, as if I thought that if I had been anybody else I might have been saved. How often I wished I had been a poor swearing, drunken man in the streets, and then I thought I might have a better chance; but as it was, I thought I was to die alone, like the deer in the shade of the forest. But well do I remember my friends singing that sweet hymn:

> His grace is sov'reign, rich and free,
>   And why, my soul, why not for thee?

One of the hymns in Denham's selection, and it ought to have been in Rippon's, as well as I can remember, ends thus:

> He shed his blood so rich and free,
>   And why, my soul, why not for thee?

That is just the question we never put to ourselves. We say, "Sure, my soul, why not for anybody else but you." Up, poor soul! If Satan is trying to tear you, tell him it is written, *He is able also to save forever those who draw near to God through Him*; that *"the one who comes to Me I will certainly not cast out"*; and it may be that thus God will deliver you from that desperate conflict into which, as a coming sinner, you have been cast.

But Satan is not very scrupulous, and he sometimes throws the coming sinner down and tears him by *telling horrible falsehoods*. Some of you may not have known this, and I thank God if you do not understand some of the things of which I am about to speak. Many a time when the soul is coming to Christ, Satan violently injects infidel thoughts. I have never been thoroughly an unbeliever but once, and that was not *before* I knew the need of a Savior, but *after* it. It was just when I wanted

Christ and panted after him, that all of a sudden the thought crossed my mind, which I despised but could not conquer, that there was no God, no Christ, no heaven, no hell; that all my prayers were but a farce, and that I might as well have whistled to the winds or spoken to the howling waves. Ah! I remember how my ship drifted along through that sea of fire, loosened from the anchor of my faith which I had received from my fathers. I doubted everything, until at last the devil defeated himself by making me doubt my own existence, and I thought I was an idea floating in the nothingness of a black hole. Then, startled with that thought, and feeling that I was substantial flesh and blood after all, I saw that God was, and Christ was, and heaven was, and hell was, and that all these things were absolute truths.

I should not be astonished if many here have been upon the very verge of infidelity, and have doubted almost everything. It is when Satan finds the heart tender that he tries to stamp his own imprint of infidelity upon the soul; but, blessed be God, he never accomplishes it in the truly coming sinner. He labors also to inject blasphemous thoughts, and then tells us they are ours. Has he not sometimes poured in most vehement torrents of blasphemy and evil imaginations into our hearts, which we ignorantly thought must be our own? Yet not one of them perhaps belonged to us. I remember I had once been alone musing on God, when all of a sudden it seemed as if the floodgates of hell had been loosened; my head became a very pandemonium; ten thousand evil spirits seemed to be holding carnival within my brain; and I held my mouth lest I should give utterance to the words of blasphemy that were poured into my ears. Things I had never heard or thought of before came rushing suddenly into my mind, and I could scarcely withstand their influence. It was the devil throwing me down and tearing me. Ah! poor soul, you will have that perhaps, but remember it is only one of the tricks of the archenemy. He drives his unclean beasts into your field and then calls them yours. Now, in old time, when tramps and vagrants troubled a parish, they whipped them and then sent them on to the next parish. So when you get these evil thoughts, give them a sound whipping and send them away; they do not belong to you if you do not indulge them. But if you fear that these thoughts are your own, you may say, "I will go to Christ, and even if these blasphemies are mine

I will confess them to the Great High Priest, for I know that all manner of sin and blasphemy shall be forgiven unto men."

Then if the devil cannot overcome you there, he tries another method. He takes all the threatening passages out of God's Word, and says they all apply to you. He reads you this passage: *"There is a sin leading to death; I do not say that he should make request for this."* "There," says the devil, "the apostle did not say he could even pray for the man who had committed certain sins." Then he reads that *"blasphemy against the Spirit shall not be forgiven."* "There," he says, "is your character; you have committed sin against the Holy Spirit, and you will never be pardoned." Then he brings another passage: *Ephraim is joined to idols; let him alone.* "There," says Satan, "you have had no liberty in prayer lately; God has let you alone, you are given unto idols, and you are entirely destroyed"; and the cruel fiend howls his song of joy, and makes a merry dance over the thought that the poor soul is to be lost. But do not believe him, my dear friends. No man has committed the sin against the Holy Spirit as long as he has grace to repent; it is certain that no man can have committed that sin if he flies to Christ and believes on him. No believing soul can commit it; no penitent sinner ever has committed it. If a man be careless and thoughtless – if he can hear a terrible sermon and laugh it off, and put away his convictions – if he never feels any strivings of conscience, there is a fear that he may have committed that sin. But as long as you have any desires for Christ, you have no more committed that sin than you have flown up to the stars and swept cobwebs from the skies. As long as you have any sense of your guilt, any desire to be redeemed, you cannot have fallen into that sin; as a repentant one you may still be saved, but if you had committed that sin, you could not be repentant.

> **No man has committed the sin against the Holy Spirit as long as he has grace to repent.**

Let me dwell for a moment or two upon the second point – the devil's design. Why does he throw the coming soul down and tear it?

First, because *he does not like to lose it.* "No king will willingly lose his subjects," said Apollyon to Christian when he stretched himself across the road, "and I swear thou shalt go no farther; here will I spill thy soul." There he stood vowing vengeance at him because he had escaped from his dominion. Do you suppose that Satan would lose his subjects one by one and not be angry? Assuredly not. As soon as he sees a soul hurrying off to the wicket gate, with his eyes fixed on the light, away go all hell's dogs after him. "There is another of my subjects going; my empire is being thinned, my family is being diminished," and he tries with his might and muscle to bring the poor soul back again. Ah! soul, don't be deceived by him; his design is to throw you down. He does not tell you these things to do you good, or to humble you, but in order to keep you from coming to Christ, and lure you into his net, where he may utterly destroy you.

Sometimes, I believe, he has the vile design of *inducing poor souls to take away themselves* before they have faith in Christ. This is an extreme case, but I have met with not a few who have been thus tempted to take away their lives, and rush before their Maker with their hands red with their own blood; for Satan knows full well that no murderer has eternal life abiding in him. But he never accomplished his design in the soul of one elect sinner yet.

Then Satan has another motive. *When the soul is coming to Christ he tries, out of spite, to worry that soul.* Satan's heart is made up of that which is just the opposite of benevolence – malevolence. He hates every thing, and loves nothing; he hates to see any creature happy, any soul glad. When he sees a soul coming to Christ, he says, "Ah! I have nearly lost him; I shall never have an opportunity of bringing thundering condemnation into his ears, and dragging him about in the flames of hell as I thought; so now, before he is gone, I will do something. The last grip shall be a hard one; the last blow shall be dealt with all my power." Then down he comes upon the poor soul, who falls wallowing upon the earth in despair and doubt; then he tears him, and will not leave him until he has worked as much of his way with him as the Lord will let him. Don't be afraid, child of God. *Resist the devil and he will flee from you;* and even though he may cast you to the ground, remember that the righteous falls many times, but he rises up again. And so shall you, and the designs of the Enemy shall be frustrated, as it is written, *"So your enemies will cringe before you."*

In the third place, there is the devil's discovery. I do not think the devil would be able to throw one poor sinner to the ground if he came as the devil; but it is seldom that he does that. He presents himself as an angel of light, or even as the Holy Spirit. He knows that the Holy Spirit does all the work of salvation, and therefore he tries to counterfeit the operations of the Holy Spirit. He knows it is the Holy Spirit's work to take away pride from man and to humble the soul. Well, Satan counterfeits that blessed work and takes away *hope* from man as well as pride. Under the pretense of humbling the poor sinner, and telling him that he ought to lie lower in the dust, he not only humbles the poor soul, but he also puts it down so low that he dishonors God too in the sinner's estimation, by telling him that God himself cannot save him. Satan will try, if he can, to mar God's work while it is still upon the potter's wheel, by putting on his own instrument while the clay is whirling around upon the wheel, so that it may not assume the Holy Spirit's shape, but that there may be some marks of the devil's workmanship in the article. Sometimes you ask God that you may be able to agonize in prayer. "That is right," says Satan, "agonize in prayer; but remember you must *now* receive the mercy, or you are lost." So he glides in and adds a little piece to the truth, making you believe it is an impulse of the Holy Spirit, while it is, after all, a deception of the Father of Lies. The Holy Spirit tells you that you are a lost sinner and undone. "Ah!" says the devil, "you are, and you cannot be saved"; and thus again under the very garb of the Spirit's operations he deceives the soul. It is my firm belief that very much of the experience of a Christian is not Christian experience. Many Christians experience things that have nothing to do with Christianity, but more to do with demonology. When you read the convictions of John Bunyan, you may think that all that terror was the fruit of the Holy Spirit; but be assured it was the fruit of satanic influence. You may think it is God's Holy Spirit that drives sinners to despair and keeps them shut up in the iron cage for so long. Not at all. There was God's Holy Spirit, and then Satan came in to mar the work if he could.

Now I will give the poor sinner a means of detecting Satan so that he may know whether his convictions are from the Holy Spirit, or merely the bellowing of hell in his ears. In the first place, *you may be always sure that that which comes from the devil will make you look at yourselves and not at Christ.* The Holy Spirit's work is to turn our eyes from ourselves to Jesus Christ, but the Enemy's work is the very opposite. Nine out of ten of the insinuations of the devil have to do with ourselves. "You are guilty," says the devil – *that is self.* "You have not faith" – that is self. "You do not repent enough" – that is self. "You have got such a wavering hold of Christ" – that is self. "You have none of the joy of the spirit, and therefore cannot be one of his" – that is self. Thus the devil begins picking holes in us, whereas the Holy Spirit takes self entirely away, and tells us that we are "nothing at all," but that "Jesus Christ is all in all."

Satan brings the carcass of self and pulls it about, and because it is corrupt, he tells us that most assuredly we cannot be saved. But remember, sinner, it is not your *hold* of Christ that saves you – it is Christ. It is not your *joy* in Christ that saves you – it is Christ. It is not even faith in Christ, though that is the instrument – it is Christ's blood and merits; therefore, look not so much to your hand with which you are grasping Christ, as to Christ; look not to your hope, but to Christ, the source of your hope; look not to your faith, but to Christ, the author and finisher of your faith. And if you do this, ten thousand devils cannot throw you down, but as long as you look at yourself, the meanest of those evil spirits may tread you beneath his feet.

> The Holy Spirit's work is to turn our eyes from ourselves to Jesus Christ, but the Enemy's work is the very opposite.

You may discern the devil's insinuations in another way: that *they generally reflect upon some attribute of God.* Sometimes they reflect upon his love, and tell you that God will not save you; sometimes upon his longsuffering, and they tell you that you are too old, and that God won't save you; sometimes upon his sovereignty, and they tell you that God does not choose as he wills, but that he has respect to characters, and takes men according to their merits. Sometimes they reflect upon God's truth, and they tell you that he will not keep his promise; alas, and sometimes they reflect upon the very being of God, and tell you that there is not such a one. But O poor trembling soul, Satan shall not get an advantage over you, but take care – detect him; and when you have found out the devil, you have frustrated his aims as far as you are yourself concerned.

Now, in the last place, we have to consider the devil's defeat. How was he defeated? Jesus rebuked him. Beloved, there is no other way for us to be saved from the castings down of Satan but by the rebuke of

Jesus. "Oh," says one poor soul, "many months and years have I been distressed for fear I should not be saved. I have gone from place to place in hopes that some minister might say something which would rebuke the evil spirit." Sister, or beloved brother, have you not been doing wrong? Is it not Jesus who rebukes the evil spirit? Or perhaps you have been trying to rebuke the evil spirit yourself; you have tried to argue and dispute with him; you have said that you are not so vile as he described you to be. Beloved, have you not been doing wrong? It is not your business to rebuke Satan. *"The Lord rebuke you!"* is what you should say. Oh! if you had looked to Jesus and said, "Lord, rebuke him," he would have only had to say, "Hush!" and the demon would have been still in a moment, for he knows how omnipotent Jesus is, since he feels his power. But you strive to pacify your own heart when you are under these temptations, instead of remembering that it is Jesus only who can remove the affliction.

If I had one here who suffered the most from this ailment – the possession of Satan – I would tell him to sit down and remember Jesus; go to Gethsemane, and depend upon it that the devil will never stay there with you. Think on the agonies of your Savior covered with his blood; the devil cannot bear Christ's blood – he goes howling away at the very thought of it. Go to the pavement where Christ endured the accursed whipping; the devil will not stay long there with you; and if you sit at the foot of his cross and say,

> Oh! how sweet to view the flowing,
>   Of his ever-precious blood,

You will not long find the devil vexing you. The way to overcome Satan and to have peace with God is through Christ. *"I am the way"*; if you would know the way, come to Christ. "I am the truth"; if you would refute the devil's lies, come to the truth. "I am the life"; if you would be spared from Satan's killing, come to Jesus.

There is one thing which all of us too much blur in our preaching, though I believe we do it very unintentionally – namely, the great truth that it is not prayer, it is not faith, it is not our doings, it is not our feelings upon which we must rest, but it is upon Christ, and on Christ alone. We are apt to think that we are not in a right state or that we do not feel enough, instead of remembering that our business is not with self, but with Christ. Our business is only with Christ. O soul, if you could fix your soul on Jesus, and neglect everything else – if you could but despise good works, and anything else, so far as they relate to your salvation, and look wholly, simply on Christ, I tell you Satan would soon give up throwing you down. He would find it would not answer his purpose, for you would fall on Christ, and like the giant who fell upon his mother, the earth, you would rise up each time stronger than before. Have I then within hearing one poor tested, tempted, and devil-dragged soul? Has Satan been pulling you through the thorns, and briers, and thickets, until you are scarred and bruised? Come now, I have tried to preach a rough sermon to you because I knew I had rough work to do with roughly used souls. Is there nothing here, poor sinner, that you can lay hold upon? Are you so locked up that not one ray of light comes through the iron bars? What! Are you so chained that you cannot move hand or foot? Why, man, I have brought you a pitcher and a piece of bread today even in your dungeon. Though you are cast down, there is a little here to comfort you in what I have said. But oh! If my Master would come he would bring more than that, for he would rebuke the unclean spirit, and it would immediately depart from you. Let me implore you, look only to Christ. Never expect deliverance from self, from Satan, from ministers, or from means of any kind apart from Christ. Keep your eye simply on him, and let his death, his agonies, his groans, his sufferings, his merits, his glories, and his intercession be fresh upon your mind. When you wake in the morning, look for him; when you lie down at night, look for him. Oh! let not your hopes or fears come between you and Christ; seek only Christ. Let the hymn we sang be your hymn and your prayer:

> Lord, deny me what thou wilt,
>   Only ease me of my guilt,
> Prostrate at thy feet I lie.
>   Give me Christ, or else I die.

And then, even though the devil throws you down and tears you, it would be better that he should do so now than that he should tear you forever.

I have some here, however, who will laugh at what I have been preaching. Ah! sirs, you may do so; but bitter though my text may be, I wish you had it in your mouths. Though sad be the experience of being torn when coming to Christ, I would rather see you so than see you whole and away from Christ. It is better to be torn in pieces coming to the Savior, than to have a sound, whole heart away from him. Tremble, sinner, tremble, for if you come not to Christ, he shall tear you at last; his eye shall not pity, neither shall his hand spare you. He has said, *"Now consider this, you who forget God, or I will tear you in pieces, and there will be none to deliver."* Sirs, within another hour, and some of you may know this, certainly before long there are some who will be torn in pieces by the wrath of God. Why will you die? *Why* will you die? You cannot answer the question, I think, but let it rest upon your hearts. What profit will you have in your own blood? What will you profit if you gain the whole world and lose your own soul? Remember, Jesus Christ can save even you. Believe on his name, you convinced sinners, believe on Christ. The Lord bless you, for Jesus' sake! Amen.

Chapter 13

The Devil's Last Throw

While he was still approaching, the demon slammed him to the ground and threw him into a convulsion. (Luke 9:42)

Our Lord Jesus Christ taught the people much by his words, but he taught them even more by his actions. He was always preaching. His whole life was a heavenly discourse on divine truth, and the miracles which he worked were not only the proofs of his deity, but also the illustrations of his teaching. His wonders of mercy were, in fact, acted sermons, truths embodied, pictorial illustrations appealing to the eye, and thus setting forth gospel teaching quite as clearly as vocal speech could have done. When we read of the miracles of our Lord, we should not only accept them as proofs of his deity and seals of his commission, but also as instructions as to the manner of his gracious working. What he did of old to the bodies of men should be received as a prophecy of what he is today prepared to do to the souls of men. I am sure I shall not be straining the meaning of the text, or the intention of the miracle, if, instead of preaching about the youth possessed of the devil, and dwelling only upon that wonderful display of power, I endeavor to show that there are parallel cases at this time in the world of the mind. Jesus is able to work in the unseen spirit world miracles such as were foreshadowed by those which he worked in the visible natural world.

I suppose that we have never seen satanic possession, although I am not quite sure about it, for some men exhibit symptoms which are very much like it. The present existence of demons within the bodies of men I shall neither assert nor deny; but certainly, in our Savior's day it was very common for devils to take possession of men and torment them greatly. It would seem that Satan was let loose while Christ was here below so that the Serpent might come into personal conflict with the appointed seed of the woman, that the two champions might stand foot to foot in solemn duel, and that the Lord Jesus might win a glorious victory over him. Ever since his defeat by our Lord, and by his apostles, it would seem that Satan's power over human bodies has been greatly limited; but we have still among us the same thing in another and worse shape, namely, the power of sin over men's minds. That this is akin to the power of the devil over the body is clear from Holy Scripture. *The god of this world has blinded the minds of the unbelieving. The spirit that is now working in the sons of disobedience,* says the apostle Paul. Satan works in all ungodly men, as a blacksmith at his shop; do you wonder that they sometimes curse and swear? These are only the sparks from the shop below, flying out of the chimney. The Evil One is found cooperating with evil natures, finding fire for their tinder, blowing up the flame that is within them, and in every way assisting them and exciting them to do evil, so that, even though men are not possessed of devils in the sense in which they were so in Christ's day, yet the Evil One still has power over them and leads them to whatever place he desires. Do we not constantly meet with persons of this kind? I do. I know passionate men in whom the fiercest of devils appear to rave and rage; and I could point out others whose love of lying betrays the presence of the Father of Lies. One blasphemes and uses such filthy language that we are sure his tongue is set on the fire of hell, even if the prince of devils is not ruling it. A man says, "Drink is ruining me, body and soul. I know that it is shortening my life. I have had delirium tremens, and I know that I shall have it again if I continue as I am; but I cannot leave the drink. Sometimes the craving comes over me and I seem as if I must swallow the intoxicating draft, whether I will or not." Whether this is the devil, or whether it is altogether the man himself, I am not going to argue; but the drink devil, whose name is legion, is certainly among us to this day, and we hear persons tell us that they are anxious to escape from its power, and yet they return to it, rushing to intoxication as the swine rushed into the sea when the demons had entered into them.

Need I mention another form of this evil in the shape of unchastity? How many a man there is – alas, it is true of women too – struggling against a fierce passion, and yet that passion conquers them. The unclean desire comes upon them like a hurricane bearing all before it, and they yield to it as the dry leaf yields to the blast. No, more than that, they rush into a sin which they themselves condemn, of which already they have tasted the bitter fruit; they could not be more eager for it if it were the purest of all enjoyments. As the moth dashes again into the candle which has burned its wings, so do men hurry into the vice which has filled them with misery. They are possessed and domineered by the spirit of lust, and they return to their crimes as the oxen return to the stream.

> Unless Christ has set us free we are all in some shape or other under the dominion of the Prince of Darkness.

I need not go further into details, for one man falls into sin in one way, and another falls after quite a different fashion. All devils are not alike – though they are alike evil. Anger differs from lust, and immorality laughs at covetousness, yet are they all of one brood, privates in the same dreadful legion. Men practice differing sins, but their sins all manifest the same evil power. Unless Christ has set us free we are all in some shape or other under the dominion of the Prince of Darkness, the master of the forces of evil.

This poor young man of whom we are to talk today was brought into a most horrible condition through the influence of a satanic spirit.

He was a lunatic: reason had been dethroned. He was an epileptic, so that if left alone he would fall into the fire or into the water. You have yourself seen persons in fits of epilepsy, and you know how dreadful would be their danger if they were taken in a fit in the middle of a street, or by the side of a river. In this youth's case the epilepsy was only the means by which the demon exercised his power, and this made his condition sevenfold worse than if it had been simply a disease. This afflicted one had become deaf and mute besides, and very violent, so that he was capable of doing a great deal of mischief. In all the Holy Land there was only one who could do anything for him! There was one name by which he could be cured, and only one. It was the name of Jesus. The Lord Jesus had disciples who had worked miracles in his name, but they were baffled by this extraordinary case. They tried what they could do, but they were utterly defeated, and gave up the task in despair; and now there remained only one person beneath the canopy of heaven that could touch this child's case and drive out the devil. Only one person could now answer the poor father's prayers; every other hope was dead. That is just the state in which we are: there is but one name under heaven whereby we must be saved. Many are the pretended salvations, but only one is real.

> There is a name high over all,
>   In hell, and earth, and sky.
> Angels and men before it fall,
>   And devils fear and fly.

That one name is the name of Jesus, the Son of God, to whom all power is given. He is God, and he can deliver any man from the dominion of evil, whatever form it may have assumed, and however long established the dominion may be. A cure besides this there is none. Nothing else can rescue a man from the enslavement of his sin but the word of Jesus. When the word of power is spoken from his divine mouth all things obey; but none out of the ten thousand voices of earth can deliver us from evil. We are shut up to heaven's unique remedy. God grant that, being so shut up, we may avail ourselves of it.

This poor lad, although nobody could cure him except Jesus, had a father who loved him, and nobody could tell the sorrow of that father's heart because of his poor son. The father had a sharp struggle to get his son to the disciples, for epileptic persons who are also insane are hard to manage. I cannot tell how many round about assisted in holding him, all pitying the poor creature. Alas, the Lord Jesus Christ was away! The parent's heart was heavy when he found that the great Healer to whom he looked was for a while absent. But when Jesus came down from the mountaintop the poor demoniac had this one great advantage – he had friends to aid in bringing him to Christ. I hope that all here who are not saved are privileged with a relationship with some friend who seeks their salvation. Perhaps it is a wife who cannot bear that her husband should remain out of Christ, or a husband who languishes till his spouse is turned unto the Lord; and in either case it is a great help. How often a mother bears a secret anguish in her breast for her unconverted sons and daughters! I have known a sister in the family to be the only one who knew the Lord, and she has pleaded with the Lord day and night, entreating him to bless the whole of her household. Frequently a servant in the house becomes its best helper, or it may be a neighbor who has seen the ungodly conduct of his neighbors and never ceases to pray for them. When some few get together to bring a specially hard case before Jesus, it is blessed work, for desperate cases grow hopeful under the influence of prayer. Come, you saved ones, pray with me now for these unrenewed sinners, that at this moment they may feel the power of our Lord Jesus.

So then, my first point shall be that our hopes are all awakened. Here is a poor youth, but bad as he is, terribly possessed as he is, he is coming to Christ! Prayer has been offered for him by his father, and Jesus is near. All looks well! We will take the case of a sinner who is in a similar condition: prayer has been offered for him, and that prayer has, in some measure, been heard. We have in this congregation, I trust, some who are coming to Christ, and I am very glad of it. Coming to Christ is not the best possible condition, for the best condition is to have already come to him. For a hungry man to be coming to a dinner is not enough; he must actually reach the table and eat. For a sick man to be coming to a notable physician is hopeful, but it is not enough; he must get to that physician, take his medicine, and be restored. That is the point. To be coming to Christ is not enough: you must have actually come to him, and really received him; for to such only does he give power to become the sons of God.

This poor child was coming, and so are some here. That is to say, they have begun to hear the gospel with attention. They did not formerly go anywhere on the Sabbath, nor did they get up very early on a Sunday morning. I can see a man who seldom rose on a Sunday morning, and when he did, he read his newspaper. You might see him anytime before one o'clock in his shirtsleeves. Half this city of London is in that condition every Sunday morning, because they look upon the day as simply their own day and not the Lord's Day. They have very short memories, and do not *"remember the sabbath day, to keep it holy."* They forget all about its being the Lord's Day and do not reverence it. This is shameful conduct towards God. If a man on the road were to meet with a poor beggar, and give him six out of seven shillings which he had with him, the beggar would be a wicked wretch if he afterwards knocked the man down and stole the other shilling. Yet there are multitudes of people to whom God gives six days out of seven, and nothing will satisfy them but that they must have the seventh day all to themselves, and rob God of it. The man I refer to is repenting of this wrong, and so you see him coming upon the Sunday morning to hear the gospel. He hears it very attentively; he leans forward to catch every word, and he treasures up what he hears.

We are sure that he is coming to Christ, for when he gets home he reaches for his Bible. He has begun to read the Word of God in an earnest way. He thought at one time that it was about the dullest book in the world. He even dared to turn it into a jest, and all because he never read it; for those who deny the inspiration of Scripture are almost always people who have never read it for themselves. It is a book which carries conviction within itself to candid minds when they carefully peruse it. Assuredly this man is coming to Christ, for he searches the Scriptures.

I feel sure he is coming to Christ, for he has begun to mend in many respects. He has dropped his frequent attendance at his usual place of worship, namely, the tavern. He keeps himself more at home, and is therefore sober. Plenty of people in London need no bell to fetch them into the temples of their gods. We see in some of our churches and chapels persons going in twenty minutes or half an hour after the service begins; but look at the temples of Bacchus at one o'clock, and at six in the evening, and see how punctual are his followers! The worshipers of liquid fire stand outside till the shrine is opened; they are afraid of being late; they are so thirsty that they long for the time of the deadly drink. Drink seems to be the water of life to them, poor creatures that they are! But now our friend of whom we are so hopeful is not seen waiting at the posts of the doors – the "Blue Posts," I mean. Thank God, he is looking to another fountain for comfort.

Note also that he has dropped his blasphemy and his impurity. He is a purer man in mouth and body than he used to be. He is coming to Christ. But, as I said, coming is not enough. The thing is really to reach the Lord Jesus and to be healed by him. I pray you, do not rest short of this.

Still, this is all hopeful, very hopeful. The man is a hearer; he is also a reader of the Scriptures. He has begun to mend a bit, and now he is a thinker too, and he begins to be a little careful about his soul. While he is at his labor, you can see that there is something working in his brain, though once it was filled with pride and wickedness. He has a weight, too, on his heart, and a burden on his mind. He is evidently in earnest; so far as he knows the teaching of Scripture he is deeply affected by it. He has learned that he will not cease to exist when he dies; but that he will continue to be when yonder sun becomes black as a burnt-out coal. He knows that there will be a day of judgment, when throngs upon throngs, yes, all the dead, shall stand before the judgment seat of Christ to give an account of the things which they have done in the body; he thinks this over, and he is alarmed. He chews the cud upon divine truth, and finds time for solitary meditation. That man is coming to Christ, for there is no better evidence of the face being set towards Christ and heaven than a thoughtful state of mind.

> I know that he is coming to Christ, for prayer is a sure token.

And I have heard – of course, I cannot tell, for I was not there to see – I have heard, I say, that the other night he began to pray. If so, I know that he is coming to Christ, for prayer is a sure token. He has not yet cast himself fully at the feet of Jesus, but he cries, "Lord, save me." He is coming, and I am as glad as the birds on a spring morning. The angels are watching; they are leaning from the battlements of heaven to see whether it will end rightly, and you and I are very hopeful, especially those of us who have been praying for this man. For since we see that there is some change in him, and he begins to think and pray, we look for his salvation as men look for flowers when April showers are falling. So, you see, our hopes are excited.

And now I will read the text again – *While he was still approaching, the demon slammed him to the ground and threw him into a convulsion.* By this our fears are aroused. What a sight it must have been! Here is the poor father bringing his lunatic son, and friends are helping him. They are getting him near the Savior, and he is just coming to him who can cure him, when, all of a sudden, he is taken in a fearful fit, worse than he had ever suffered before. He is cast down, thrown about, dashed to and fro; he wallows on the ground; he seems to be flung up and down as by an unseen hand, and we fear that he will be torn to pieces. See! he falls down like a dead man, and there he lies. As the crowd gathers around him, people cry, "He is dead." Does it not seem a dreadful thing that when hope was at its brightest all should be dashed aside?

I have observed this thing scores of times; I might say, I think without exaggeration, hundreds of times. I have seen men, just when they were beginning to hear and beginning to think, taken all of a sudden with such violence of sin, and so fearfully carried away by it, that if I had not seen the same thing before I would have despaired of them. But, having often seen it, I know what it means, and I am not so dismayed as a raw observer might be, though I must confess that it half breaks my heart when it happens to some hopeful convert whom I hoped to receive into the church and to rejoice over. We mourn when we hear that the man who was somewhat impressed has become worse than he was formerly, and has gone back to the very vice from which he had been rescued. The case runs on the same lines as our text – *While he was still approaching, the demon slammed him to the ground and threw him into a convulsion.*

How does the devil do this? Well, we have seen it done in this way: when the man had almost believed in Christ, but not quite, Satan seemed to multiply his temptations around him and bring his whole force to bear upon him. There is a wicked man in the shop, and the devil says to him, "Your mate is beginning to be serious; ridicule him. Tempt him all you can. Treat him to a strong drink. Get him away to the theater, the music hall, or the brothel." It is astonishing how the ungodly will lay all kinds of traps for one who is escaping from his sins. They are fearfully set on keeping him from Christ. This is a free country, is it not? A wonderfully free country when a Christian man in the workshop has to run the gauntlet for his very life to this day. A man may swear, and drink, and do what he likes that is detestable, and never is there a word of rebuke for him; but the moment he begins to be serious and thoughtful, the wicked are down upon him like so many dogs on a rat. The devil finds willing servants, and they worry the poor awakened one. Is there any wonder that, as he has not yet found Christ and is not yet saved, he should for the time be carried away by these assaults, and feel as if he could not go further on the right road?

I have known in addition to all this that Satan has stirred up the anxious one's bad passions. Passions that lay asleep have suddenly been aroused. Moreover, the man has become thoughtful, and from that very fact doubts which he never knew before have come upon him. He begins to mend, and now he finds a difficulty in getting his needle through where the tear was made. He finds that tearing is easier work than mending, and that running into sin is a much more easy thing than rising out of the black ditch into which he has fallen. So now, with those around him tempting him, his bad passions responding to the temptation and his doubts overclouding everything, it is not a marvelous thing that the poor creature grows worse before he gets better. The disease which before had been concealed in more hidden and vital parts, seems to be thrown out upon the surface, and the sight is sickening. This, however, is not always a bad sign. Doctors rather prefer it to an inward festering.

So have I seen it when men have been coming to Christ; their boat has been tossed with a tempest, and they have been driven far out upon a raging sea.

Yes, and I will tell you what I have seen. I have seen a man almost converted – almost a believer in Christ, all of a sudden become more obstinate in his opposition to the gospel than he ever was before. A man who was quiet and harmless and inoffensive before has, under the influence of Satan, just when we hoped the best things of him, turned around in a rage against the people who sought to do him good, and he has spoken abusively of the gospel which a little while before he seemed eager to understand. Sometimes such persons act as if they were reckless and profane, just as boys, when they go through a graveyard, whistle to keep their courage up. Many a man says big things against the gospel when he is pretty nearly caving in, and he does not like anybody to know that he is beaten. He is coming to Jesus; but still he does not want anybody to see that he is so, and therefore he pretends to an opposition of it, which is not sincere. Have you not discovered that a man is never so violent against a thing as when he is unwillingly convinced of the truth of it? He has to try and demonstrate to himself that he does not believe it by being very loud in his declarations. A secret something in his soul makes him believe, and he is mad because he cannot resist the inward conviction.

Do not be astonished – you that are trying to bring men to Christ – if it should often happen that these lunatics break loose, that these epileptics have a worse fit just before Christ cures them than ever you knew them to have had before.

I will describe the usual way in which the devil throws men down and tears them. You need not listen to this unless you want to, because it does not relate to all of you here; but it is true of a sufficient number to render it needful for me to speak of it. It is a very curious thing that if there is a poor soul in London that is nearly insane through despair of heart, he wants to talk to me. I am often sorely burdened by the attempt to sympathize with the distracted. I do not know why they should be attracted to me, but they come to tell me of their evil state of mind – people who have never seen me before. This fact gives me a wide field of actual practice and careful observation. I frequently meet with persons who are tempted with blasphemous thoughts. They have not yet laid hold on Christ, but they are trying to do so; and at this stage of their experience, most-horrible thoughts pass through their minds. They cannot prevent it. They hate the thoughts, and yet they come, till they are ready to lose their reason. I will tell you what happened to me.

I was engaged in prayer alone in a quiet place one day when I had just found the Savior, and while I was in prayer a most horrible stream of blasphemies came into my mind, till I clapped my hand to my mouth for fear that I should utter any one of them. I was so brought up that I do not remember ever hearing a man swear while I was a child; yet at that moment I seemed to know all the swearing and blasphemy that ever was in hell itself, and I wondered at myself. I could not understand from where this foul stream proceeded. I wrote to my venerable grandfather who was for sixty years a minister of the gospel, and he said to me, "Do not trouble about it. These are no thoughts of yours; they are injected into your mind by Satan. The thoughts of men follow one another like the links of a chain, one link draws on another; but when a man is in prayer, the next natural thought to prayer is not blasphemy; it is not, therefore, a natural succession of our own thoughts. An evil spirit casts those thoughts into the mind." I read also in an old book what they used to do years ago in our parishes in the "good old times" when nobody had any sense of humanity. If a poor wretch came to a parish begging, they whipped him through the place and sent him on to his own parish. Thus should we treat these diabolical thoughts. Whip them by hearty repentance, and send them off to where they came from, back to their own parish, which is far down in the deeps.

Thoughts of this sort, seeing you loathe them, are none of yours. Do not let Satan lay his brats at your door, but send them packing. Perhaps when you know this, it may help to break the chain; for the devil may not think it worth his while to worry you in this way anymore. When he cannot by this means lead you to despair, he seldom wastes his time in spreading nets when the bird can see them. Therefore, tell Satan to depart, for you can see him, and you are not going to let him deceive you. It may be he will take the hint and depart.

Diabolical thoughts, seeing you loathe them, are none of yours.

When this does not work, I have known Satan to throw the coming sinner down and tear him in another way. "There," says he, "did you not hear the preacher speaking about election? You are not one of the elect." "Perhaps I am not," says one. Perhaps you are, say I, and I think that whether you are one of the elect or not, you had better come, on the ground that Jesus says, *"The one who comes to Me I will certainly not cast out."* If you come, he will not cast you out, and then you will find that you are one of the elect. You need not trouble yourself about predestination, for you will see *that* clearly enough very soon. If any man had a ticket to go to a meeting, and he said, "I do not know whether I am ordained to get in or not," I would think it very probable that he was not ordained to enter if he sat at home in the chimney corner and did not make the attempt to go; but if, having his ticket, he walked to the place and went in, I would feel sure that he was ordained to go in. You will know your election when you have obeyed your calling. Go you to Christ because you are commanded and invited, and leave the deeper question to be answered by the facts.

Satan will throw men down and tear them in another way. "Ah!" says he, "you are too big a sinner." I make short work of that. No man is too big a sinner. *Any sin and blasphemy shall be forgiven people.*

"Oh but," says Satan, "it is too late." Another lie of his. It is never too late so long as we are in this world and come to Jesus for pardon. Generally, in the case of young people he puts the clock back and says, "It is too soon," and then when they get old he puts the clock on and says, "It is too late." It is never too late as long as Jesus lives and the sinner repents. If a sinner were as old as Methuselah, if he came to Christ and trusted him, he would be saved.

"Oh but," the devil says, "it is no use your trying at all. The gospel is not true." Alas, but it is true, for some of us have proved it. I could bring before you today, if it were necessary, men and women who lived in sin and wallowed in it, and yet the Lord Christ has saved them by his precious blood. They would rejoice to tell you how they have been delivered from the reign of sin by faith in Jesus, though they could never have delivered themselves. The gospel is true. Our converts prove it. Conversion is the standing miracle of the church; and while we see what it does every day in the week, we are confident and sure. When men that were passionate, dishonest, impure, and covetous become holy, gracious, loving, pure, and generous, then we know that the gospel is true by the effect which it produces. A lie would never produce holiness and love. Out of the way, devil! It is all in vain for you to come here with your falsehoods; we know the truth about you, and about the gospel, and you shall not deceive us.

And then the devil will come with this – "It is of no use. Give it up, give it up." Many and many a man who has been on the brink of eternal life has been thrown down and torn with this: "It is of no use; give it up. You have prayed, and you have not been answered, so never pray again. You have attended the house of God, and you have become more miserable than ever, so never go again. Ever since you have been a thinking man and a sober man, you have had more trouble than ever you had. See," says the devil, "what comes of your religion." Thus he tries to induce the newly awakened to give it up. But oh, in God's name let me implore you do not turn from it, for you are on the brink of the grand discovery. Another turf turned, and there is the golden treasure. After all your striving – your long striving – never give up the search until you have found your Savior, for your Savior is to be found. Trust in him this night, and he is yours forever.

I shall not detain you much longer. But as our hopes have been awakened and our fears have been aroused, let us look on the scene till our wonder is excited. Did you notice when I was reading in the ninth chapter of Mark how Jesus healed this poor child? He did *heal* him; he healed him of all that complication, healed him of the devil's domination, healed him of the epilepsy, healed him of being deaf and mute, healed him of being a lunatic, healed him of pining away; and in one moment that young man was completely saved from all his ills. He could speak; he could hear; he was cured of his epilepsy, and was no more a lunatic, but a happy, rational being. The whole thing was done at once. Wonder, and never leave off wondering!

"Can a man be changed all at once? It must take a long time," says one. I admit there are certain qualities which come only by education and patient watchfulness. There are certain parts of the Christian character that come from culture and must be watered with tears and prayer. But let me assure you, not as a matter of theory but as a matter which I have seen for thirty years, that a man's character may be totally changed in less time than it takes me to tell you of it. There is such power in the name of Christ that if that name be preached and the Spirit of God applies it, men can be turned right around. There can be a total reversal of all their conduct, and, what is more than that, of all their inclinations, and desires and wishes, and delights and hates; for God can take away the heart of stone and give a heart of flesh. The child of darkness can be transformed into the kingdom of light. The dead heart can be revived into a spiritual existence, and that in a single moment, by faith in Jesus Christ. When that poor epileptic child was healed, it is said that the people were amazed. But how much greater will be our amazement if we see the Lord Jesus work such a miracle upon you. You have struggled to get better, you have prayed to get better, and all seems to be not helping. Now, just trust Christ, the blessed Son of God who reigns in heaven, who died for sinners, and now lives for sinners. Only trust him, and this blessed deed is done; you become a new creature in Christ Jesus, and commence a holy life which shall never end. This wonder can be performed *now*.

This cure was perfected at once, and it remained with the youth. The most charming point about it was that the Lord Jesus said, *"You deaf and mute spirit, I command you, come out of him and do not enter him again." "Do not enter him again"* – there is the glory of it! Though the epileptic fit was ended, yet the young man would not have been cured if the devil had returned to take possession of him again. The Savior's cures endure the test of years. *"Do not enter him again"* preserved the young man by a lifelong word of power.

I never dare to preach to anybody a temporary salvation. *"Believe in the Lord Jesus, and you will be saved,"* not for today merely, but forever. When God saves a man, he is saved: not for weeks and years, but eternally. If Christ turns the devil out of him, he shall enter into that man no more forever. Now, this is a salvation that is worth your having, and worth my preaching. A temporary, I would almost say, a senseless, salvation, that saves a man for a few months and then lets him perish, is not worth preaching or having; but that which so makes a man new as to put into him *"a well of water springing up to eternal life"* – that is worth worlds. I will tell you a story of Christmas Evans which I like to tell on this point. Christmas Evans was once describing the prodigal's coming back to his father's house, and he said that when the prodigal sat at the father's table, his father put upon his plate all the daintiest bits of meat that he could find; but the son sat there and did not eat, and every now and then the tears began to flow. His father turned to him and said, "My dear son, why are you unhappy? You spoil the feasting. Do you not know that I love you? Have I not joyfully received you?" "Yes," he said, "dear father, you are very kind, but have you really forgiven me? Have you forgiven me altogether, so that you will never be angry with me for all I have done?" His father looked on him with unspeakable love and said, "I have blotted out your sins and your iniquities, and will remember them no more forever. Eat, my dear son." The father turned around and waited on the guests, but by and by his eyes were on his boy; they could not be removed from him for very long. There was the son weeping again, but not eating. "Come, dear child," said his father, "come. Why are you still mourning? What is it that you want?" Bursting into a flood of tears a second time, the son said, "Father, am I always to stop here? Will you never turn me out of doors?" The father replied, "No, my child, you shall go no more out forever, for a son abides forever." Still the son did not enjoy the banquet; there was still something rankling within him, and again he wept. Then his father said, "Now, tell me, tell me, my dear son, all that is in your heart. What do you desire more?" The son answered, "Father, will you make me stop here? Father, I am afraid lest, if I were left to myself, I might play the prodigal again. Oh, constrain me to stay here forever!" The father said, "I will put my fear in your heart, and you shall not depart from me." "Ah! then," the son replied, "it is enough," and merrily he feasted with the rest. So I preach to you just this – that the great Father when he takes you to himself will never let you go away from him again.

Whatever your condition, if you trust your soul to Jesus, you shall be saved, and saved forever.

> Once in Christ, in Christ forever:
> Nothing from his love can sever.

"But what if we fall into great sin?" says one. You shall not abide in great sin. You shall be kept and preserved by that same power which has begun the good work, for it will surely carry it on even to the end.

Just two or three sentences and I will be finished. I have been speaking about the devil throwing some down and tearing them when they are coming to Christ. Are there any of you who do not know anything about that? Well, I am glad that you do not. If you come to Christ without being thrown down and torn, I am glad of it. I have endeavored to help those that are terribly tormented; but if you are not so tested, do not wish to be. There were here this morning two or three of the good fishpeople from Newhaven, and when I saw them in their picturesque costumes they reminded me of a story that I heard about an old fishwife who used to live near Edinburgh. A young man visited her, and began speaking to her about her soul. She was going out, and she took up her great load of fish to carry on her back, much more than most men would like to carry. The young man said to her, "Well, you have got a great burden there, good woman. Have you ever felt a spiritual burden?" She put down her load and said, "You mean that burden which John Bunyan speaks about in the *Pilgrim's Progress,* do you not?" "Yes," he said. "Well," she said, "I felt that burden before you were born, and I got rid of it too; but I did not go exactly the same way to work that John Bunyan's pilgrim did." Our young friend thought that she could not be up to the mark to talk so, for he imagined that John Bunyan could not make a mistake. "Well," she said, "John Bunyan says that Evangelist pointed the man with the burden on his back to the wicket gate, and when he could not see the gate, Evangelist said, 'Do you see that light?' And he looked till he thought he saw something like it. 'You are to run that way – the way of that light and that wicket gate.' Why," she said, "that was not the right direction to give a poor burdened soul. Much good he got out of it; for he had not gone far before he fell into the Slough of Despond, up to his neck in the mire, and would have been swallowed up. Evangelist ought to have said, 'Do you see that cross? Do not run an inch, but stand where you are, and look to that; and as you look your burden will be gone. I looked to the cross at once and lost my load.'" "What!" said the young man, "did you never go through the Slough of Despond?" "Yes," she said, "I have been through it far too many times; but let me tell you, young friend, that it is a great deal easier to go through the Slough of Despond with your burden off than it is with your burden on." There is much blessed truth in this story. Do not any of you be saying to yourselves, "How I wish I could get into the Slough of Despond!" If you say that, you will get in, and then you will say, "How I wish I could get out of the Slough of Despond!" I have met with persons who fear that they never were saved because they have not experienced much terror. I meet with others who say that they cannot be saved because they experience too much terror. There is no pleasing people. Oh, that they would look to Jesus either way!

After I was preaching Jesus Christ from this platform once, there came a man into the vestry who said to me, "Blessed be God that I entered this tabernacle. I come from Canada, sir. My father, before he found true religion, had to be locked up in a lunatic asylum, and I always thought that I must undergo a similar terror before I could be saved." I said, "No, no, my dear friend, you are to believe in the Lord Jesus Christ, and if you do that, despond or not despond, you are a saved man." This gospel I preach to you. Believe in the Lord Jesus Christ. Trust him quietly, humbly, simply, and immediately. Trust him to make you a holy man – to deliver you from the power of the devil and the power of sin, and he will do it. I will be bound for him that he will keep his word. Jesus is truth itself, and he never breaks his word. He never boasts that he can do what he cannot do. He has gone into heaven, and he is therefore *able also to save forever those who draw near to God through Him, since He always lives to make intercession for them.* Only trust him. Trust him to overcome the evil you have to fight with. You will conquer it, man, if you will only trust Jesus. Woman, there is hope for you if you will trust the wounded, bleeding, dying, risen, and living Savior. He will battle for you, and you shall get the victory.

God bless you, everyone, and may we all meet in heaven to praise the Son of God forever and ever.

> Jesus never boasts that he can do what he cannot do.

Charles H. Spurgeon – A Brief Biography

Charles Haddon Spurgeon was born on June 19, 1834, in Kelvedon, Essex, England. He was one of seventeen children in his family (nine of whom died in infancy). His father and grandfather were Nonconformist ministers in England. Due to economic difficulties, eighteen-month-old Charles was sent to live with his grandfather, who helped teach Charles the ways of God. Later in life, Charles remembered looking at the pictures in *Pilgrim's Progress* and in *Foxe's Book of Martyrs* as a young boy.

Charles did not have much of a formal education and never went to college. He read much throughout his life though, especially books by Puritan authors.

Even with godly parents and grandparents, young Charles resisted giving in to God. It was not until he was fifteen years old that he was born again. He was on his way to his usual church, but when a heavy snowstorm prevented him from getting there, he turned in at a little Primitive Methodist chapel. Though there were only about fifteen people in attendance, the preacher spoke from Isaiah 45:22: *Look unto me, and be ye saved, all the ends of the earth.* Charles Spurgeon's eyes were opened and the Lord converted his soul.

He began attending a Baptist church and teaching Sunday school. He soon preached his first sermon, and then when he was sixteen years old, he became the pastor of a small Baptist church in Cambridge. The church soon grew to over four hundred people, and Charles Spurgeon, at the age of nineteen, moved on to become the pastor of the New Park Street Church in London. The church grew from a few hundred attenders to a few thousand. They built an addition to the church, but still needed more room to accommodate the congregation. The Metropolitan Tabernacle was built in London in 1861, seating more than 5,000 people. Pastor Spurgeon preached the simple message of the cross, and thereby attracted many people who wanted to hear God's Word preached in the power of the Holy Spirit.

On January 9, 1856, Charles married Susannah Thompson. They had twin boys, Charles and Thomas. Charles and Susannah loved each other deeply, even amidst the difficulties and troubles that they faced in life, including health problems. They helped each other spiritually, and often together read the writings of Jonathan Edwards, Richard Baxter, and other Puritan writers.

Charles Spurgeon was a friend of all Christians, but he stood firmly on the Scriptures, and it didn't please all who heard him. Spurgeon believed in and preached on the sovereignty of God, heaven and hell, repentance, revival, holiness, salvation through Jesus Christ alone, and the infallibility and necessity of the Word of God. He spoke against worldliness and hypocrisy among Christians, and against Roman Catholicism, ritualism, and modernism.

One of the biggest controversies in his life was known as the "Down-Grade Controversy." Charles Spurgeon believed that some pastors of his time were "down-grading" the faith by compromising with the world or the new ideas of the age. He said that some pastors were denying the inspiration of the Bible, salvation by faith alone, and the truth of the Bible in other areas, such as creation. Many pastors who believed what Spurgeon condemned were not happy about this, and Spurgeon eventually resigned from the Baptist Union.

Despite some difficulties, Spurgeon became known as the "Prince of Preachers." He opposed slavery, started a pastors' college, opened an orphanage, led in helping feed and clothe the poor, had a book fund for pastors who could not afford books, and more.

Charles Spurgeon remains one of the most published preachers in history. His sermons were printed each week (even in the newspapers), and then the sermons for the year were re-issued as a book at the end of the year. The first six volumes, from 1855-1860, are known as *The Park Street Pulpit*, while the next fifty-seven volumes, from 1861-1917 (his sermons continued to be published long after his death), are known as *The Metropolitan Tabernacle Pulpit*. He also oversaw a monthly magazine-type publication called *The Sword and the Trowel*, and Spurgeon wrote many books, including *Lectures to My Students, All of Grace, Around the Wicket Gate, Advice for Seekers, John Ploughman's Talks, The Soul Winner, Words of Counsel for Christian Workers, Cheque Book of the Bank of Faith, Morning and Evening*, his autobiography, and more, including some commentaries, such as his twenty-year study on the Psalms – *The Treasury of David*.

Charles Spurgeon often preached ten times a week, preaching to an estimated ten million people during his lifetime. He usually preached from only one page of notes, and often from just an outline. He read about six books each week. During his lifetime, he had read *The Pilgrim's Progress* through more than one hundred times. When he died, his personal library consisted of more than 12,000 books. However, the Bible always remained the most important book to him.

Spurgeon was able to do what he did in the power of God's Holy Spirit because he followed his own advice – he met with God every morning before meeting with others, and he continued in communion with God throughout the day.

Charles Spurgeon suffered from gout, rheumatism, and some depression, among other health problems. He often went to Menton, France, to recuperate and rest. He preached his final sermon at the Metropolitan Tabernacle on June 7, 1891, and died in France on January 31, 1892, at the age of fifty-seven. He was buried in Norwood Cemetery in London.

Charles Haddon Spurgeon lived a life devoted to God. His sermons and writings continue to influence Christians all over the world.

Other Similar Titles

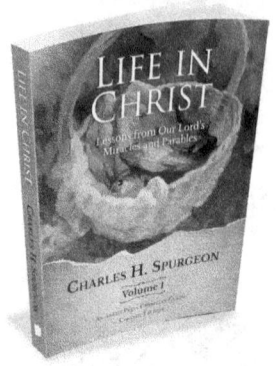

Life in Christ (Vol. 1 - 6),
by Charles H. Spurgeon

Men who were led by the hand or groped their way along the wall to reach Jesus were touched by his finger and went home without a guide, rejoicing that Jesus Christ had opened their eyes. Jesus is still able to perform such miracles. And, with the power of the Holy Spirit, his Word will be expounded and we'll watch for the signs to follow, expecting to see them at once. Why shouldn't those who read this be blessed with the light of heaven? This is my heart's inmost desire.

– Charles H. Spurgeon

Available where books are sold.

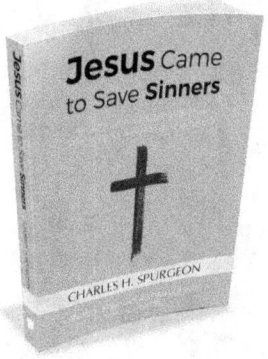

***Jesus Came to Save Sinners,* by Charles H. Spurgeon**

This is a heart-level conversation with you, the reader. Every excuse, reason, and roadblock for not coming to Christ is examined and duly dealt with. If you think you may be too bad, or if perhaps you really are bad and you sin either openly or behind closed doors, you will discover that life in Christ is for you too. You can reject the message of salvation by faith, or you can choose to live a life of sin after professing faith in Christ, but you cannot change the truth as it is, either for yourself or for others. As such, it behooves you and your family to embrace truth, claim it for your own, and be genuinely set free for now and eternity. Come and embrace this free gift of God, and live a victorious life for Him.

Available where books are sold.

**Words of Warning,
by Charles H. Spurgeon**

This book, *Words of Warning*, is an analysis of people and the gospel of Christ. Under inspiration of the Holy Spirit, Charles H. Spurgeon sheds light on the many ways people may refuse to come to Christ, but he also shines a brilliant light on how we can be saved. Unsaved or wavering individuals will be convicted, and if they allow it, they will be led to Christ. Sincere Christians will be happy and blessed as they consider the great salvation with which they have been saved.

Available where books are sold.

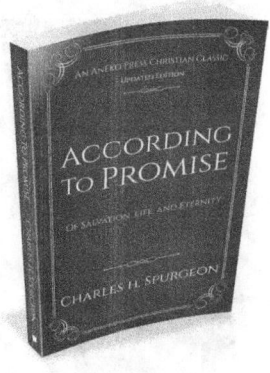

According to Promise,
by Charles H. Spurgeon

The first part of this book is meant to be a sieve to separate the chaff from the wheat. Use it on your own soul. It may be the most profitable and beneficial work you have ever done. He who looked into his accounts and found that his business was losing money was saved from bankruptcy.

The second part of this book examines God's promises to His children. The promises of God not only exceed all precedent, but they also exceed all imitation. No one has been able to compete with God in the language of liberality. The promises of God are as much above all other promises as the heavens are above the earth.

Available where books are sold.

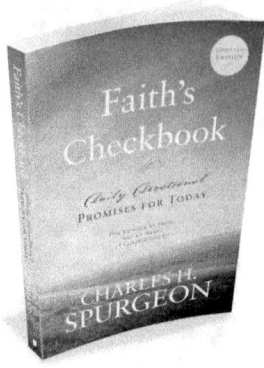

Faith's Checkbook, by Charles H. Spurgeon

Faith's Checkbook is a one-year devotional meant to encourage you to take God at His Word – to take hold of God's promises by faith. Each day you will be presented with a specific promise from the Bible, along with accompanying exhortation by Charles Spurgeon.

This is your "spiritual checkbook," if you will. God's bank account of provision is ample, and it cannot be overdrawn. Every situation you might face is equally met with a promise that, if accepted, will sufficiently see you through.

"God has given no promise that He will not redeem. He does not offer hope that He will not fulfill. To help my brethren believe this, I have prepared this little volume." – Charles H. Spurgeon

Available where books are sold.

Morning by Morning, by Charles H. Spurgeon

Charles H. Spurgeon's devotionals *Morning by Morning* and *Evening by Evening* have inspired, encouraged, and challenged Christians for generations. Spurgeon, with his masterful hand, carefully selected his text from throughout the Bible and covered a broad range of topics, in order to present a well-balanced and fruitful daily devotional for readers both young and old.

Now updated into more-modern English for today's readers, and again separated into two volumes as originally published, with morning devotionals in one volume and evening devotionals in the second. We chose a 11-point font for the sake of legibility, and formatted the devotionals so each fits on a single page.

Available where books are sold.

Faithful to Christ, by Charles H. Spurgeon

I believe that many Christians get into a lot of trouble by not being honest in their convictions. For instance, if a person goes into a workshop, or a soldier into a barracks, and if he does not fly his flag from the beginning, it will be very difficult for him to run it up afterwards. But if he immediately and boldly lets them know, "I am a Christian, and there are certain things that I cannot do to please you, and certain other things that I cannot help doing even though they might displease you" – when that is clearly understood, after a while the peculiarity of the thing will be gone, and the person will be let alone.

However, if he is a little dishonest and thinks that he is going to please the world and please Christ too, he can depend on it that he is in for a rough time. If he tries the way of compromise, his life will be like that of a toad under a harrow or a fox in a dog kennel. That will never do. Come out. Show your colors. Let it be known who you are and what you are. Although your course will not be smooth, it will certainly not be half as rough as if you tried to run with the hare and hunt with the hounds, which is a very difficult piece of business.

Available where books are sold.

Following Christ, **by Charles H. Spurgeon**

You cannot have Christ if you will not serve Him. If you take Christ, you must take Him in all His qualities. You must not simply take Him as a Friend, but you must also take Him as your Master. If you are to become His disciple, you must also become His servant. God-forbid that anyone fights against that truth. It is certainly one of our greatest delights on earth to serve our Lord, and this is to be our joyful vocation even in heaven itself: *His servants shall serve Him: and they shall see His face* (Revelation 22:3-4).

Available where books are sold.

www.ingramcontent.com/pod-product-compliance
Lightning Source LLC
Chambersburg PA
CBHW070133080526
44586CB00015B/1677